AAT

INTERMEDIATE
NVQ LEVEL 3 DIPLOMA
FOR ACCOUNTING TECHNICIANS (QCF)

REVISION COMPANION   Units 6 & 7

Costing & Reports and Returns

BPP LEARNING MEDIA

Ninth edition June 2009
First published 2001

ISBN 9780 7517 6716 2 (previous ISBN 9780 7517 4634 1)

British Library Cataloguing-in-Publication Data
A catalogue record for this book is available from the British Library

Published by

BPP Learning Media Ltd
BPP House
Aldine Place
London W12 8AA

www.bpp.com/learningmedia

Printed in the United Kingdom

> Your learning materials, published by BPP Learning Media Ltd, are printed on paper sourced from sustainable, managed forests.

All our rights reserved. No part of this publication may be reproduced, stored in a retrieval system or transmitted, in any form or by any means, electronic, mechanical, photocopying, recording or otherwise, without the prior written permission of BPP Learning Media Ltd.

We are grateful to the AAT for permission to reproduce sample simulations and simulations and examples from previous assessments. The answers to the sample simulations for Units 6 and 7 have been published by the AAT. All other answers have been prepared by BPP Learning Media Ltd.

©
BPP Learning Media Ltd
2009

CONTENTS

Introduction (v)

Chapter activities   Questions   Answers

Unit 6 Recording Cost Information

1	Costing information	1	307
2	Materials costs	5	317
3	Labour costs and expenses	15	329
4	Overheads	19	333
5	Absorption costing and marginal costing	25	339
6	Costing systems	27	343
7	Cost bookkeeping	31	347
8	Short-term decision making	35	351
9	Long-term decision making	39	357

Unit 7 Preparing Reports and Returns (NVQ only)

10	Internal information	43	361
11	Performance measures	45	363
12	Writing a report	49	367
13	Tables and diagrams	51	371
14	Reporting figures over time	57	379
15	External reporting	65	389
16	Value added tax	71	395
17	VAT records	77	397

Practice assessments

Unit 6

Practice Exam 1 – Fly 4 Less plc	85	403
Practice Exam 2 – Premier Labels Ltd	103	415
Practice Exam 3 – Stow Solvents Ltd	121	427
Practice Exam 4 – Eastern Bus Company plc	139	437
Practice Exam 5 – Breckville Dairies Ltd	157	449
AAT Sample Simulation – Quality Candles Ltd	175	457
Practice Simulation – High Heat Ltd	213	473

Unit 7 (NVQ only)

AAT Sample Simulation – Homer Ltd	255	493
Practice Simulation – Donald Ratherson & Co	277	503

MCQ/OT questions and answers	519	541

INTRODUCTION

This is BPP Learning Media's AAT Revision Companion for Unit 6, Recording Cost Information and Unit 7 (of the NVQ), Preparing Reports and Returns. It is part of an integrated package of AAT materials.

It has been written in conjunction with the BPP Course Companion, and has been carefully designed to enable students to practise all aspects of the requirements of the Standards of Competence and performance criteria. It is fully up to date as at April 2009 and reflects the revised Standards of Competence.

This Revision Companion contains these key features:

- graded activities corresponding to each chapter of the Course Companion
- the AAT's sample simulations and answers for Units 6 and 7
- a further practice simulation and answers for Units 6 and 7
- five Unit 6 exams set between December 2006 and December 2008, with full answers
- A bank of MCQ/OT questions at the back of the Revision Companion. Starting in 2009, Unit 6 will be assessed by MCQ/OT as well as the current longer questions if students opt for this.

The emphasis in all activities and questions is on the practical application of the skills acquired. All activities, practice assessments and simulations have full answers prepared by BPP Learning Media.

Tutors adopting our Companions (minimum of ten Course Companions and ten Revision Companions per Unit, or ten Combined Companions as appropriate) are entitled to free access to the Lecturers' Area resources, including the Tutor Companion. To obtain your log-in, e-mail lecturersvc@bpp.com.

Home Study students are also entitled to access to additional resources. You will have received your log-in details on registration.

VAT

You will find examples and questions throughout this companion which need you to calculate or be aware of a rate of VAT. This is stated at 17.5% in these examples and questions. Please use this rate and not the temporary rate of 15% that applies at present.

If you have any comments about this book, please e-mail helendarch@bpp.com or write to Helen Darch, AAT range manager, BPP Learning Media Ltd, BPP House, Aldine Place, London W12 8AA.

introduction

> **Diploma Pathway**
>
> Please note that under the Diploma Pathway students do not need to study Unit 7, as the content is included in Diploma Unit 34, Supplying and Presenting Financial Data. Diploma Pathway students, therefore, need only study Chapters 1 to 9 of this book.

chapter 1:
COSTING INFORMATION

1   Explain the main differences between financial accounting and cost accounting.

2   Explain how cost information can be used to assist in the three main roles of management – decision making, planning and control.

3   Explain how costs are classified in the following ways:

   a)   Capital and revenue costs
   b)   According to function
   c)   Direct and indirect costs
   d)   According to behaviour

4   Show whether each of the following costs would be treated as capital or revenue costs:

	Capital	Revenue
Purchase of a car for resale by a car dealer		
Purchase of a car for use by a salesman		
Road tax payable on purchase of a car for use by a salesman		
Redecorating head office		
Installing new machinery		
Cleaning of new machinery after initial use		

costing information

5 Show how each of the following costs would be classified by function:

	Production cost	Selling and distribution cost	Administration cost
Depreciation of salesmen's cars			
Production manager's salary			
Depreciation of machinery			
Rent of office space			
Depreciation of delivery vans			
CD-Roms for office computer			

6 Show how each of the following costs would be classified as either a direct cost or an indirect cost:

	Direct cost	Indirect cost
Wages of factory supervisor		
Hire of plant for construction of a building by a building firm		
Cleaning materials used in the factory		
Factory rent		
Wages of a trainee accountant in an accountancy firm		
Cement used for construction of a building by a building firm		

7 Classify each of the following costs according to their behaviour:
   a) Telephone bill for line rental and call charges
   b) Factory rent and rates
   c) Materials used in production
   d) Supervisor's salary
   e) Warehouse rental where additional space is rented when stock levels are high

costing information

8   Given below are the output levels and associated production costs for a factory for the last six months:

	Output in units	Cost £
February	125,000	375,000
March	142,000	418,000
April	110,000	340,000
May	120,000	362,000
June	145,000	424,000
July	130,000	394,000

Use the high(–)/low method to estimate the variable cost per unit and the overall fixed costs of the factory.

9   A factory produces a single product which has a raw materials input of £3.80 per unit, labour costs of £1.40 per unit and packaging costs of £0.30 per unit. The factory rent is currently £150,000 per annum but if production levels rise above 120,000 units then additional factory space must be rented at an additional cost of £40,000 per annum. The depreciation of the machinery is £30,000 per annum.

The factory production for the forthcoming year will depend upon the outcome of a promotion of this product and the management hope that production will be for 180,000 units. However if the promotion is not quite as successful as hoped then production will be only 130,000 units. If the promotion is not successful then production will only be for 80,000 units.

Produce a schedule showing the total production costs at each possible level of production.

10 Suggest the cost units which would be appropriate for management information systems in the following industries.

a)   A building contractor
b)   An airline

11 Wheely Wheels Ltd is a successful wheel making company which makes wheels for a variety of uses: wheelbarrows; carts; toys and so on.

The production operation consists of three departments: bending; cutting and assembly. The bending and cutting departments have general purpose machinery which is used to manufacture all the wheels produced.

Complete the table below by analysing the cost items for Wheely Wheels Ltd into the appropriate columns and agreeing the balances.

3

costing information

	Total £	Prime cost £	Production expense £	Admin. expense £	Selling and distribution expense £
Wages of assembly employees	6,750				
Wages of stores employees	3,250				
Tyres for toy wheels	1,420				
Safety goggles for operators	810				
Job advert for new employees	84				
Depreciation of delivery vehicles	125				
Depreciation of production machines	264				
Cost of trade exhibition	1,200				
Computer stationery	130				
Course fee for AAT training	295				
Royalty for the design of wheel 1477	240				
	14,568				

12 You are required to show a separate sketch graph of the cost behaviour patterns for each of the listed items of expense. The vertical axis of each graph should be total cost. You should label the horizontal axis of each graph clearly.

   a) Electricity bill: a standing charge is paid for each period plus a charge for each unit of electricity consumed.

   b) Supervisory labour.

   c) Production bonus, which is payable when output in a period exceeds 10,000 units. The bonus amounts in total to £20,000 plus £50 per unit for additional output above 10,000 units.

   d) Sales commission, which amounts to 2% of sales turnover.

   e) Machine rental costs of a single item of equipment; the rental agreement is that £10 should be paid for every machine hour worked each month, subject to a maximum monthly charge of £480.

13 Prepare a report for the managing director of your company explaining how costs may be classified by their behaviour, with particular reference to the effects of changes in activity both on total costs and on unit costs.

   Your report should:

   a) explain why it is necessary to classify costs by their behaviour; and
   b) be illustrated by sketch graphs within the body of the report.

chapter 2:
MATERIALS COSTS

1 Complete the following sentences.

    a) The three main categories of stock for a manufacturing business are ...., ... and ....

    b) The internal document used to record the quantity of materials received from a supplier is known as a ....

    c) The initial internal document that starts the purchasing process for materials is known as a ....

    d) A .... is the document that is sent to a supplier to request the supply of materials

    e) When materials are required from stores by the factory a .... is filled out

    f) A .... is the document received from a supplier of materials requesting payment

2 Given below is a stock card for one of the materials used by a manufacturing business. During the month of June the following goods received notes and materials requisitions for this material were completed:

Goods received notes:

3 June	GRN 0326	340 units
12 June	GRN 0348	300 units
28 June	GRN 0363	320 units

Materials requisitions:

5 June	MR 0295	150 units
10 June	MR 0307	190 units
20 June	MR 0315	180 units
25 June	MR 0320	100 units

Write up the stock card for the month of June.

materials costs

STOCK CARD

Description: 23 Electrical component EC23

Bin No: 413

Code No:

Receipts			Issues			Balance
Date	Reference	Quantity	Date	Reference	Quantity	Quantity
1 June						50

3   Martin Ltd uses the weighted average cost method to value stock issues and closing stocks. Fill in the shaded boxes in the stores ledger account shown below for stock item LRM.

STORES LEDGER ACCOUNT

Stock item ____LRM____

Code ____8888____

Date	Receipts Qty	Receipts Unit price £	Receipts £	Issues Qty	Issues Unit price £	Issues £	Balance Qty	Balance Unit cost £	Balance £
Op bal							100	2.00	
3 Sept	400	2.10					500		
4 Sept				200			300		
9 Sept	300	2.12					600		
11 Sept				400			200		
18 Sept	100	2.40					300		
20 Sept				100			200		

4   Given below are the purchases and issues to production of material XK2 for the month of July:

4 July	Issue	MR 416	320 kg
7 July	Purchase	GRN 668	500 kg @ £3.20 per kg
12 July	Issue	MR 422	180 kg
16 July	Issue	MR 428	300 kg
19 July	Purchase	GRN 674	500 kg @ £3.50 per kg
23 July	Issue	MR 433	230 kg
28 July	Issue	MR 440	300 kg

Opening stock at 1 July consists of 400 kg all purchased at a price of £3.00 per kg.

You are required to write up the stores ledger accounts given below for this material for the month of July on the following bases:

a)   First in first out (FIFO)
b)   Last in first out (LIFO)
c)   Average cost (AVCO)

materials costs

STORES LEDGER ACCOUNT

Stock item XK2

Code 041861

FIFO basis

Date	Receipts				Issues				Balance	
	GRN	Qty	Unit price £	£	Req No	Qty	Unit price £	£	Qty	£
1 July									400	1200.00

STORES LEDGER ACCOUNT

Stock item   XK2

Code   041861

LIFO basis

| Date | Receipts ||||| Issues ||||| Balance ||
	GRN	Qty	Unit price £	£	Req No	Qty	Unit price £	£	Qty	£
1 July									400	1200.00

materials costs

STORES LEDGER ACCOUNT

Stock item XK2

Code 041861

AVCO basis

Date	Receipts				Issues				Balance	
	GRN	Qty	Unit price £	£	Req No	Qty	Unit price £	£	Qty	£
1 July									400	1200.00

5   Given below are the stock movements for component JJ41 for the month of July:

1 July	Opening balance	220 units @ £5.60
3 July	Issue	160 units
7 July	Purchases	300 units @ £6.00
10 July	Issue	170 units
15 July	Issue	100 units
20 July	Purchases	250 units @ £6.30
24 July	Issue	200 units

You are required to calculate:

a)   the cost of issues
b)   the value of closing stock

in the month of July using FIFO, LIFO and AVCO methods of stock valuation.

6   Describe the FIFO and LIFO methods of stock valuation, and state the advantages and disadvantages of each method.

7   During the month of September a manufacturing business made purchases of materials on credit totalling £83,469. Stocks of raw materials at 1 September were valued at £12,523. During September issues of £79,247 were made to the factory for direct production and £6,248 of indirect materials were also issued to the factory.

Write up the cost ledger accounts to reflect these transactions.

8   At a time of rapidly rising prices a manufacturing company decides to change from a FIFO system to a LIFO system of pricing material issues. What would be the effect on the following?

a)   Stock valuation
b)   Cost of materials charged to production

9   Protective gloves are used in the production departments of Flimsey Ltd and are drawn from stores at regular intervals. Records show the following for November.

1 November	Opening stock	100 pairs @ £2 each
7 November	Purchases	200 pairs @ £1.90 each
18 November	Issues	150 pairs

Calculate the value of the closing stock of gloves given that the FIFO system of valuing issues is used.

materials costs

10. Wiggles plc, a printing company, specialises in producing accounting manuals for several accountancy training companies. The manuals are written by the training companies and passed to Wiggles plc for printing. The company uses three main stages in producing the manuals.

a) The preparation of the text
b) The printing of the text
c) The assembly and binding of the manuals

Write up the following information on the stock card using the AVCO (average cost) method to value the issues.

Material: Paper – Code 1564A
Opening stock: 10,000 sheets – value £3,000

Purchases			Issues	
3 May	4,000 sheets	£1,600	6 May	7,000 sheets
12 May	10,000 sheets	£3,100	15 May	6,000 sheets
25 May	10,000 sheets	£3,200	22 May	7,200 sheets

Calculate the average cost to two decimal places of a £ and the value of the issues to the nearest £.

STOCK RECORD CARD

Material description: _Paper_

Code no: _1564A_

		Receipts		Issues			Balance	
Date	Details	Sheets	£	Sheets	Unit price £	£	Sheets	£

11 Roman Ltd sells and services cars.

Complete the following extract from the stock record card for May and calculate the quantity and value of stock on 24 May using the Last In, First Out (LIFO) method of stock valuation.

STOCK RECORD CARD

Product: Motor oil

Centre: Servicing

Date	Receipts Quantity	Receipts Cost per litre	Receipts Total cost	Issues Quantity	Issues Cost per litre	Issues Total cost	Balance Quantity	Balance Total cost
	litres	£	£	litres	£	£	litres	£
B/f May							2,100	2,100
4 May	2,400	1.20	2,880					
8 May				3,300				
10 May	3,000	1.10						
11 May				3,200				
17 May	5,000	1.00						
18 May				5,400				
23 May	6,400	0.95						
24 May				4,420				

chapter 3:
LABOUR COSTS AND EXPENSES

1 A business pays its employees on a time rate basis with time and half for any hours worked over 37 hours per week. George is paid a basic rate of £6.80 per hour and during the week ending 31 July he worked for 43 hours.

   Calculate the following figures for the week:

   a) George's total gross pay;
   b) the overtime payment;
   c) the overtime premium.

2 An employee is paid on a differential piecework system on the following basis:

   Up to 300 units produced a week – £1.00 per unit

   Units over 300 and up to 400 – £1.15 per unit

   Any units over 400 – £1.35 per unit

   In the week ending 28 June the employee produced 430 units. What is his total gross pay for the week?

3 A business has a number of different types of employees who are remunerated by different methods. Harry is paid on a piecework basis as follows:

   Per unit of product A produced   £10.40
   Per unit of product B produced   £18.60

   Stella is paid on a time rate basis at £8.40 per hour for 35 hours a week. For any hours over 35 each week she is paid overtime at the rate of time and a third.

   Yvette is paid a salary of £20,000 per annum.

   During the week ending 30 June Harry produced 22 units of product A and 7 units of product B and Stella worked for 43 hours. Yvette is paid her salary monthly and for the month of June a performance bonus of 5% of total salary is to be paid to all salaried employees.

   Calculate the following figures:

   a) Harry's gross pay for the week;
   b) Stella's gross pay for the week;
   c) Yvette's gross pay for the month of June.

labour costs and expenses

4   The payroll records for a business for the week ending 15 July show the following details:

	£
Net pay	24,700
PAYE and NIC deductions	6,200
Company pension scheme deductions	2,400
Gross pay	33,300

The payroll analysis also shows that of this total £20,900 relates to direct labour costs and the remainder to indirect labour costs.

Write up the cost ledger accounts to reflect this.

5   A company owns three classes of fixed assets:

- A freehold building which was purchased for £450,000 including land which was valued at £50,000. Land is not depreciated but the building is depreciated on the basis that it has a remaining useful life of 40 years.

- Machinery with an original cost of £220,000. When the machinery was purchased it was estimated that it would have a life of 32,000 hours and would be sold for scrap at the end of this period for £20,000. During the current year the machinery was used for 4,200 hours.

- A fleet of cars for the sales team, which originally cost £120,000 and which have been depreciated by £52,500 at the start of the year. The cars are depreciated on the reducing balance basis at a rate of 25%.

What is the depreciation charge for each class of fixed assets for the current year?

6   During the month of October a manufacturing business incurred general production overheads of £39,256. It also paid £7,200 of hire costs in order to replace a machine that had broken down.

Write up the cost ledger accounts to reflect this.

labour costs and expenses

7 The production manager of your organisation wishes to know the direct labour cost of jobs N172, N174 and M215 performed on 14 May. You have reviewed the time sheets of those direct employees who allocated their hours to those job numbers.

Using the information on the time sheets below, calculate the direct labour cost of jobs N172, N174 and M215.

Time Sheet No.	15				
Employee Name	N Davies	Clock Code	412	Dept	15
Date	14/5/??	Week No.	7		

Job No.	Start time	Finsih time	Quantity	Checker	Hours	Rate	Extension
AB 64	0800	0830				6.60	
N172	0930	1145				6.60	
M215	1450	1650				6.60	

Time Sheet No.	19				
Employee Name	Y Chang	Clock Code	476	Dept	1
Date	14/5/??	Week No.	7		

Job No.	Start time	Finsih time	Quantity	Checker	Hours	Rate	Extension
FJ15	0730	1030				6.50	
NI64	1045	1230				6.50	
AB64	1230	1630				6.50	
M215	1700	1830				6.50	

Time Sheet No.	20				
Employee Name	J Pitman	Clock Code	31	Dept	3
Date	14/5/??	Week No.	7		

Job No.	Start time	Finsih time	Quantity	Checker	Hours	Rate	Extension
NI74	1200	1800				10.00	

labour costs and expenses

Time Sheet No.		17						
Employee Name		R Khan		Clock Code	183		Dept	8
Date		14/5/??		Week No.	7			

Job No.	Start time	Finsih time	Quantity	Checker	Hours	Rate	Extension
NI68	0900	1200				6.80	
NI72	1200	1300				6.80	
M215	1430	1815				6.80	

8 a) Most expenses are direct costs.   True/False?
    b) Most expenses are not related to the production side of an organisation.   True/False?
    c) The cost of the power to run machines is always a direct expense.   True/False?
    d) Cleaners not on an organisation's payroll are an indirect expense.   True/False?

chapter 4:
OVERHEADS

1   A manufacturing organisation has two production cost centres, the assembly department and the finishing department and two service cost centres, stores and the maintenance department.

The budgeted overheads for the following six month period was as follows:

	Total £	Assembly £	Finishing £	Stores £	Maintenance £
Indirect materials	18,700	16,500	2,200		
Indirect labour	22,800	7,500	6,200	4,500	4,600
Rent and rates	10,000				
Heat and light	7,400				
Supervisor's wages	9,880				
Depreciation of machinery	8,400				

You are also provided with the following information:

	Total	Assembly	Finishing	Stores	Maintenance
Floor area (sq m)	20,000	6,000	4,000	5,000	5,000
Net book value of machinery	£240,000	£150,000	£50,000	£15,000	£25,000
Supervisor's time in each department (hours)	38	22	16		
Materials requisitions	300	220	80		
Maintenance hours	1,200	700	500		

You are required to:

a)   apportion the overheads to each of the production and service cost centres;

b)   reapportion the service cost centre costs to the production cost centres (the stores and maintenance cost centres do not provide any services to each other).

overheads

2   A manufacturing organisation has two production departments, A and B, and two service cost centres, stores and the canteen.

The budgeted overheads for the next period are as follows:

	Total £	A £	B £	Stores £	Canteen £
Indirect wages	75,700	7,800	4,700	21,200	42,000
Rent	24,000				
Buildings insurance	2,000				
Power	6,400				
Heat and light	4,000				
Supervisor's wages – Dept A	10,000				
Machinery depreciation	3,200				
Machinery insurance	2,200				

You are also provided with the following information:

	Total	A	B	Stores	Canteen
Net book value of machinery	£300,000	£140,000	£120,000	£15,000	£25,000
Power usage (%)	100%	45%	30%	5%	20%
Number of employees	126	70	40	10	6
Supervisor's hours	40	25	15		
Floor area (sq m)	30,000	12,000	8,000	4,000	6,000
Materials requisitions	500	300	200		

The stores staff use the canteen but the canteen makes no use of the stores services.

You are required to:

a) allocate or apportion the overheads to each of the production and service cost centres on a fair basis;

b) reapportion the service cost centre costs to the production cost centres using the step down method.

overheads

3 The overheads for a business have already been apportioned to its two production and two service cost centres for manufacturing as follows:

	Total £	Assembly £	Polishing £	Stores £	Maintenance £
	130,000	60,000	40,000	20,000	10,000

You are also given the following information:

	Total	Assembly	Polishing	Stores	Maintenance
Number of materials requisitions	400	200	160		40
Maintenance hours required	1,000	600	400		

You are required to reapportion the service cost centre costs using the step down method.

4 The budgeted overheads of a manufacturing business have been allocated and apportioned to the two production cost centres as follows:

Cutting £58,600
Finishing £42,400

The two production cost centres are budgeted to produce 10,000 units in the next period.

You are also provided with the following further information:

	Cutting	Finishing
Direct labour hours	4,000	24,000
Machine hours	12,000	2,000
Direct labour cost	£24,500	£168,000
Direct materials cost	£180,000	£25,000
Prime cost	£204,500	£193,000

You are required to calculate overhead absorption rates on each of the following bases and to state in what circumstances each absorption rate would be appropriate:

a) rate per unit
b) rate per direct labour hour
c) rate per machine hour

21

overheads

5   The budgeted overheads apportioned to a business's two production cost centres, C and D, together with the budgeted labour hours and machine hours, are given below:

	C	D
Overheads	£125,000	£180,000
Direct labour hours	12,000	80,000
Machine hours	100,000	10,000

Production cost centre C is a highly mechanised department with only a few machine operatives whereas production cost centre D is a highly labour intensive department.

a) You are to calculate separate departmental overhead absorption rates for each production cost centre using an appropriate basis and to justify the basis that you have used.

b) Each unit of Product P spends the following hours in each production department:

	C	D
Direct labour hours	1	7
Machine hours	5	2

Determine how much overhead will be included in the cost of each unit of product P.

6   In each of the following situations calculate any under- or over-absorption of overheads and state how they would be dealt with in the profit and loss account:

a) Budgeted production is 1,200 units and budgeted overheads were £5,400. Overheads are to be absorbed on a unit basis. The actual production was 1,000 units and the overheads incurred were £5,000.

b) Budgeted production was 600 units to be produced in 1,800 labour hours. Budgeted overheads of £5,040 are to be absorbed on a direct labour hour basis. The actual production for the period was 700 units in 2,200 labour hours and the actual overheads were £5,100.

c) Budgeted production was 40,000 units and the budgeted machine hours per unit was 2 hours per unit. Budgeted overheads were £320,000 and were to be absorbed on a machine hour basis. The actual overheads incurred were £320,000 and the production was 42,000 units. The total machine hours were 82,000.

7   Using the data from the previous activity write up the production overhead control account in each case clearly showing the transfer to the profit and loss account for under-/over-absorption of overheads.

8   Explain what is meant by under- and over-absorption of overheads, and how they occur.

9   The overhead absorption rate for the machining department at Jefferson Ltd is £5 per direct labour hour. During the year to 31 December 1,753 direct labour hours were worked and overheads incurred were £9,322.

You are are required to calculate the under- or over-absorption of overheads in the twelve-month period.

overheads

10 Happy Ltd manufactures and sells furnishing fabrics and its operations are organised by departments, as follows.

- Administration
- Manufacturing
- Sales
- Warehouse

The budgeted and actual fixed overheads of the company for November were as follows.

	£
Depreciation	14,600
Rent	48,000
Other property overheads	12,800
Administration overheads	28,800
Staff costs:	
Warehouse	4,800
Indirect manufacturing	14,340
Sales	12,250
Administration	8,410
Total actual fixed overheads	144,000

The following information is also relevant.

Department	% of floor space occupied %	Net book value of fixed assets £'000
Warehouse	20	160
Manufacturing	65	560
Sales	5	40
Administration	10	40
	100	800

Overheads are allocated and apportioned between departments using the most appropriate basis.

You are required to complete the following table showing the allocation and apportionment of fixed overheads between the four departments.

Actual fixed overheads for November	Basis	Total £	Warehouse £	Manufacturing £	Sales £	Administration £
Depreciation		14,600				
Rent		48,000				
Other property overheads		12,800				
Administration overheads		28,800				
Staff costs		39,800				
		144,000				

chapter 5:
ABSORPTION COSTING AND MARGINAL COSTING

1   The following information relates to Trident Ltd for the month of March.

    Note. There were no opening or closing stocks.

    Sales revenue – March

    4,000 units were sold at a selling price of £40 per unit.

    Production costs – March

    Direct material costs – £25,000
    Direct labour costs – £50,000
    Variable overhead costs – £15,000
    Fixed costs – £30,000

    You are required to, using the information given above, calculate the total contribution earned for the month of March.

2   A business produces a single product in its factory which has two production departments, cutting and finishing. In the following quarter it is anticipated that 120,000 units of the product will be produced. The expected costs are:

Direct materials		£12 per unit
Direct labour		2 hours cutting @ £7.40 per hour
		1 hour finishing @ £6.80 per hour
Variable overheads	cutting	£336,000
	finishing	£132,000
Fixed overheads	cutting	£144,000
	finishing	£96,000

    Overheads are absorbed on the basis of direct labour hours.

    What is the unit cost under:

    a) absorption costing
    b) marginal costing?

absorption costing and marginal costing

3 Given below are the budgeted production and sales figures for the single product that a business makes and sells for the months of July and August.

	July	August
Production	24,000 units	24,000 units
Sales	22,000 units	25,000 units

There were stocks of 1,500 units of the product at the start of July.

The expected production costs for each of the two months are as follows:

Direct materials	£6.80 per unit
Direct labour	£3.60 per unit
Variable production costs	£32,400
Fixed production costs	£44,400

Overheads are absorbed on the basis of the budgeted production level and the product is sold for £16 per unit.

a) Prepare the budgeted profit and loss account for the two months using:

    i) absorption costing
    ii) marginal costing

b) Prepare a reconciliation explaining any difference in the two profit figures in each of the two months.

4 You are given the budgeted data about the production of a business's single product for the following quarter:

Opening stock	840 units
Production	8,000 units
Sales	8,200 units
Direct materials	£23.60
Direct labour	4 hours @ £5.80 per hour
Variable overheads	£88,000
Fixed overheads	£51,200

Overheads are absorbed on the basis of units of production The product has a selling price of £70 per unit.

a) Prepare the budgeted profit and loss account for the quarter using:

    i) absorption costing
    ii) marginal costing

b) Prepare a reconciliation explaining any difference in the profit using absorption costing and profit using marginal costing.

5 Explain why marginal costing may be a more appropriate method than absorption costing for costing and reporting purposes.

chapter 6:
COSTING SYSTEMS

1 Fill in the missing words.

Batch costing is a form of costing that is similar to _____ costing except that costs are collected for _____. The cost unit is the _____. A cost per unit is calculated by _____.

2 Suggest appropriate costing methods for the following organisations.

a) A plumbing business
b) A clothing manufacturer
c) A caterer

3 Explain when the use of job costing is appropriate.

4 A manufacturer of custom-made bedroom furniture has been asked to supply bedroom fittings for a customer. The estimated costs are given below:

Materials for units – £2,800
Direct labour for fitting units – 27 hours @ £19.50 per hour
Overheads are absorbed on the basis of £8.70 per direct labour hour
Profit on each job is 20% of total costs
VAT is charged at 17.5%

You are to prepare a job costing schedule showing how much the bedroom fittings will cost the customer.

costing systems

5   Given below is a job costing schedule based on the estimates made which is still to be completed.

JOB NUMBER 2856

	Budget £	Actual £	Variance £
Direct materials			
■ wood	1,650.00		
■ components	830.00		
■ plastic	320.00		
Direct labour			
■ Grade I – 30 hours	414.00		
■ Grade III – 12 hours	132.00		
Direct expenses			
■ hire of equipment	300.00		
Overheads			
Total cost			
Profit			
VAT @ 17.5%			

Overheads are absorbed into the cost of jobs at a rate of £4.60 per direct labour hour. Profit on jobs is 25% of total cost.

On the completion of the job the cost of the wood was £1,830.00, the components £755.00 and the plastic £300. In total 33 hours of Grade I labour were charged to the job at a rate of £14.50 per hour and 7 hours of Grade III labour were charged at an hourly rate of £11.00. The equipment hired had to be kept for an additional two days increasing the hire cost to £380.

You are required to:

a)   complete the costing of the job to show the price to be charged to the customer;

b)   compare the actual costs to the budgeted costs showing the variances;

c)   complete the job costing schedule at the end of the job showing the final profit that was actually earned on the job.

6   Given below are the details for a process for the month of May:

Direct materials	100,000 kg	£287,000
Direct labour		£138,000
Overheads		£82,600
Normal loss		6%
Output		92,000 kg

Write up the ledger accounts to record the process results for the month.

Question 7

Workings:

- Input: 18,000 litres
- Normal loss (5%): 900 litres
- Expected output: 17,100 litres
- Actual output: 17,500 litres
- Abnormal gain: 400 litres

Total cost = £35,800 + £7,200 + £11,720 = £54,720

Cost per litre = £54,720 / 17,100 litres = £3.20 per litre

Process Account

	Litres	£		Litres	£
Direct materials	18,000	35,800	Normal loss	900	–
Direct labour		7,200	Finished output	17,500	56,000
Overheads		11,720			
Abnormal gain	400	1,280			
	18,400	56,000		18,400	56,000

Normal Loss Account

	Litres	£		Litres	£
Process account	900	–	Abnormal gain account	400	–
			Balance	500	–

Abnormal Gain Account

	Litres	£		Litres	£
Normal loss account	400	–	Process account	400	1,280
Costing P&L account		1,280			
	400	1,280		400	1,280

chapter 7:
COST BOOKKEEPING

1. A manufacturing business absorbs production overheads into work in progress at a rate of £3.20 per direct labour hour. In the month of August the overheads incurred totalled £4,720 and the direct labour hours worked were 1,400.

   Write up the production overhead control account. Explain the accounting treatment of any balance on the account.

2. A manufacturing business absorbs production overheads at a rate of £6.45 per direct labour hour. In the month of July a total of 940 direct labour hours were worked and the production overhead incurred was £5,840.

   Write up the production overhead control account and explain the accounting treatment of any balance on the account.

3. A manufacturing business has the following transactions for the week ending 7 September:

Materials purchased on credit	£14,365
Materials requisitions from the factory	£11,632
Total payroll costs – direct factory labour	£18,375
– indirect factory labour	£2,682
Production overheads incurred	£6,243
Production overheads to be absorbed	1,530 hours @ £5.20 per hour
Transfer of production to finished goods	£36,540

   Write up the following ledger accounts in an integrated cost bookkeeping system to reflect these transactions:

   - Materials control account
   - Wages control account
   - Production overhead control account
   - Work in progress control account

cost bookkeeping

4 Given below are extracts from the trial balance of a business at 1 August:

	Debit £	Credit £
Stock:		
Raw materials	1,290	
Work in Progress	1,540	
Finished goods	1,830	
Debtors	7,200	
Creditors		5,460
Cash at bank	3,070	

You are also given a summary of some of the transactions of the business for the month of August:

	£
Materials purchased on credit	7,640
Materials requisitions – factory	6,620
– administration	990
Wages cost – direct factory labour (490 hours)	5,430
– indirect factory labour	1,460
Sales invoices issued	14,700
Cheques received from debtors	6,800
Cheques paid to creditors	4,900
Production transferred to finished goods	12,200
Production overheads paid by cheque	4,290
Administration overheads paid by cheque	1,210
Closing stock of finished goods	1,650

Production overheads are absorbed at the budgeted overhead absorption rate of £11.10 per direct labour hour.

You are required to:

a) write up the ledger accounts given below to reflect these transactions;
b) balance each of the accounts at the end of the month;
c) prepare the profit and loss account for the month.

Materials control account

£	£

Wages control account

£	£

cost bookkeeping

Production overhead control account
£	£

Work in progress control account
£	£

Finished goods control account
£	£

Debtors control account
£	£

Creditors control account
£	£

Cash at bank account
£	£

cost bookkeeping

Administration overheads account

	£		£

Sales account

	£		£

chapter 8:
SHORT-TERM DECISION MAKING

1. When making decisions about production and sales in the short term, explain why contribution per unit is a more useful figure than total production cost per unit.

2. A business sells a single product and has budgeted sales of 115,000 units for the next period. The selling price per unit is £28 and the variable costs of production are £17. The fixed costs of the business are £1,100,000.

   a) What is the breakeven point in units?

   b) Calculate the margin of safety:

   i) in units
   ii) as a percentage of budgeted sales

3. The following information relates to one period for Product D which is manufactured by Mild Ltd.

   Expected sales revenue = £160,000
   Selling price per unit = £16 per unit
   Variable cost = £8 per unit
   Fixed costs = £40,000

   You are required to calculate the breakeven point both in terms of units and sales revenue.

4. The following information relates to one period for Product V which is manufactured by Hay-on-Wye Ltd.

   Selling price per unit = £80
   Variable cost per unit = £25
   Budgeted fixed costs = £110,000
   Budgeted sales = 2,500 units

   You are required to calculate the margin of safety, in terms of both units and sales revenue.

short-term decision making

5. A business sells a single product at a selling price of £83 and the variable costs of production and sales are £65 per unit. The fixed costs of the business are £540,000.

   How many units of the product must the business sell in order to make a target profit of £300,000?

6. A business sells its single product for £40. The variable costs of this product total £28. The fixed costs of the business are £518,000.

   What is the sales revenue required in order to make a target profit of £250,000?

7. A business produces three products. Production and sales details are given below:

	Product R	Product S	Product T
Direct materials @ £5 per kg	£20	£25	£15
Direct labour @ £7 per hour	£14	£21	£21
Selling price	£45	£60	£55
Machine hours per unit	4	3	2
Maximum sales demand	20,000 units	25,000 units	8,000 units

   During the next period the supply of materials is limited to 250,000 kgs, the labour hours available are 100,000 and the machine hours available are 180,000.

   What is the production plan which will maximise contribution and what is the contribution that will be earned under that production plan?

8. Pure Delight Ltd, is a company producing and selling three types of ice-cream sauce: fudge; butterscotch and chocolate. The expected monthly costs and sales information for each sauce is as follows.

Sauce	Fudge	Butterscotch	Chocolate
Sales and production (bottles)	500	700	600
Labour hours per month	60	50	40
Total sales revenue	£1,000	£1,400	£600
Total direct materials	£100	£175	£60
Total direct labour	£300	£350	£150
Total variable overheads	£25	£70	£30

   The total expected monthly fixed costs relating to the production of all sauces is £300.

a) You are required to complete the table below to show the profit volume ratio for each sauce.

Sauce	Fudge £	Butterscotch £	Chocolate £
Selling price per bottle			
Less: Unit variable costs			
Direct materials			
Direct labour			
Variable overheads			
Contribution per bottle			
Profit volume ratio (%)			

b) If the company only manufactures chocolate sauce, calculate the sales revenue that it would need to earn each month to cover the monthly fixed costs of £300.

chapter 9:
LONG-TERM DECISION MAKING

1 Explain what is meant by the time value of money.

2 Given below are the anticipated cash flows from investment in new plant and machinery that a business is considering.

		£
1 Jan 2009	Outflow	95,000
31 Dec 2009	Inflow	15,000
31 Dec 2010	Inflow	25,000
31 Dec 2011	Inflow	35,000
31 Dec 2012	Inflow	30,000
31 Dec 2013	Inflow	30,000

   a) The business policy is only to accept projects with a payback period of 3 years or less. On this basis would you advise the managers of the business to invest in this project?

   b) The business has a cost of capital of 10%. Calculate the net present value of the project. Would you now change your advice to the managers of the business?

   c) State any assumptions that you have made in parts a) and b).

   d) What might this situation indicate about the payback period method of investment appraisal?

3 Today's date is 1 April 2007. What is the present value of each of the following independent cash flows?

   a) Payment of £24,000 on 31 March 2009 – interest rate 7%
   b) Receipt of £1,500 on 31 March 2008, 2009 and 2010 – interest rate 12%
   c) Receipt of £2,000 every 31 March from 2008 onwards – interest rate 6%
   d) Payment of £30,000 on 1 April 2007 – interest rate 8%

long-term decision making

4 A company is considering the purchase of a small sole trader's business for a cost of £84,000 on 30 June 2009. The estimated cash inflows from the purchased business are:

	£
30 June 2010	26,000
30 June 2011	30,000
30 June 2012	21,000
30 June 2013	14,000

Thereafter the purchased business will be closed down and its operations merged with the other operations of the company.

The company has a cost of capital of 7% and analyses potential investments using the net present value method.

What would your advice be to the directors of the company concerning the purchase of the sole trader's business? Justify that advice.

5 The managers of a business are considering investing in a new factory. It has been estimated that the cost now would total £355,000. The anticipated profit for the factory for each of the next five years are as follows:

	Profit
	£
Year 1	47,000
Year 2	55,000
Year 3	68,000
Year 4	53,000
Year 5	22,000

The profit figures given are after charging depreciation of £60,000 in each year. The business has a cost of capital of 12%.

a) What is the net present value of the potential investment?
b) State any assumptions that you have made in your calculations.
c) What would be your advice to the managers about this potential investment?

long-term decision making

6. The managers of a business are considering investment in a new production line which would cost £180,000 on 1 October 2009. The estimated cash cost savings from the new production line are:

	£
30 Sept 2010	42,000
30 Sept 2011	50,000
30 Sept 2012	75,000
30 Sept 2013	80,000

By the end of September 2013 the production line will require replacing.

a) Calculate the NPV of the project at the company's cost of capital of 15%, and state whether the company should accept the project. Justify your conclusion.

b) The company may be able to obtain finance for the project with an interest rate of 10%. Re-evaluate whether the project is worthwhile at this new cost of capital.

c) The internal rate of return (IRR) of the project is 12.5%. Explain the meaning of the IRR and why this can be useful in project evaluation.

7. Confectioners Unlimited is a cake and ice-cream manufacturer. The company requires an annual rate of return of 15% on any new project. The Managing Director has asked you to appraise the financial effects of setting up a new ice-cream parlour. You are given the following information relating to this project.

	Year 1 £'000	Year 2 £'000	Year 3 £'000	Year 4 £'000	Year 5 £'000
Set-up costs	(160)				
Sales revenues		60	100	320	100
Variable costs		(30)	(50)	(160)	(50)
15% present value factor	0.8696	0.7561	0.6525	0.5718	0.4972

a) Calculate the following for the new project.
   i) The payback period, where cash flows are received at the end of each year.
   ii) The net present value.

b) Use the data from a) above to prepare a report for the Managing Director on the new ice-cream parlour. Your report should:
   i) recommend whether to accept or reject the project based on its net present value
   ii) recommend whether to accept or reject the project based on its Internal Rate of Return which you are told is approximately 26%.

long-term decision making

REPORT

To:

From:

Date:

chapter 10:
INTERNAL INFORMATION

1. Knight Industrial makes a range of electronic components in its factory. The factory employees clock in and out using clock cards and work a standard 35-hour week. Any hours that are worked in excess of the 35 hours are paid at time and a half if on a week day and double time at weekends.

   What type of information about the labour force would be likely to be required by the following personnel in the organisation?

   a) The factory Supervisor
   b) The Manufacturing Director
   c) The Managing Director

2. Outline the general requirements of useful information.

3. Give four examples of internal sources of business information.

4. Cost and management accounting is concerned entirely with providing information in the form of periodic performance reports or special 'one-off' reports. Give six examples of cost and management accounting information.

5. What would be the typical type of information that might be required by the partners in a firm of solicitors in order to appraise the performance of the firm for the last month?

6. Kenzo Stores has three shops in Abberville, Bacup and Calver. Given below are the summarised profit and loss accounts for the three stores for the month of July.

	Abberville	Bacup	Calver
	£	£	£
Sales	137,489	195,374	104,328
Cost of sales	53,621	72,288	41,731
Gross profit	83,868	123,086	62,597
Expenses	33,373	37,121	22,952
Net profit	50,495	85,965	39,645

   You are required to produce the consolidated profit and loss account figures for the three stores for the month of July.

chapter 11:
PERFORMANCE MEASURES

1. Distinguish between the terms production and productivity.

2. A manufacturing business has produced 330,000 of its product in the quarter ending 30 June at a total manufacturing cost of £567,900. The budgeted production for the quarter had been 350,000 units and the actual hours worked in the quarter were 12,600.

   In the quarter ending 31 March the budgeted production was 320,000 units and actual production was 332,000 units. This production level was achieved in 12,300 hours and the total cost of production in that quarter was £580,400.

   Calculate the following performance measures for the quarter ending 30 June and compare them to the same performance measures for the previous quarter:

   - cost per unit
   - labour productivity
   - productivity index

3. A mail order manufacturing business employs 280 factory employees and 27 telephone sales staff. For the month of July the following performance figures were available:

Units produced	128,700
Budgeted units	120,000
Manufacturing cost of units produced	£557,800
Factory labour hours	39,400
Telephone orders processed	9,180
Telephone sales department costs	£14,560

   From the information given produce a schedule that summarises the performance of the factory and the telephone sales department for the month.

4. Explain the difference between avoidable and unavoidable idle time.

performance measures

5 The number of labour hours worked and the number of idle time hours for a factory for the last six months was as follows:

	Jan	Feb	Mar	Apr	May	June
Hours worked	2,100	2,050	2,220	2,200	2,310	2,250
Idle time hours	90	80	20	100	120	100

The hours worked plus the idle time hours total to the number of hours available for work in the month.

Calculate the labour utilisation percentage for each of the six months to one decimal place.

6 You are given the following information about a business for the last three months:

	May	June	July
Sales	£360,000	£402,000	£398,000
Capital	£300,000	£310,000	£320,000
NBV of fixed assets	£210,000	£190,000	£200,000
Machine hours worked	28,000	32,000	31,000

For each of the three months calculate measures to indicate the fixed asset utilisation, machinery utilisation and capital utilisation or asset turnover.

7 What do you understand by the term return on capital employed?

8 Given below are the summarised profit and loss accounts for a business for the last three months:

	May £'000	June £'000	July £'000
Sales	1,320	1,420	1,500
Cost of sales	790	850	970
	530	570	530
Expenses	290	330	290
Net profit	240	240	240

The capital of the business was as follows for the three months:

	May £'000	June £'000	July £'000
Capital	2,600	2,840	3,080

Prepare a schedule showing the gross profit margin, net profit margin and return on capital employed for each of the three months, calculated to one decimal place, making brief comment as to what the performance measures indicate about the business.

performance measures

9 Given below is a variety of information about a manufacturing business for the last three months:

	May	June	July
Sales	£595,000	£600,000	£610,000
Manufacturing cost	£416,000	£402,000	£403,000
Expenses	£131,000	£144,000	£149,000
Number of units produced	220,000	215,000	216,000
Budgeted number of units	220,000	220,000	220,000
Hours worked	1,400	1,360	1,430
Budgeted hours	1,400	1,400	1,400
Net book value of fixed assets	£320,000	£300,000	£340,000
Capital	£460,000	£508,000	£562,000

You are required to calculate the following performance measures and to comment on the results that you find:

a) Cost per unit
b) Productivity per labour hour
c) Productivity index
d) Labour utilisation percentage
e) Fixed asset utilisation
f) Asset turnover (capital utilisation)
g) Gross profit margin
h) Net profit margin
i) Return on capital employed

10 S plc compares its 2009 results with 2008 results as follows.

	2009 £	2008 £
Sales	800,000	600,000
Cost of sales		
Direct materials	200,000	100,000
Direct labour	200,000	150,000
Production overhead	110,000	100,000
Marketing overhead	210,000	175,000
	720,000	525,000
Profit	80,000	75,000

Calculate the net profit margins for S plc for 2008 and 2009.

47

chapter 12:
WRITING A REPORT

1   What are the major elements of a report?

2   Given below are the summarised profit and loss account figures for the last six months for one shop that is part of a chain of retail stores.

	Jan £'000	Feb £'000	Mar £'000	Apr £'000	May £'000	June £'000
Sales	420	450	500	550	580	630
Cost of sales	248	261	285	310	325	345
Gross profit	172	189	215	240	255	285
Expenses	110	119	145	160	165	190
Net profit	62	70	70	80	90	95
Capital	660	720	780	810	840	900

Write a report on the profitability of the shop for the last six months for the Sales Director showing any performance indicators that can be calculated in an appendix.

Today's date is 19 August 20X7.

3   Given below are productivity details of the three manufacturing divisions of an organisation, which each produce the same product, for the last quarter.

	Division A	Division B	Division C
Number of units produced	400,000	240,000	300,000
Cost of manufacture	£1,248,000	£739,200	£915,000
Hours worked	14,000	8,000	10,400
Budgeted production – units	450,000	250,000	330,000
Budgeted hours	15,000	8,333	11,000

You are required to write a report commenting to the Manufacturing Director upon the productivity of the three divisions.

Today's date is 20 July 20X7.

chapter 13:
TABLES AND DIAGRAMS

1   Significant digits

State 2,197.283 correct to:

a)   six significant digits
b)   five significant digits
c)   four significant digits

2   Decimal places

State 38.1784 correct to:

a)   three decimal places
b)   two decimal places
c)   one decimal place

3   Independent variable

What is an independent variable and which axis on a graph represents it?

4   Scattergraph

What is a scattergraph?

tables and diagrams

5 You are given the following information about a company for the last four months.

	June £	July £	Aug £	Sept £
Sales	48,700	50,200	45,600	46,800
Cost of sales	30,200	31,600	29,200	30,000
Expenses	12,200	12,500	11,400	11,700
Capital	52,500	52,500	55,000	55,000

a) Prepare a computer spreadsheet which will calculate the following performance measures by inserting appropriate formulae for:

   i) gross profit percentage
   ii) net profit percentage
   iii) return on capital employed
   iv) asset turnover

	A	B	C	D	E
1		June	July	August	September
2	Sales				
3	Cost of sales				
4	Gross profit				
5	Expenses				
6	Net profit				
7	Capital				
8	Gross profit %				
9	Net profit %				
10	ROCE				
11	Asset turnover				

b) Show the amount for these performance measures that appear once the spreadsheet is completed.

	A	B	C	D	E
1		June	July	August	September
2	Sales				
3	Cost of sales				
4	Gross profit				
5	Expenses				
6	Net profit				
7	Capital				
8	Gross profit %				
9	Net profit %				
10	ROCE				
11	Asset turnover				

tables and diagrams

6   A manufacturing business has produced 330,000 of its product in the quarter ending 30 June at a total manufacturing cost of £567,900. The budgeted production for the quarter had been 350,000 units and the actual hours worked in the quarter were 12,600.

In the quarter ending 31 March the budgeted production was 320,000 units and actual product was 332,000 units. This production level was achieved in 12,300 hours and the total cost of production in the quarter was £580,400.

Tabulate this information on a computer spreadsheet and insert appropriate formulae in order that the following performance indicators can be calculated for each quarter:

a) Cost per unit
b) Labour productivity
c) Productivity index

	A	B	C	D	E
1					
2					
3					
4					
5					
6					
7					
8					
9					
10					
11					

7   Given below are the sales figures for a business for each of the last six months.

	Feb £'000	Mar £'000	Apr £'000	May £'000	June £'000	July £'000
Sales	320	300	360	400	350	310

You are to show these sales figures in a simple bar chart.

53

tables and diagrams

8 Given below are the summarised profit and loss figures for a business for the last three years:

	30 June 20X5 £'000	30 June 20X6 £'000	30 June 20X7 £'000
Sales	280	350	400
Cost of sales	175	200	220
Gross profit	105	150	180
Expenses	60	70	80
Net profit	45	80	100

Show the sales, gross profit and net profit for each of the three years in a compound bar chart.

9 Given below are the sales figures for each of the three divisions of a company for four quarters.

	To 30 Sept 2006 £'000	To 31 Dec 2006 £'000	To 31 Mar 2007 £'000	To 30 June 2007 £'000
Division A	160	180	220	250
Division B	150	120	100	100
Division C	120	140	150	170
	430	440	470	520

You are to show the sales for each division for each quarter in a component bar chart.

10 Given below are the profit figures for three hotels owned by a business for the last three years:

	2007 £'000	2008 £'000	2009 £'000
Royal Hotel	320	350	300
Mermaid Hotel	110	70	50
Crown Hotel	290	340	320

You are to illustrate these figures in the following ways:

a) Show the total profit for the three years in a simple bar chart
b) Show the breakdown of profit between the hotels in a compound bar chart
c) Show the breakdown of the profit between the hotels in a component bar chart

tables and diagrams

11 Given below is a breakdown of the costs of a manufacturing business for the last three months:

	May £'000	June £'000	July £'000
Production costs	400	500	460
Selling and distribution costs	120	250	160
Administration costs	100	140	180
Finance costs	50	50	150
	670	940	950

You are to illustrate the breakdown of these costs in a pie chart for each of the three months.

12 Present the following information in the form of a table, including in your table the percentage changes in the volume of UK car sales of different origins of manufacture and overall between the first quarter of 2006 and the first quarter of 2007.

453,000 cars were sold in the United Kingdom during the first three months of 2007: this is an increase of 46,000 on the same period one year earlier. Of these 453,000 vehicles, 205,000 were made in Britain, with 188,000 coming from the rest of the European Union (EU). Cars built in Japan made up 41,000 of the 453,000 total. Imports from countries other than EU members and Japan comprised 19,000 cars in the first quarter of 2007. This compares with a figure of 18,000 cars originating in these other countries for the same period one year earlier. In the first quarter of 2005, 184,000 of cars built in Britain were sold in the UK. In this period, UK car sales included 166,000 vehicles imported from the rest of the EU and 39,000 vehicles imported from Japan.

tables and diagrams

13 M, N, O, P, Q and R are operatives employed in the sheet metal work department of AT Engineering Ltd, whose records for the week ended 12 June show their attendance, in hours, as follows.

	Mon	Tue	Wed	Thu	Fri	Sat
M	8	8	9	9	8	4
N	9	8	10	8	4	
O	8	8	8	8	8	
P	9	10	9	10	9	4
Q	10	9	10	9	10	4
R	8	4	6	8	8	

Hours worked in excess of eight on Mondays to Fridays are paid at basic hourly rate plus one third, and all hours worked on Saturdays are paid at double the basic rate.

The basic hourly rates for each operative are as follows.

M, O and R   £7.20
N and P   £7.50
Q   £8.40

a) Prepare a statement showing the wages of each of the six operatives and the total wages for the week ended 12 June.

b) Using the total wages of all six operatives, calculate the weighted average wages cost, to the nearest penny, per operative hour.

chapter 14:
REPORTING FIGURES OVER TIME

1 Averages

Write brief notes explaining the following terms to a colleague.

a) The mean
b) The median
c) Time series

2 Given below are the number of customers served in a restaurant each day for the last seven days:

Sunday	159
Monday	62
Tuesday	55
Wednesday	86
Thursday	104
Friday	168
Saturday	192

What is the average number of customers each day?

3 Given below are the monthly sales figures for a business during a certain period:

	£
July 2006	337,600
August 2006	415,300
September 2006	289,500
October 2006	266,400
November 2006	198,700
December 2006	258,600
January 2007	177,200
February 2007	199,300
March 2007	222,900
April 2007	256,100
May 2007	265,800
June 2007	365,700

Calculate a three-month moving average for these sales figures.

reporting figures over time

4 Given below are the weekly production costs for the first 16 weeks of the year for a manufacturing business:

Week	Costs £
1	128,500
2	195,400
3	148,600
4	177,800
5	137,500
6	165,700
7	148,200
8	183,400
9	177,300
10	164,700
11	155,400
12	193,600
13	158,100
14	174,500
15	162,900
16	159,400

Calculate a four-week moving average for these production figures.

5 Using the figures from the previous activity, prepare a computer spreadsheet to calculate the four-week moving average.

	A	B	C	D
1				
2				
3				
4				
5				
6				
7				
8				
9				
10				
11				
12				
13				
14				
15				
16				
17				
18				
19				
20				
21				
22				
23				
24				
25				
26				
27				
28				
29				
30				
31				

reporting figures over time

6 Given below are the monthly production cost figures for a small manufacturing business:

20X6	£
January	55,600
February	52,700
March	56,100
April	56,800
May	58,300
June	60,500
July	58,900
August	59,200
September	61,300
October	62,100
November	63,400
December	62,700

20X7	
January	61,300
February	62,500
March	64,100
April	65,200
May	64,900
June	66,700

You are required to:

a) calculate a three-month moving average in order to show the trend of these figures
b) plot the monthly figures and the trend line on a graph.

7 Explain the difference between interpolation and extrapolation.

8 What is a price index?

reporting figures over time

9 Given below are the sales figures for a business for the last year:

20X6	£
August	527,500
September	513,400
October	556,700
November	523,400
December	582,300
20X7	
January	561,300
February	532,600
March	524,300
April	515,700
May	529,600
June	538,200

Using August 20X6 as the base month with an index of 100, show the index for each of the subsequent month's sales.

10 Sales for V plc over five years were as follows.

Year	Sales
	£'000
2003	35
2004	42
2005	40
2006	45
2007	50

V plc's Managing Director decides that he wants to set up a sales index (ie an index which measures how sales have done from year to year), using 2003 as the base year. The £35,000 of sales in 2003 is given the index 100%. What are the indices for the other years?

reporting figures over time

11 Given below are the sales for a business for the first eight months of the year together with the Retail Price Index for that month:

	£	RPI
January	162,400	171.1
February	163,800	172.0
March	165,900	172.2
April	167,200	173.0
May	166,200	172.1
June	164,100	171.3
July	162,300	171.0
August	160,500	170.3

a) Calculate the RPI adjusted sales figures for the eight months with prices being reflected in terms of January prices.

b) Using the RPI adjusted sales figures produce an index for the sales for each month with January as the base period.

c) Prepare a computer spreadsheet which will calculate the RPI adjusted index by inserting appropriate formulae.

	A	B	C	D	E
1					
2					
3					
4					
5					
6					
7					
8					

12 The following data relates to an express passenger coach service operator over the three years 2005 to 2007. The operation faced new competition on its main routes from another coach company in 2007.

	2005	2006	2007
Total passenger kilometres	54,748,148	61,273,617	64,788,492
Total loaded coach kilometres	1,921,261	1,964,325	1,981,380
Total receipts (fares) (£)	3,119,842	3,799,421	4,145,014
Total operating expenses (£)	2,327,452	2,458,123	2,531,770

Notes. Loaded coach kilometres represent distance travelled when coaches are in service. Coaches have a full capacity of either 46 or 48 passengers.

reporting figures over time

You are required from the information above, calculate the following performance indicators for each of the three years.

a) Receipts per loaded coach kilometre (in pounds, to two decimal places)

b) Receipts per passenger kilometre (in pence, to one decimal place)

c) Passenger kilometres per loaded coach kilometre (average coach load) (in number of passengers, to one decimal place)

d) Total operating expenses per loaded coach kilometre (in pounds, to two decimal places)

13 a) Adjust the indicators you have calculated in Activity 12 to real terms, where it is appropriate to do so, using the following price index.

	Index
2005	93.2
2006	96.1
2007	100.0

b) Comment briefly on trends in the performance indicators you have calculated.

chapter 15:
EXTERNAL REPORTING

1 Name as many of the thirteen 'themes' included in the government's National Statistics as you can remember.

2 Given below is a grant application form for a grant from the local authority:

BARDEN LOCAL DISTRICT COUNCIL
GRANT APPLICATION

PART 1 BUSINESS DETAILS

Business name ....

....

Business address ....

....

....

Business telephone ....

Business fax ....

Owner's name ....

....

E-mail address ....

Type of business ....

....

....

....

PART 2 FINANCIAL DETAILS

2A TURNOVER AND PROFIT

Figures are to be provided for annual turnover and reported net profit for the last three complete financial years

Financial year ended:	UK turnover £	Export turnover £	Net profit £
Month Year			

2B WORKING CAPITAL

Figures are to be provided for working capital at the end of the most recent financial year.

Year ending:

£

Current assets   ....

Minus: current liabilities   ....

Working capital   ....

2C FIXED ASSETS

Figures are to be provided for fixed asset totals at the end of the most recent financial year.

Year ending:

£

Land and buildings   ....

Plant and machinery   ....

Other   ....

Total fixed assets   ....

PART 3 NON FINANCIAL DETAILS

3A EMPLOYMENT DETAILS

Figures are to be provided for the number of employees for the last three financial years.

Financial year ended:	Number of full time employees	Number of part time employees
Month Year		

3B BUSINESS DETAILS

Date business started: ....

Business type -   Sole trader   ☐
                  Partnership   ☐
                  Company   ☐

PART 4 GRANT APPLICATION

Indicate in the space provided the reasons for the grant application. If the grant application is processed further more detail will be requested at a later date.

....
....
....
....
....
....
....

external reporting

You work for a partnership called D & G Harper which was set up in 1998 by David and Gareth Harper to manufacture curtains and blinds, largely for businesses. The business is run on a day-to-day basis by David Harper and in the year ended 30 June 2007 employed 14 full-time employees and three part-time employees. The business expanded in the year ended 30 June 2006 and in that year five more full-time employees were taken on and two part-time employees.

The grant application is for £15,000 to help fund additional factory space and the potential employment of potentially six additional full-time employees.

The business is run from Harper House, East Park Road, Barden, BD4 6GK and the telephone number and fax number are 02185 3743 and 02185 3264 respectively. The e-mail address used by David and Gareth is dgh@dandgharper.co.uk.

You have been asked to complete the grant application form prior to it being signed and checked by David Harper. From the accounting records you have been able to find summaries of the profit and loss accounts for the last three years and a summarised balance sheet as at 30 June 2007.

Summarised profit and loss accounts

	Y/e 30 June 2005 £	Y/e 30 June 2006 £	Y/e 30 June 2007 £
UK sales	378,690	735,400	882,400
Export sales	10,580	38,600	48,340
	389,270	774,000	930,740
Cost of sales	210,580	387,400	446,750
	178,690	386,600	483,990
Expenses	104,580	224,060	279,220
Net profit	74,110	162,540	204,770

Summarised balance sheet as at 30 June 2007

	£	£	£
Fixed assets:			
Land and buildings			184,500
Machinery			190,400
Cars			84,500
Office equipment			13,200
			472,600
Current assets:			
Stock of fabrics		28,400	
Debtors		65,400	
Cash at bank		3,670	
		97,470	
Current liabilities:			
Trade creditors	38,600		
PAYE/NIC	3,570		
		42,170	
			55,300
			527,900

You are required to complete the grant application form ready for checking and signature.

external reporting

3 You work as an Accounting Technician for a medium-sized building firm with a turnover for the year ended 30 June 2009 of £367,400 and for the previous year of £283,400. The net profit made in the year ended 30 June 2007 was £48,414 compared to £39,382 for the previous year. The owner of the business is confident that turnover and profits will continue to increase in the foreseeable future. All of the business takes place in the UK.

You are required to complete the Chamber of Commerce Annual Economic Review that has been sent to your business in order to aid in the collection of National Statistics.

CHAMBER OF COMMERCE
ANNUAL ECONOMIC REVIEW

Please tick the appropriate box in answer to each question – all answers will be treated in the strictest confidence. All answers should be based upon the business performance for the last full financial year.

1 BUSINESS DETAILS

End of last full financial year:

Turnover range:

Up to £50,000 ☐
£50,000 - £100,000 ☐
£100,000 - £250,000 ☐
£250,000 - £500,000 ☐
£500,000 - £1,000,000 ☐
Over £1,000,000 ☐

Main business activity:

Engineering	☐	Health	☐
Construction	☐	Art and design	☐
Agriculture	☐	Transport	☐
Energy	☐	Tourism	☐
Retail	☐	Other (please state)	
Education	☐	....	

external reporting

2 TURNOVER

Percentage of total turnover accounted for by export sales:

0%	☐	30% to 50%	☐
up to 10%	☐	50% to 75%	☐
10% to 20%	☐	75% to 100%	☐
20% to 30%	☐		

Percentage increase/decrease in turnover compared to previous financial year:

Decrease Up to 20%	☐	Increase Up to 20%	☐
Decrease of 20% to 50%	☐	Increase of 20% to 50%	☐
Decrease of more than 50%	☐	Increase of more than 50%	☐

Percentage increase/decrease in net profit compared to previous financial year:

Decrease Up to 20%	☐	Increase Up to 20%	☐
Decrease of 20% to 50%	☐	Increase of 20% to 50%	☐
Decrease of more than 50%	☐	Increase of more than 50%	☐

3 BUSINESS CONFIDENCE

Do you consider that over the following 12 months:

Turnover	will increase	☐	Profitability	will increase	☐
	remain the same	☐		remain the same	☐
	decrease	☐		decrease	☐

chapter 16:
VALUE ADDED TAX

1 Complete the following sentences:

a) From 1 May 2009 the VAT registration threshold is £ ....

b) From 1 May 2009 the VAT deregistration limit is £ .... for taxable supplies

c) VAT on purchases is known as .... tax

d) VAT on sales is known as .... tax

e) A VAT return is normally completed every .... months

2 What are the three rates of VAT in the UK currently?

....

....

....

3 A business has made purchases during a month of £13,500 plus VAT. What is the total cost of these purchases for each of the following businesses and why?

a) A business that makes exempt supplies

b) A business that makes zero-rated supplies

....

....

4 Why might a business register for VAT even if its turnover has not reached the VAT registration limit?

....

....

....

value added tax

5 A VAT registered business has made the following purchases:

    a) A car for use by the Sales Manager for £14,200 plus VAT
    b) A business lunch for clients costing £120 plus VAT.

What is the cost to the business of each of these expenses and why?

....

....

6 What is the tax point in each of the following situations and is it a basic tax point or an actual tax point?

    a) An invoice is dispatched to a customer on 13 August 2009 and the goods are delivered the following day.

    b) Goods are delivered on 15 August 2009 and the invoice is sent to the customer on 31 August 2009.

    c) Services are provided to a customer on 8 August 2009 and an invoice is sent out on 12 August 2009.

    d) A customer pays for goods on 20 August 2009 and the goods are delivered two days later.

....

....

....

....

7 Calculate the amount of VAT that should be charged in each of the following situations:

    a) Goods sold for £146.80 plus VAT

    b) Goods sold for £220.00 plus VAT less a trade discount of 10%

    c) Goods sold for £200.00 plus VAT with a settlement discount of 3% offered

    d) Goods sold for £320.00 plus VAT less a trade discount of 20% and a settlement discount of 2%

....

....

....

....

value added tax

8 Calculate the VAT and the net of VAT amount in each of the following.

a) £432.16 including VAT
b) £262.77 including VAT
c) £216.90 including VAT
d) £310.18 including VAT

....

....

....

....

9 Explain what details would appear on a less detailed VAT invoice for a retail sale of less than £100.00.

....

....

....

....

10 Clipper Ltd holds the following invoices from suppliers.

a)

VAT reg no 446 9989 57	Jupiter plc
Date: 4 January 2008	1 London Road
Tax point: 4 January 2008	Reading
Invoice no.	RL3 7CM

Clippers Ltd
13 Gale Road
Chester-le-Street
NE1 1LB

Sales of goods

Type	Quantity	VAT rate %	Net £
Earrings @ £0.5 per unit	2,700	17.5	1,350.00
Earring studs @ £0.5 per unit	2,800	17.5	1,400.00
			2,750.00
VAT at 17.5%			457.19
Payable within 60 days			3,207.19
Less 5% discount if paid within 14 days			137.50
			3,069.69

73

value added tax

b)

HILLSIDE LTD
'The Glasgow Based Supplier of Quality Jewellery Items'

VAT reg no 337 4849 26

Clipper Ltd
13 Gale Road
Chester-le-Street
NE1 1LB

Invoice no. 0010
Date: 10 August 2008
Tax point: 10 August 2008

	£
Sale of 4,000 Jewellery boxes @ £2 per unit	8,000
VAT at 17.5%	1,450
Total	9,450

Terms: strictly net 30 days

c)

GENEROUS PLC

11 Low Fell
Leeds
LS1 XY2

Clipper Ltd
13 Gale Road
Chester-le-Street
NE1 1LB

Invoice no: 2221
Date: 12 December 2008
Tax point: 12 December 2008

	Net £	VAT £	Total £
4,000 Earrings @ £0.5 per unit	2,000.00	350.00	2,350.00
8,000 Brooches @ £0.3125 per unit	2,500.00	437.50	2,937.50
2,500 'How to make Jewellery' books @ £2 per book	5,000.00	0.00	5,000.00
	9,500.00	787.50	10,287.50

d)
> **JEWELS & CO**
>
> 101 High Street, Gateshead NE2 22P
>
> VAT reg no 499 3493 27
>
> Date: 2 January 2008
>
> 30 necklaces sold for £4 each totalling £120.00 including VAT at 17.5%.

For each of the above invoices, state whether it is a valid VAT invoice. Give your reasons.

chapter 17:
VAT RECORDS

1 Peter Perfect runs a retail business supplying both tradespeople and the general public, and is registered for VAT. He does not use the cash accounting scheme or any retail scheme.

Peter had the following transactions in the quarter ended 31 March 2009.

Date	Type	Net amount £	VAT rate %
2 January	Sale	6,237	17.5
4 January	Purchase	9,950	17.5
4 January	Sale	14,850	0.0
7 January	Purchase	5,792	17.5
10 January	Sale	19,008	17.5
21 January	Sale	2,079	0.0
2 February	Sale	29,700	0.0
14 February	Purchases returned	743	17.5
14 February	Sale	3,416	0.0
16 February	Purchase	8,168	17.5
27 February	Sales returned	1,188	0.0
1 March	Sale	1,084	17.5
13 March	Purchases returned	178	17.5
17 March	Sale	2,525	0.0
31 March	Sales returned	505	17.5

All returns of goods are evidenced by credit notes for both the net price and (where applicable) the VAT. All returns related to current period transactions, except for the return on 14 February.

On the previous period's VAT return, output VAT was overstated by £700 and input VAT was understated by £800. These errors are to be corrected through the VAT account for this quarter.

You are required to prepare Peter's VAT account for the quarter.

VAT records

2 In the quarter ended 31 March 2009, Control plc made sales as follows. All amounts given exclude any VAT.

	£
Standard rated sales	6,000,000
Zero rated sales	1,500,000
Exempt sales	2,800,000

The VAT on purchases attributable to standard rated and zero rated sales was £600,000. The VAT on purchases attributable to exempt sales was £258,000. In addition, VAT on purchases not attributable to any particular type of sale was £96,000.

Included in standard rated sales was £20,000 for the sale of plant no longer required by the business.

You are required to compute the amount payable to or recoverable from HM Revenue & Customs in respect of the quarter.

3 Given below is information about the VAT of a business that has been taken from the books of prime entry:

VAT figures

	£
From the sales day book	3,474.89
From the sales returns day book	441.46
From the purchases day book	2,485.61
From the purchases returns day book	210.68
From the cash receipts book	993.57
From the cash payments book	624.78
EU acquisitions	925.47

Write up the VAT control account.

VAT account	
£	£

4 Given below is information about the VAT of a business taken from the books of prime entry:

	£
From the sales day book	6,275.78
From the sales returns day book	726.58
From the purchases day book	4,668.14
From the purchases returns day book	510.36
From the cash receipts book	1,447.30
From the cash payments book	936.47
EU acquisitions	772.46
Bad debt relief	284.67
VAT underpaid in a previous period	126.57
VAT overpaid in a previous period	221.68

You are to write up the VAT control account.

VAT account

	£		£

VAT records

5 Given below are extracts from the books of prime entry for a business Waltzer Enterprises, Adam Industrial Park, Yarden, LR3 9GS. The business's VAT registration number is 234 4576 12 and the tax period is April 2009 to June 2009.

Sales day book summary

	Zero-rated sales £	Standard rated sales £	VAT £	Total £
Total	3,628.47	57,615.80	10,082.76	71,327.03

Purchases day book summary

	Zero-rated purchases £	Standard rated purchases £	VAT £	Total £
EU acquisitions		1,572.45	275.17	1,847.62
UK purchases	2,636.47	33,672.57	5,892.69	42,201.73

Sales returns day book summary

	Zero-rated sales £	Standard rated sales £	VAT £	Total £
Total	236.34	4,782.57	836.94	5,855.85

Purchases returns day book summary

	Zero-rated purchases £	Standard rated purchases £	VAT £	Total £
Total	125.34	3,184.57	557.29	3,867.20

Cash receipts book summary

	Net £	VAT £	Total £
Cash sales	5,325.65	931.98	6,257.63

Cash payments book summary

	Net £	VAT £	Total £
Cash purchases	3,157.46	552.55	3,710.01

You are required to complete the VAT return given.

Value Added Tax Return
For the period
01 04 09 to 30 06 09

For Official Use

Registration number | Period

You could be liable to a financial penalty if your completed return and all the VAT payable are not received by the due date.

Due date:

For Official Use

If you have a general enquiry or need advice please call our National Advice Service on 0845 010 9000

ATTENTION

If this return and any tax due are not received by the due date you may be liable to a surcharge.

If you make supplies of goods to another EC Member State you are required to complete an EC Sales List (VAT 101).

Before you fill in this form please read the notes on the back and the VAT Leaflet "*Filling in your VAT return*" and "*Flat rate schemes for small businesses*", if you use the scheme. Fill in all boxes clearly in ink, and write 'none' where necessary. Don't put a dash or leave any box blank. If there are no pence write "00" in the pence column. Do not enter more than one amount in any box.

For official use			£	p
	VAT due in this period on sales and other outputs	1		
	VAT due in this period on acquisitions from other EC Member States	2		
	Total VAT due (the sum of boxes 1 and 2)	3		
	VAT reclaimed in this period on purchases and other inputs (including acquisitions from the EC)	4		
	Net VAT to be paid to Customs or reclaimed by you (Difference between boxes 3 and 4)	5		
	Total value of sales and all other outputs excluding any VAT. Include your box 8 figure	6		00
	Total value of purchases and all other inputs excluding any VAT. Include your box 9 figure	7		00
	Total value of all supplies of goods and related services, excluding any VAT, to other EC Member States	8		00
	Total value of all acquisitions of goods and related services, excluding any VAT, from other EC Member States	9		00

If you are enclosing a payment please tick this box.

DECLARATION: You, or someone on your behalf, must sign below.

I, _____ declare that the
(Full name of signatory in BLOCK LETTERS)
information given above is true and complete.

Signature _____ Date _____ 20 ____

A false declaration can result in prosecution.

VAT records

6 What would you do if you discovered that your business had made an error on an earlier VAT return which was more than £10,000 (and 1% of turnover)?

....
....
....
....
....
....

7 Explain how the annual accounting scheme for VAT works.

....
....
....
....
....
....
....
....
....
....
....
....
....
....
....
....
....
....
....
....

VAT records

8 Zag plc had the following sales and purchases in the three months ended 30 June 2009. All amounts exclude any VAT, and all transactions were with United Kingdom traders.

	£
Sales	
Standard-rated	877,500
Zero-rated	462,150
Exempt	327,600
Purchases	
Standard-rated	
Attributable to taxable supplies	585,000
Attributable to exempt supplies	146,250
Unattributable	468,000
Zero-rated	8,190
Exempt	15,405

You are required to compute the figures which would be entered in boxes 1 to 5 of Zag plc's VAT return given for the period.

VAT records

Value Added Tax Return
For the period
01 04 09 to 30 06 09

For Official Use

Registration number | Period

You could be liable to a financial penalty if your completed return and all the VAT payable are not received by the due date.

Due date:

For Official Use

ATTENTION

If this return and any tax due are not received by the due date you may be liable to a surcharge.

If you make supplies of goods to another EC Member State you are required to complete an EC Sales List (VAT 101).

If you have a general enquiry or need advice please call our National Advice Service on 0845 010 9000

Before you fill in this form please read the notes on the back and the VAT Leaflet "*Filling in your VAT return*" and "*Flat rate schemes for small businesses*", if you use the scheme. Fill in all boxes clearly in ink, and write 'none' where necessary. Don't put a dash or leave any box blank. If there are no pence write "00" in the pence column. Do not enter more than one amount in any box.

			£	p
For official use	VAT due in this period on sales and other outputs	1		
	VAT due in this period on acquisitions from other EC Member States	2		
	Total VAT due (the sum of boxes 1 and 2)	3		
	VAT reclaimed in this period on purchases and other inputs (including acquisitions from the EC)	4		
	Net VAT to be paid to Customs or reclaimed by you (Difference between boxes 3 and 4)	5		
	Total value of sales and all other outputs excluding any VAT. Include your box 8 figure	6		00
	Total value of purchases and all other inputs excluding any VAT. Include your box 9 figure	7		00
	Total value of all supplies of goods and related services, excluding any VAT, to other EC Member States	8		00
	Total value of all acquisitions of goods and related services, excluding any VAT, from other EC Member States	9		00

If you are enclosing a payment please tick this box.

DECLARATION: You, or someone on your behalf, must sign below.

I, _____ declare that the
(Full name of signatory in BLOCK LETTERS)
information given above is true and complete.

Signature_____ Date _____ 20 _____
A false declaration can result in prosecution.

PRACTICE EXAM 1
UNIT 6

FLY 4 LESS PLC

These tasks were set by the AAT in December 2008.

Time allowed: 3 hours plus 15 minutes' reading time

practice exam 1 – unit 6

This exam paper is in TWO sections.

You must show competence in BOTH sections. So, try to complete EVERY task in BOTH sections.

Section 1 contains 6 tasks and Section 2 contains 5 tasks.

You should spend about 90 minutes on each section.

You should include all essential workings and calculations in your answers.

Both Sections 1 and 2 are based on the information below about Fly 4 Less plc (F4L).

DATA

For the past three years you have been employed as an accounting technician with Fly 4 Less plc (F4L).

The company is an airline that provides low cost scheduled and charter flights throughout Europe.

You report to the Chief Accountant.

F4L recovers its costs on the basis of the number of air miles flown. Its profit per mile is the difference between its income from fares and its total operating costs.

It has two profit and three cost centres that relate to its operations:

Flights' profit centres

- **Scheduled services**
  Scheduled services operate on a fixed daily timetable and are available for anyone to book directly via the company's website or indirectly through a travel agent or other third party.

- **Charter flights**
  Charter flights are flights that are exclusively booked by a holiday travel operator. The travel operator's customers are flown to and from their holidays as part of an overall holiday package.

Support cost centres

- Aircraft maintenance and repairs
- Fuel and parts store
- General administration

The company's year end is 30 November.

The data and tasks cover activities during November and December 2008.

SECTION 1 (Suggested time allowance: 90 minutes)

Task 1.1

The stock record card, shown below, for aviation fuel has only been fully completed up until 26 November.

a) Enter the following two transactions in the stock record card (showing the cost per litre in pence to 2 decimal places)

    27 November: received 200,000 litres at a total cost of   £184,000
    28 November: issued 180,000 litres to the fleet with a total cost of   £162,000

b) Identify the stock issue method being used for costing issues of aviation fuel to the fleet.

_____

_____

c) Complete ALL entries in the stock record card for the remaining two transactions in the month and for the closing balance at the end of November.

Stock record card for aviation fuel

Date	Receipts Quantity Litres	Receipts Cost per Litre (£)	Receipts Total cost (£)	Issues Quantity Litres	Issues Cost per Litre (£)	Issues Total cost (£)	Balance Quantity Litres	Balance Total cost £
Balance as at 26 Nov							220,000	198,000
27 Nov							420,000	382,000
28 Nov								
29 Nov	100,000		94,000					
30 Nov				260,000				

practice exam 1 – unit 6

DATA

The following extracts are from F4L's stock control policy:

- Aviation fuel should be re-ordered in quantities between 100,000 and 200,000 litres depending on the Economic Order Quantity (EOQ) at the time.
- The minimum balance of aviation fuel to be held in stock is 150,000 litres.

Task 1.2

Write an email to the Chief Accountant in which you explain:

a) whether F4L's stock control policy for aviation fuel re-ordering has been complied with

b) the purpose of calculating an EOQ (you are NOT required to produce either a formula or calculations).

Email

To:
From:
Subject:
Date:

practice exam 1 – unit 6

DATA

The payroll for maintenance employees for the week ending 30 November has been completed. The following payments are to be made:

	£
Net wages/salaries to pay to employees	10,000
Income tax and national insurance contributions (NIC) to pay to HMRC	2,000
Pension contributions to pay to F4L pension scheme	1,000
Gross payroll costs	13,000

The payroll for the week is analysed as:

	£
Direct labour costs	7,000
Indirect labour costs	4,000
Maintenance administration labour costs	2,000
Gross payroll costs	13,000

The following cost account codes are used to record maintenance labour costs:

Code	Description
6200	Maintenance direct labour
6400	Maintenance overheads
6600	Maintenance administration
8200	Wages control

Task 1.3

a) Complete the wages control account entries in the account shown below:

Wages control account

Debit	£	Credit	£
Bank (net wages/salaries)		Maintenance (direct labour)	
HMRC (income tax and NIC)		Maintenance overheads	
Pension contributions		Maintenance administration	
	13,000		13,000

practice exam 1 – unit 6

b) Complete the table below to show how the gross payroll cost for the week is charged to the various cost accounts of the business:

Date	Code	DR	CR
30 November			
30 November			
30 November			
30 November			
30 November			
30 November			

DATA

F4L has budgeted for the following overheads for its two profit and three cost centres for Quarter 1 of the next financial year:

	£'000	£'000
Depreciation of aircraft		36,400
Aviation fuel and other variable costs		42,200
Pilots and aircrew salaries:		
Scheduled services	5,250	
Charter flights	4,709	
Total pilots and aircrew salaries		9,959
Rent and rates and other premises costs		12,600
Indirect labour costs:		
Aircraft maintenance and repairs	9,600	
Fuel and parts store	3,200	
General administration	7,800	
Total indirect labour cost		20,600

The following information is also available:

Profit/cost centre	Net book value of aircraft £000	Planned number of miles flown	Floor space (square metres)	Number of employees
Scheduled services	1,080,000	215,600		105
Charter flights	720,000	176,400		96
Aircraft maintenance and repairs			190,000	260
Fuel and parts store			114,000	146
General administration			76,000	220
Total	1,800,000	392,000	380,000	827

Primary allocations or apportionments are made on the most appropriate basis. The support cost centres are then reapportioned to the two flight profit centres using the direct method.

- The Aircraft maintenance and repairs cost centre spends 60% of its time maintaining the aircraft in the scheduled services profit centre and the remainder in the charter flights profit centre.
- 55% of the issues from the Fuel and parts store cost centre is made to the scheduled services profit centre and the remainder to the Charter flights profit centre.
- The Scheduled services profit centre and the Charter flights profit centre both incur general administration costs equally.
- The three support cost centres are not involved in reciprocal servicing.

Task 1.4

Use the following table to allocate or apportion the overheads between the profit/cost centres, using the most appropriate basis.

	Basis of apportionment	Scheduled services £000	Charter flights £000	Aircraft maintenance and repairs £000	Fuel and parts store £000	General admin £000	Totals £000
Depreciation of aircraft							
Aviation fuel and other variable costs							
Pilots' and aircrews' salaries							
Rent and rates and other premises costs							
Indirect labour							
Totals							
Reapportion aircraft maintenance and repairs							
Reapportion fuel and parts store							
Reapportion general admin							
Total overheads to profit centres							

Task 1.5

Both profit centres absorb (recover) their overheads on the basis of the cost per planned mile flown.

Using your answers from Task 1.4 and the information above, calculate the overhead absorption rates for both profit centres (to the nearest whole £).

Workings

practice exam 1 – unit 6

DATA

During the first week of December 2008 the actual number of miles flown by one of the charter flights' aircraft was 6,890 miles.

The actual overheads incurred were £2,079,000.

Task 1.6

a) Using the information above and your answers from Task 1.5, calculate the actual overhead absorbed by the aircraft in the first week of December 2008 (to the nearest whole £).

b) Calculate the under- or over-absorbed overheads for the week (to the nearest whole £). Clearly state whether the overheads are under- or over-absorbed.

c) Explain how the under- or over-absorbed overheads will be recorded in the company's profit and loss account in December, and what effect this will have on the reported profit.

practice exam 1 – unit 6

SECTION 2 (Suggested time allowance: 90 minutes)

DATA

The charter flights profit centre has just revised its forecasts for the number of miles it expects to fly during the next month on a particular charter contract. Originally it expected the contract would be for flights totalling 5,000 miles. F4L now expects that the total miles to be flown will increase to either 6,000 or 7,000 miles.

Notes

- The company chartering the flights has negotiated with F4L a reduction of 10% per mile, paid on all miles flown in excess of the 5,000 miles agreed in the original contract.
- Landing and servicing fees are a semi-variable cost. There is a fixed charge of £600,000 plus £50/mile.

Task 2.1

a) Use the table below to estimate the profit per mile (in pounds, to 2 decimal places) of this contract at both 6,000 and 7,000 miles flown.

Likely miles	5,000	6,000	7,000
	£'000	£'000	£'000
Sales revenue	2,500		
Variable/semi-variable costs:			
Aviation fuel	400		
Landing and servicing fees	850		
Other variable overheads	135		
Fixed costs:			
Wages and salaries	420		
Other fixed overheads	625		
Total cost	2,430		
Total profit	70		
	£	£	£
Profit per mile flown	14.00		

95

practice exam 1 – unit 6

b) i) Explain the terms 'relevant' and 'irrelevant' costs.

___

ii) Identify which of the costs in Task 2.1 a) are 'relevant' and which are 'irrelevant', in the short term, in reviewing this contract.

___

Workings

practice exam 1 – unit 6

DATA

Based on the information provided in Task 2.1, F4L has decided that it now requires the charter flights profit centre to make a target profit of £60,000 on this contract.

Task 2.2

Use the table below and the information given in Task 2.1 for the original 5,000 likely miles option, to calculate the required number of miles to be flown to achieve the target profit on this contract. (Round to the nearest mile.)

Calculation of required number of miles

Fixed costs (£000)	
Target profit (£000)	
Sales revenue (£000)	
Less variable costs (£000)	
Contribution (£000)	
Contribution per mile (£000)	
Required number of miles to achieve target profit	

Workings

practice exam 1 – unit 6

DATA

BALPA, the airline pilots' trade union has informed F4L of a planned three-day strike, as part of a dispute concerning pension rights. During these three days only those pilots who are not in BALPA will be available to fly. As a result there will be only 124 hours of pilots' flying time available between three of the scheduled services' routes, A, B and C.

The following information is available about these routes:

Scheduled route	A	B	C	Total
	£'000	£'000	£'000	£'000
Contribution	6,200	5,200	7,320	18,720
Fixed costs	1,100	1,100	1,100	3,300
Profit	5,100	4,100	6,220	15,420
Total number of miles in the route	20,000	16,000	24,000	
Number of pilot hours required	50	52	48	

Task 2.3

Complete the table below to recommend which route(s) should be operated on the three days of the strike to maximise profits on those days.

Scheduled route	A	B	C	Total
Contribution per mile (£)				
Contribution per pilot hour (£'000)				
Route ranking				
Pilot hours available				
Pilot hours allocated to each route				
Number of miles to fly in the route				
Total contribtuion earned (£'000)				
Less: fixed costs (£'000)				
Profit/loss made (£'000)				

DATA

F4L is due to replace several of its scheduled services' aircraft, and has produced the following estimates of capital expenditure, revenue and operating costs for replacements by either Airbus (A) or Boeing (B). Whichever fleet of aircraft is chosen, it will be sold at the end of its three-year economic life:

Aircraft A	Year 0 £ million	Year 1 £ million	Year 2 £ million	Year 3 £ million
Capital expenditure	350			
Disposal proceeds				50
Revenue		735	820	910
Operating costs		455	495	574

Aircraft B	Year 0 £ million	Year 1 £ million	Year 2 £ million	Year 3 £ million
Capital expenditure	300			
Disposal proceeds				35
Revenue		695	790	880
Operating costs		460	515	565

F4L's cost of capital is 16%.

Present value (PV) factors for a 16% discount rate are:

	Year 0	Year 1	Year 2	Year 3
PV factors	1.00000	0.86207	0.74316	0.64066

Task 2.4

Use the tables below to calculate the net present value for both types of aircraft. (Round the discounted cash flows to the nearest £million.)

The net present value of aircraft A

	Year 0 £ million	Year 1 £ million	Year 2 £ million	Year 3 £ million
Capital expenditure/disposal				
Revenue				
Operating costs				
Net cash flows				
PV factors				
Discounted cash flows				
Net present value				

The net present value of aircraft B

	Year 0 £ million	Year 1 £ million	Year 2 £ million	Year 3 £ million
Capital expenditure/disposal				
Revenue				
Operating costs				
Net cash flows				
PV factors				
Discounted cash flows				
Net present value				

Task 2.5

Using the information given in Task 2.4 and your own calculations for this task, write a report to the Chief Accountant in which you:

a) advise, with a supporting reason, which of the two types of aircraft to buy

b) explain whether increasing the company's cost of capital to 18% would make capital investments more or less viable

c) identify another investment appraisal technique that shows how quickly the initial capital expenditure costs can be recovered.

Report

To: The Chief Accountant
From:
Subject:
Date:

This page is for the continuation of your report. You may not need all of it.

PRACTICE EXAM 2
UNIT 6

PREMIER LABELS LTD

These tasks were set by the AAT in June 2008.

Time allowed: 3 hours plus 15 minutes' reading time

practice exam 2 – unit 6

This exam paper is in TWO sections.

You must show competence in BOTH sections. So, try to complete EVERY task in BOTH sections.

Section 1 contains 6 tasks and Section 2 contains 6 tasks.

You should spend about 85 minutes on Section 1 and about 95 minutes on Section 2.

Both Sections 1 and 2 are based on the business described below.

DATA

You are employed as an accounting technician with Premier Labels Ltd, a company that manufactures and sells a wide range of specialist own-labelled packaging for the food and drink industry. Its customers are mainly manufacturers of soft drinks, fast foods, tinned foods and pet foods.

You report to the Management Accountant.

SECTION 1 (Suggested time allowance: 85 minutes)

Task 1.1

The stock record card shown below for plastic part AT3 for May 2008 has only been partially completed.

a) Identify the stock issue method being used for valuing issues to production.

b) Complete the remaining entries in the stock record card using this method. Round the costs per kg to 4 decimal places.

Stock record card for plastic part AT3

	Receipts			Issues			Balance	
Date	Quantity kgs	Cost per kg (£)	Total cost (£)	Quantity kg	Cost per kg (£)	Total cost (£)	Quantity kg	Total cost £
Balance at 1 May							6,000	16,800
6 May	10,000	3.0000	30,000				16,000	46,800
17 May				7,000	2.9250	20,475		
23 May	10,000	3.3525						
30 May				12,000				

DATA

The company's stock control policy for plastic part AT3 is that:

- This part should be re-ordered when the stock balance falls to 4,000 kgs
- The re-order quantity should be 8,000 kgs.

Task 1.2

Write a brief e-mail to the Management Accountant to explain:

a) whether the stock control policy has been complied with, using examples to help your explanation

b) the financial implications for the company if employees do not comply with its stock control policy.

practice exam 2 – unit 6

Email

To: AATStudent@Premier.net
From: ManagementAccountant@Premier.net
Subject: Compliance with stock control policy
Date: 16 June 2008

DATA

The following information relates to direct labour costs incurred in producing 57,600 labelled soft drink bottles during May 2008:

Normal time hours worked	900 hours
Overtime at time and a half worked	180 hours
Overtime at double time worked	135 hours
Total hours worked	1,215 hours

Normal time hourly rate £8 per hour

Overtime premiums paid are included as part of direct labour cost.

practice exam 2 – unit 6

A trainee accounts clerk has produced the following incorrect calculation of the total cost of direct labour used to produce these bottles:

		£
Cost at normal rate	1,215 hours at £8 =	9,720
Cost at time and a half	135 hours at £12 =	1,620
Cost at double time	180 hours at £16 =	2,880
Total direct labour cost		14,220

Task 1.3

a) Calculate the correct total cost of direct labour used to produce the soft drink bottles during May 2008.

b) Calculate the direct labour cost per soft drink bottle.

DATA

Premier Labels Ltd has the following departments involved in producing labelled plastic food containers:

- Plastics Moulding
- Labelling
- Stores
- Equipment Maintenance

The budgeted overheads relating to these departments for the next quarter are shown below, together with their behaviour and how they are apportioned to departments.

practice exam 2 – unit 6

Budgeted cost	Cost behaviour		Comments
Heat and lighting	Semi-variable	60,000	Apportion fixed element of £24,000 equally between all four departments. Apportion variable element according to floor area.
Power for machinery	Variable	28,000	Apportion 70% to Plastics Moulding, and 30% to Labelling.
Supervision	Fixed	120,000	Apportion to the two production departments pro rata to direct labour costs.
Stores wages	Fixed	72,000	
Equipment Maintenance salaries	Fixed	188,200	
Depreciation of fixed assets	Fixed	84,000	Apportion according to net book value of fixed assets.
Other overhead costs	Dependant on specific cost	128,000	Apportion 60% to Plastics Moulding, 20% to Labelling, and 10% each to Stores and Equipment Maintenance.

The following information is also available:

Department	Square metres occupied	Net book value of fixed assets (£)	Number of material requisitions	Direct labour costs (£)
Plastics Moulding	320,000	160,000	162,750	100,000
Labelling	180,000	80,000	56,000	140,000
Stores	80,000	30,000		
Equipment Maintenance	20,000	10,000		

Task 1.4

Use the following table to allocate or apportion the overheads between the production departments, using the most appropriate basis. Round to the nearest £ throughout.

Note:

The Equipment Maintenance department's total costs should be apportioned equally to the other three departments. Then the total of the Stores department's costs should be apportioned according to the number of material requisitions.

practice exam 2 – unit 6

Overhead	Basis of allocation	Plastics Moulding £	Labelling £	Stores £	Equipment Maintenance £	Total £
Heat and lighting fixed cost						
Heat and lighting variable cost						
Power for machinery						
Supervision						
Stores' wages						
Equipment Maintenance salaries						
Depreciation of fixed assets						
Other overhead costs						
Total of primary apportionments						
Reapportion Equipment Maintenance						
Reapportion Stores						
Total Production Department overheads						

109

practice exam 2 – unit 6

DATA

The Plastics Moulding department recovers its overheads on the basis of the budgeted machine hours. The Labelling department, however, recovers its overheads on the basis of the budgeted direct labour hours.

The following information relates to these two departments for July 2008:

	Plastics moulding department	Labelling department
Budgeted machine hours	8,404	6,500
Budgeted direct labour hours	10,005	16,250

Task 1.5

Using the above information and your calculations from Task 1.4, calculate the budgeted overhead recovery (absorption) rate for:

a) the Plastics Moulding department

b) the Labelling department

DATA

The following information relates to the manufacture of labelled pet food tins:

	£
Direct materials	14,870
Direct labour	42,206
Total variable overheads	48,064
Total fixed overheads	75,100
Number of batches produced	15,020

Task 1.6

Calculate the following costs per batch of labelled pet food tins:

a)   Prime cost

b)   Variable (marginal) cost

c) Full absorption cost

Post exam note (at August 2008)

The wording of the data for Task 1.6 shown here is different to that in the actual paper. The version in the paper read:

	£
Direct materials per batch	14,870
Direct labour per batch	42,206

This should have read as shown on page 111:

	£
Direct materials	14,870
Direct labour	42,206

The marking scheme was amended to give full credit whether candidates used the figures per batch or per total. The Chief Assessor re-examined all unsuccessful scripts to ensure that no candidate was penalised by the error in terms of either credit or time.

SECTION 2 (Suggested time allowance: 95 minutes)

Task 2.1

Premier Labels Ltd has produced three forecasts of activity levels for the next period for one of its labelled drinks cans. The original budget involved producing 50,000 cans, but sales and production levels of between 60,000 and 70,000 cans are now more likely.

a) Complete the table below to estimate the production cost per can of the labelled drinks can at the three different activity levels.

Cans made	50,000	60,000	70,000
Costs:	£	£	£
Variable costs:			
▪ direct materials	5,250		
▪ direct labour	2,250		
▪ overheads	11,100		
Fixed costs:			
▪ indirect labour	9,200		
▪ overheads	15,600		
Total cost	43,400		
Cost per can	0.868		

b) Explain why the cost per can changes as the number of cans made increases.

_____

_____

_____

_____

_____

practice exam 2 – unit 6

c) If the production volume for this product were to increase to 150,000 cans per period, explain what the likely effect would be on the fixed costs and cost per can.

Workings

DATA

The following budgeted annual sales and cost information relates to labelled food containers types A and B:

Product	A	B
Units made and sold	300,000	500,000
Machine hours required	60,000	40,000
Sales revenue (£)	450,000	600,000
Direct materials (£)	60,000	125,000
Direct labour (£)	36,000	70,000
Variable overheads (£)	45,000	95,000

Total fixed costs attributable to A and B are budgeted to be £264,020.

114

Task 2.2

Complete the table below (to 2 decimal places) to show the budgeted contribution per unit of A and B sold, and the company's budgeted profit or loss for the year from these two products.

	A(£)	B(£)	Total (£)
Selling price per unit			
Less: variable costs per unit			
▪ direct materials			
▪ direct labour			
▪ variable overheads			
Contribution per unit			
Sales volume (units)			
Total contribution			
Less: fixed costs			
Budgeted profit or loss			

Task 2.3

ADDITIONAL DATA

The £264,020 of fixed costs attributed to products A and B can be split between the two products: £158,620 to A and £105,400 to B.

The latest sales forecast is that 250,000 units of product A and 400,000 units of product B will be sold during the year.

a) Using your calculations from Task 2.2 and the additional data above, complete the table below to calculate:

    i)   the budgeted break-even sales, in units, for each of the two products
    ii)   the margin of safety (in units) for each of the two products
    iii) the margin of safety as a percentage (to 2 decimal places).

Product	A	B
Fixed costs (£)		
Unit contribution (£)		
Breakeven sales (units)		
Forecast sales (units)		
Margin of safety (units)		
Margin of safety (%)		

practice exam 2 – unit 6

b) Explain which of the two products, A or B, has the better margin of safety and why.

___

Task 2.4

Due to a machine breakdown the number of machine hours available for products A and B has now been reduced to only 70,000 during the year.

Given this limitation and your calculations from Task 2.2, complete the table below to recommend how many units of products A and B Premier Labels Ltd should now make in order to maximise the profit from these two products for the year.

	A	B	Total
Contribution/unit (£)			
Machine hours/unit			
Contribution/machine hour (£)			
Product ranking			
Machine hours available			
Machine hours allocated to: Product ... Product ...			
Total contribution earned (£)			
Less: fixed costs (£)			
Profit/loss made (£)			

practice exam 2 – unit 6

DATA

The company is negotiating with a potential new customer to supply them with a labelled plastic food container. The following estimates of capital expenditure, sales and costs have been produced. The contract is for three years, and at the end of that time – if it is not renewed – the capital equipment will be sold for £100,000.

	Year 0 £'000	Year 1 £'000	Year 2 £'000	Year 3 £'000
Capital expenditure/disposal	(600)			100
Other cash flows:				
Sales income		900	1,350	750
Operating costs		710	895	560

The company's cost of capital is 11%.

Present value (PV) factors for an 11% discount rate are:

	Year 0	Year 1	Year 2	Year 3
PV factor	1.000	0.9009	0.8116	0.7312

Task 2.5

Calculate both the net present value (NPV) and the payback period for the proposed new contract.

a) **The net present value (NPV)**

	Year 0 £'000	Year 1 £'000	Year 2 £'000	Year 3 £'000
Capital expenditure/disposal				
Sales income				
Operating costs				
Net cash flows				
PV factors				
Discounted cash flows				
Net present value				

b) **The payback period**

Task 2.6

Using the data given in Task 2.5 and your calculations for this task, write a report to the Management Accountant in which you:

a) recommend whether the proposed new plastic food container should be introduced. (This should be based on your calculations of the net present value and the payback period.)

b) identify TWO commercial factors that are also relevant to this decision.

c) explain the meaning of the term "internal rate of return".

Report

To: The Management Accountant
From:
Subject:
Date:

This page is for the continuation of your report. You may not need all of it.

PRACTICE EXAM 3
UNIT 6

STOW SOLVENTS LTD

These tasks were set by the AAT in December 2007.

Time allowed: 3 hours plus 15 minutes' reading time

practice exam 3 – unit 6

This exam paper is in TWO sections.

You have to show competence in BOTH sections. So, try to complete EVERY task in BOTH sections.

Section 1 contains 6 tasks and Section 2 contains 5 tasks.

You should spend about 90 minutes on each section.

Both sections are based on Stow Solvents Ltd.

You should include all essential calculations in your answers.

DATA

You are employed as an accounting technician with Stow Solvents Ltd, a medium-sized chemical processing company. The company manufactures a range of industrial solvents that it sells to manufacturers of paint and chemical products.

The company operates a process costing system.

You report to the Chief Accountant.

The stock record card shown below refers to entries for chemical RC976 for November 2007. This chemical has been steadily increasing in price over the past few weeks.

The card has been partially written up using the First In First Out (FIFO) method of stock issue and valuation, rather than the Weighted Average Cost (AVCO) method that should have been used.

STOCK RECORD CARD FOR RC976

Date	Receipts Quantity Litres	Receipts Cost per Litre (£)	Receipts Total cost (£)	Issues Quantity Litres	Issues Cost per Litre (£)	Issues Total cost (£)	Balance Quantity Litres	Balance Total cost £
Balance as of 1 Nov							8,000	3,200
5 Nov	4,000	0.52	2,080				12,000	5,280
12 Nov				5,000	0.40	2,000	7,000	3,280
18 Nov	4,000	0.55	2,200					
28 Nov				6,000				

practice exam 3 – unit 6

SECTION 1 (Suggested time allowance: 90 minutes)

Task 1.1

a) Redraft the stock record card below for the entries up to and including those on 12 November, using the Weighted Average Cost (AVCO) method.

b) Complete the entries for the rest of the month.

	\multicolumn{3}{c	}{STOCK RECORD CARD FOR RC976}					
	\multicolumn{3}{c	}{Receipts}	\multicolumn{3}{c	}{Issues}	\multicolumn{2}{c	}{Balance}
Date	Quantity Litres	Cost per Litre (£)	Total cost (£)	Quantity Litres	Cost per Litre (£)	Total cost (£)	Quantity Litres	Total cost £
Balance as of 1 Nov								
5 Nov								
12 Nov								
18 Nov								
28 Nov								

c) FIFO, AVCO and standard costing are methods of stock issue and valuation. Name ONE other method based on historical cost.

d) Would the method you identified in c) lead to a lower or higher valuation of the stock balance at the end of November (as compared to AVCO)?

123

practice exam 3 – unit 6

ADDITIONAL DATA

Chemical RC976 issued on 12 November was used to make solvent S123, while that issued on 28 November was used to make solvent S456.

The following cost accounting codes are used:

Code	Description
1953	Stocks of chemical RC976
3265	Work in progress – solvent S123
3341	Work in progress – solvent S456
0080	Creditors Control

Task 1.2

Complete the Journal below to record separately the FOUR cost accounting entries for the two receipts and two issues during November.

JOURNAL

Date	Code	DR (£)	CR (£)
5 November			
5 November			
12 November			
12 November			
18 November			
18 November			
28 November			
28 November			

ADDITIONAL DATA

The following data relates to direct labour costs incurred in producing solvent S789 during November:

Normal time hours worked	260 hours
Overtime at time and a half worked	40 hours
Overtime at double time worked	30 hours
Total hours worked	330 hours
Normal time hourly rate	£10 per hour

Overtime premiums paid are included in the direct labour cost.

Task 1.3

a) Calculate the total cost of direct labour for solvent S789 for November.

practice exam 3 – unit 6

ADDITIONAL DATA

The following data relates to work in progress stocks of solvent S789 during November:

Opening work in progress	Nil
Finished output to next process	7,000 litres
Closing work in progress	1,200 litres
Degree of completion – direct materials	100%
Degree of completion – direct labour	50%

Task 1.3 continued

b) Using the additional data above and your answer to Task 1.3 a), calculate the direct labour cost per litre of solvent S789 of the equivalent finished production.

practice exam 3 – unit 6

ADDITIONAL DATA

Stow Solvents Ltd. has the following departments involved in one of the stages of solvent production:

- Chemical mixing
- Solvent bottling
- Maintenance

The budgeted fixed overheads relating to the departments for the next quarter are:

	£	£
Insurance of machinery		50,400
Rent and rates		136,800
Indirect labour costs:		
Chemical mixing	53,625	
Solvent bottling	131,175	
Maintenance	18,375	
Total		203,175
Total fixed overheads		390,375

Department	Net book value of fixed assets £'000	Square metres occupied	Number of employees
Chemical mixing	432	660	14
Solvent bottling	216	480	48
Maintenance	72	60	6
Total	720	1,200	68

Fixed overheads are allocated or apportioned to the departments on the most appropriate basis.

The total maintenance overheads are then reapportioned to the two production departments. The maintenance department spends 80% of its time maintaining equipment in the chemical mixing department.

Task 1.4

Use the following table to allocate or apportion the fixed overheads between the production departments, using the most appropriate basis.

Fixed overhead	Basis of allocation or apportionment	Chemical mixing £	Solvent bottling £	Maintenance £	Total cost £
Insurance of machinery					
Rent and rates					
Indirect labour costs					
Sub-total					
Reapportionment of maintenance					
Total					

Workings

practice exam 3 – unit 6

ADDITIONAL DATA

The chemical mixing department is highly automated, and operates with expensive machinery. The solvent bottling department, on the other hand, is highly labour intensive.

The following budgeted data relates to the next quarter:

	Chmical mixing	Solvent bottling
Number of machine hours	5,237	3,624
Number of labour hours	4,806	17,256

Task 1.5

Refer to your calculations in Task 1.4 and to the data above.

For each of the following departments, calculate the budgeted fixed overhead absorption rates (recovery rates) for the next quarter using the most appropriate basis of absorption. (Give your answers to the nearest whole pound):

a) **The chemical mixing department**

b) **The solvent bottling department**

129

practice exam 3 – unit 6

ADDITIONAL DATA

The following planning data relates to the production of solvent S258 in the first month of the next financial year in the chemical mixing department.

Budgeted machine hours	460
Actual machine hours now expected to be worked	480
Actual overheads now expected to be incurred	£16,200

Task 1.6

Refer to your calculations in Task 1.5 and to the data above.

Calculate the overhead under- or over-absorption now expected in the first month of the next financial year. (Clearly state whether under- or over-absorption is expected.)

_____
_____
_____
_____
_____
_____
_____

SECTION 2 (Suggested time allowance: 90 minutes)

Task 2.1

The company has produced three forecasts of demand levels for the next quarter for solvent S468. The original budget was to produce 10,000 litres per quarter, but demand levels of 14,000 litres and 18,000 litres are also now feasible.

a) Complete the table below to estimate the production cost per litre of S468 at the three different demand levels.

Litres	10,000	14,000	18,000
Costs:	£	£	£
Variable costs:			
▪ direct materials	1,200		
▪ direct labour	1,000		
▪ overheads	1,600		
Fixed costs:			
▪ indirect labour	700		
▪ overheads	1,600		
Total cost	6,100		
Cost per litre	0.61		

b) Explain why the cost per litre of S468 changes with the increase in the number of litres made.

practice exam 3 – unit 6

ADDITIONAL DATA

The production manager now thinks the £2,300 of fixed costs attributable to solvent S468 may be a stepped fixed cost instead. He believes that this cost is stepped at each activity level of 10,000 litres per quarter.

c) i) Explain what is meant by a stepped fixed cost.

ii) Explain what effect the above additional data would have on the cost per litre at activity levels of 14,000 and 18,000 litres. (You are NOT required to calculate these costs.)

ADDITIONAL DATA

Solvent S468 will be sold for £0.88/litre at the budgeted 10,000 litres activity level.

Task 2.2

a) Calculate the budgeted break-even sales, in litres, for this solvent.

_____

_____

_____

_____

_____

_____

b) Complete the table below to:

   i) Calculate the margin of safety (in litres) at each of the three feasible activity levels, by comparing the level of sales forecast with the break-even level

   ii) Calculate the margin of safety as a percentage (to the nearest whole number) for each of the three activity levels.

Forecast sales litres	10,000	14,000	18,000
Breakeven sales (litres)			
Margin of safety (litres)			
Margin of safety (%)			

practice exam 3 – unit 6

ADDITIONAL DATA

The company produces solvent S782 in a single production process. During October 2007 the input to the process was 18,000 litres of raw materials at a cost of £9,000. There were no opening or closing stocks and all output was fully completed.

The table below shows the actual process results for the month:

Input Litres	Output Litres	Normal loss Litres	Abnormal loss Litres	Abnormal gains Litres	Scap value of all losses £ per litre
18,000	15,000	3,000	0	0	£0.20

Task 2.3

a) Calculate the cost per litre of output.

_____

_____

_____

_____

_____

_____

b) Complete the entries in the solvent S782 process account below:

Description	Litres	Unit cost £	Total cost £	Description	Litres	Unit cost £	Total cost £
Input to process				Normal loss			
				Output from process			

134

ADDITIONAL DATA

The company is faced with a problem involving a limiting factor and seeks your advice. This problem arises because another solvent, S893, has become available. It uses the same mixing machine as S782. However, the number of available hours for this particular mixing machine is limited to only 6,000 during the next quarter.

The following data is available:

	S782	S893
Selling price per thousand litres (£)	1,200	1,600
Marginal cost per thousand litres (£)	800	1,000
Machine hours required per thousand litres	2	5
Demand (forecast sales next quarter in thousand litres)	2,000	3,000
Total fixed costs for both solvents (£)	640,000	

Task 2.4

Using the data given above complete the table below. This is to recommend how many thousand litres of solvents S782 and S893 should be made in order to maximise profits based on the machine hours available.

	S782	S893	Total
Contribution per thousand litres (£)			
Machine hours per thousand litres			
Contribution per machine hour (£)			
Solvent ranking			
Machine hours available			
Machine hours allocated to: Solvent .... Solvent			
Litres produced ('000)			
Total contribution earned (£)			
Less: fixed costs (£)			
Profit/loss made (£)			

practice exam 3 – unit 6

ADDITIONAL DATA

The company is considering investing in a new mixing machine that will cost £3,000,000 but will reduce operating costs. The following information is relevant to this decision:

- The payback period would be 2.4 years. The company's policy is for projects to pay back within 3 years.

- The net present value is £400,000 negative.

- The internal rate of return is 14%. The company's cost of capital is 16%.

Task 2.5

Based on the data given above, write a BRIEF report to the Chief Accountant in which you advise on the basis of EACH of the THREE criteria above whether the proposed investment should be made. Make an overall accept or reject recommendation.

Report

To: AATStudent@Premier.net
From: ManagementAccountant@Premier.net
Subject: Compliance with stock control policy
Date: 16 June 2008

This page is for the continuation of your report. You may not need to use all of it.

PRACTICE EXAM 4
UNIT 6

EASTERN BUS COMPANY PLC

These tasks were set by the AAT in June 2007.

Time allowed: 3 hours plus 15 minutes' reading time

practice exam 4 – unit 6

This examination paper is in TWO sections.

You must show competence in BOTH sections. So, try to complete EVERY task in BOTH sections.

Section 1 contains 6 tasks and Section 2 contains 5 tasks.

You should spend about 90 minutes on each section.

You should include all essential calculations in your answers.

Both Sections 1 and 2 are based on the information below about Eastern Bus Company plc (EBC).

SECTION 1 (Suggested time allowance: 90 minutes)

DATA

You are employed as an accounting technician with Eastern Bus Company plc (EBC).

The company operates a fleet of buses, providing scheduled and contract bus services throughout the eastern counties of England.

You report to the Management Accountant.

EBC recovers its costs on the basis of the number of miles travelled – calculating its profitability as the difference between the fares and government subsidies it receives and its operating costs per mile.

It has five profit and cost centres that relate to the delivery of its services:

Bus service profit centres

- **Scheduled Services**

    The scheduled services are used as required by the general public and operate on a fixed daily timetable.

- **Contract Services**

    The contract services are where buses are hired out to a third party, such as to the local authority for transporting children to and from school.

Support Departments' cost centres

- Vehicle Maintenance and Repairs
- Fuel and Parts Store
- General Administration

The company's year end is 31 May.

The data and tasks cover activities during May and June 2007.

practice exam 4 – unit 6

Task 1.1

The stock record card shown below for diesel for the month of May 2007 has only been fully completed for the first three weeks of the month.

a) Complete ALL entries in the stock record card (showing the cost per litre in pence to 2 decimal places) for the following two transactions:

- 24 May: received   100,000 litres at a total cost of   £32,440
- 26 May: issued   80,000 litres to the fleet with a total cost of   £25,600

b) Identify the stock issue method being used for costing issues of diesel to the fleet.

_____

_____

c) Complete ALL entries in the stock record card for the remaining two transactions in the month and for the closing balance at the end of May.

Stock record card for diesel

	Receipts			Issues			Balance	
Date	Quantity Litres	Cost per litre p	Total cost £	Quantity Litres	Cost per Litre p	Total cost £	Quantity Litres	Total cost £
Balance as at 22 May							22,000	6,600
24 May							122,000	39,040
26 May								
28 May	50,000		16,276					
30 May				80,000				

141

practice exam 4 – unit 6

ADDITIONAL DATA

- Both receipts of diesel were bought on 30 day credit terms.
- The diesel issued on 26 May was to the Scheduled Services fleet.
- The diesel issued on 30 May was to the Contract Services fleet.

The following are extracts from the accounting codes used:

Code	Description
200	Stocks of diesel fuel
300	Bank current account
501	Scheduled Services profit centre
502	Contract Services profit centre
600	Creditors Control

Task 1.2

Complete the Journal below to record separately the FOUR cost accounting entries in respect of the two receipts and two issues of diesel fuel.

Date	Code	DR (£)	CR (£)
24 May			
24 May			
26 May			
26 May			
28 May			
28 May			
30 May			
30 May			

practice exam 4 – unit 6

ADDITIONAL DATA

Below is a weekly timesheet for one of the Scheduled Services bus drivers. These drivers work as follows.

- They have to work a basic six-hour shift every day from Monday to Friday, paid at basic pay.
- If they work for more than six hours, on any day from Monday to Friday, the extra hours are paid at time-and-a-half (basic pay plus an overtime premium equal to half of basic pay).
- They also have to work for three hours on a Saturday morning, paid at basic pay.
- If they work for more than three hours on Saturday, the extra hours are paid at double time (basic pay plus an overtime premium equal to basic pay).
- Any hours worked on Sunday are paid at double time (basic pay plus an overtime premium equal to basic pay).

Task 1.3

Complete the columns headed Basic pay, Overtime premium and Total pay.

Note. The employee's total pay for the week was £570.

practice exam 4 – unit 6

Driver's weekly timesheet for week ending 7 June 2007

	Hours spent driving	Hours worked on indirect work	Notes	Basic pay £	Overtime premium £	Total pay £
Employee: S Moss			**Profit Centre:** Scheduled Services			
Employee number: D104			**Basic pay per hour:** £12.00			
Monday	6	–				
Tuesday	3	3	12am – 3pm customer care course			
Wednesday	8					
Thursday	6					
Friday	6	1	2–3pm health and safety briefing			
Saturday	5					
Sunday	3					
Total	37	4				

144

practice exam 4 – unit 6

ADDITIONAL DATA

The budgeted overheads for the five profit and cost centres for Quarter 1 of the next financial year are:

	£	£
Depreciation of buses		3,216,600
Diesel fuel and other variable overheads		2,860,000
Rent and rates of premises		418,000
Light, heat and power at premises		92,400
Indirect labour costs:		
Vehicles Maintenance and Repairs	404,600	
Fuel and Parts Store	96,200	
General Administration	308,400	
Total indirect labour cost		809,200

The following information is also available:

Department	Net book value of buses £	Planned number of miles	Floor space (square metres)	Number of direct labour hours
Scheduled services	22,400,000	34,320		
Contract services	9,600,000	22,880		
Vehicle maintenance and repairs			14,000	3,800
Fuel and parts store			8,400	980
General administration			5,600	2,620
Total	32,000,000	57,200	28,000	7,400

Overheads are allocated or apportioned on the most appropriate basis. The total overheads of the Support Departments' cost centres are then reapportioned to the two Bus Service profit centres using the direct method.

- 75% of the Vehicle Maintenance and Repairs department's time is spent maintaining the buses in the Scheduled Services profit centre and the remainder in the Contract Services profit centre.

- The Fuel and Parts Store department makes 55% of its issues to the Scheduled Services profit centre and 45% to the Contract Services profit centre.

- General Administration supports the Scheduled Services profit centre and the Contract Services profit centre equally.

- There is no reciprocal servicing between the three Support Department cost centres.

practice exam 4 – unit 6

Task 1.4

Use the following table to allocate or apportion the overheads between the cost centres, using the most appropriate basis.

	Basis of apportionment	Scheduled services £	Contract Services £	Vehicle maintenance and repairs £	Fuel and parts store £	General admin £	Totals £
Depreciation of buses							
Diesel fuel and other variable overheads							
Rent and rates							
Light, heat and power							
Indirect labour							
Totals							
Reapportion Aircraft maintenance and repairs							
Reapportion Fuel and parts store							
Reapportion General admin							
Total overheads to profit centres							

146

Task 1.5

Both the Scheduled Services and Contract Services profit centres absorb (recover) their overheads on the basis of a cost per planned mile travelled.

Using the information above and your answers from Task 1.4, calculate the overhead absorption rates for both profit centres (to the nearest penny).

Workings

practice exam 4 – unit 6

ADDITIONAL DATA

The following information relates to a contract for transporting school children during May 2007:

	£
Fuel and other variable overheads	9,200
Fixed costs:	
■ Drivers' wages, pension and national insurance	3,220
■ Other fixed overheads	23,000
	Miles
Number of miles travelled	4,600

Task 1.6

Calculate the cost per mile under:

a) Variable (marginal) costing

b) Full absorption costing

practice exam 4 – unit 6

SECTION 2 (Suggested time allowance: 90 minutes)

DATA

Eastern Bus Company (EBC) has produced three forecasts of miles to be driven during the next three months for a particular contract. The original contract is for journeys totalling 10,000 miles. It now seems likely, however, that the total journeys involved will increase to either 12,000 or 14,000 miles.

Notes

- The rate charged by EBC per mile will stay the same irrespective of the total mileage.
- Drivers on this contract are paid entirely on a per mile driven basis.

Task 2.1

a) Complete the table below in order to estimate the profit per mile (in pounds, to 3 decimal places) of this contract for the three likely mileages.

Likely miles	10,000	12,000	14,000
	£	£	£
Sales revenue	100,000		
Variable costs			
■ fuel	8,000		
■ drivers' wages and associated costs	5,000		
■ overheads	6,000		
Fixed costs			
■ indirect labour	10,600		
■ overheads	25,850		
Total cost	55,450		
Total profit	44,550		
Profit per mile	4.455		

149

b) Briefly explain why the profit per mile changes as the number of miles travelled increases.

Workings

Task 2.2

Using the information provided in Task 2.1 and your own calculations for that task, calculate:

- the budgeted breakeven mileage for the contract
- the margin of safety, in number of miles and sales revenue, for the two forecast journey mileages shown below
- the margin of safety, as a percentage (to 1 decimal place), for the two forecast journey mileages shown below

Forecast number of miles		12,000	14,000
Sales revenue	£		
Fixed costs	£		
Contribution	£		
Contribution per mile	£		
Breakeven number of miles	Miles		
Breakeven sales revenue	£		
Margin of safety in number of miles	Miles		
Margin of safety in sales revenue	£		
Margin of safety	%		

Workings

practice exam 4 – unit 6

ADDITIONAL DATA

The drivers' trade union has just informed the company of a planned one day strike in support of a pay claim. On this day only the non-unionised drivers will report for work. This means that there will be only 620 hours of driving time available between three of the company's scheduled routes, X, Y and Z.

The Management Accountant has given you the following information about these routes:

Scheduled route	X	Y	Z	Total
	£	£	£	£
Contribution	6,400	4,800	8,400	19,600
Fixed costs allocated or apportioned	2,100	2,100	2,100	6,300
Profit	4,300	2,700	6,300	13,300
Number of miles in the route	5,000	4,000	6,000	
Number of driver hours required	400	200	420	

Task 2.3

On the basis of the information above, complete the table below to recommend which route(s) should be operated on the day of the strike to maximise profits on that day.

Scheduled route	X	Y	Z	Total
Contribution per mile (£)	1.28	1.20	1.40	
Driver hours per mile	0.08	0.05	0.07	
Contribution per driver hour (£)	16	24	20	
Route ranking	3	1	2	
Driver hours available				620
Driver hours allocated to each route	0	200	420	620
Number of miles in the route	0	4,000	6,000	
Total contribution earned (£)	0	4,800	8,400	13,200
Less: fixed costs (£)				6,300
Profit/loss made (£)				6,900

ADDITIONAL DATA

EBC is considering replacing its ticket issuing machines, and has produced the following estimates of capital expenditure and operating costs for two types of machine. Both machines are expected to have a three-year economic life:

Machine A	Year 0	Year 1	Year 2	Year 3
	£'000	£'000	£'000	£'000
Capital expenditure	800			
Operating costs		365	380	405

Machine B	Year 0	Year 1	Year 2	Year 3
	£'000	£'000	£'000	£'000
Capital expenditure	650			
Operating costs		460	470	480

The company's cost of capital is 14%.

Present value (PV) factors for a 14% discount rate are:

	Year 0	Year 1	Year 2	Year 3
PV factors	1.00000	0.87719	0.76947	0.67497

Task 2.4

Calculate the net present cost for both types of machine. Round the discounted cash flows to the nearest £.

The net present cost of machine A

	Year 0	Year 1	Year 2	Year 3
	£'000	£'000	£'000	£'000
Capital expenditure				
Operating costs				
Net cash flows				
PV factors				
Discounted cash flows				
Net present cost				

The net present cost of machine B

	Year 0	Year 1	Year 2	Year 3
	£'000	£'000	£'000	£'000
Capital expenditure				
Operating costs				
Net cash flows				
PV factors				
Discounted cash flows				
Net present cost				

Task 2.5

Based on the information given in Task 2.4 and your own calculations for this task, write a report to the Management Accountant in which you:

a) recommend, with a supporting reason, which of the two alternative ticket issuing machines to buy
b) identify TWO commercial issues that are relevant to making this decision
c) identify ONE other method of investment appraisal that is used by organisations

Report

To: The Management Accountant
From:
Subject:
Date:

This page is for the continuation of your report. You may not need to use all of it.

PRACTICE EXAM 5
UNIT 6

BRECKVILLE DAIRIES LTD

These tasks were set by the AAT in December 2006.

Time allowed: 3 hours plus 15 minutes' reading time

practice exam 5 – unit 6

This examination paper is in TWO sections.

You have to show competence in BOTH sections.

You should therefore attempt and aim to complete EVERY task in EACH sections.

Section 1 contains 6 tasks and Section 2 contains 5 tasks.

All essential workings should be included within your answers, where appropriate.

You should spend about 85 minutes on Section 1 and about 95 minutes on Section 2.

Both sections are based on Breckville Dairies Ltd.

SECTION 1 (Suggested time allowance: 85 minutes)

DATA

You work as an accounting technician at Breckville Dairies Ltd, a large processing company. The business buys milk and other farm produce from farmers and then converts these into dairy products such as cheese, butter and yoghurt. It then sells these on to high street retail chains.

The company operates a process costing system.

The Chief Accountant has given you the following tasks.

DATA FOR TASK 1.1

The stock record card shown below refers to entries for bio-protein additive for the month of November 2007. This commodity has been rapidly increasing in price over the past few weeks. The card has been partially written up using the First In First out (FIFO) method of stock issue and valuation, rather than the Weighted Average Cost (AVCO) method which should have been used.

STOCK RECORD CARD

Date	Receipts Quantity (litres)	Receipts Cost per litre (£)	Receipts Total cost (£)	Issues Quantity (litres)	Issues Cost per litre (£)	Issues Total cost (£)	Balance Quantity (litres)	Balance Total cost £
Balance as at 1 Nov							2,000	4,000
6 Nov	1,000	2.60	2,600				3,000	6,600
14 Nov				1,000	2.00	2,000	2,000	4,600
22 Nov	1,000	3.40	3,400					
27 Nov				2,000				

practice exam 5 – unit 6

Task 1.1

a) Redraft the stock record card on the previous page for the entries up to and including that on 14 November 2007.

b) Complete the entries for the rest of the month.

	\multicolumn{3}{c	}{Receipts}	\multicolumn{3}{c	}{Issues}	\multicolumn{2}{c	}{Balance}
Date	Quantity (litres)	Cost per litre (£)	Total cost (£)	Quantity (litres)	Cost per litre (£)	Total cost (£)	Quantity (litres)	Total cost £
Balance as at 1 Nov								
6 Nov								
14 Nov								
22 Nov								
27 Nov								

c) Identify ONE other method (that is, other than FIFO and AVCO) of stock issue and valuation based on historical cost (excluding standard costing).

_____

d) State whether this method would lead to a lower or higher valuation of the stock balance at 27 November (as compared to AVCO).

_____

practice exam 5 – unit 6

ADDITIONAL DATA

The issue of bio-protein additive on 14 November was for use in the production of product X, while that on 27 November was for the production of product Y.

The following cost accounting codes are used:

Code	Description
2004	Stocks of bio-protein additive
7012	Work in progress – Product X
7039	Work in progress – Product Y
6030	Creditors Control

Task 1.2

Complete the Journal below to record separately the FOUR cost accounting entries for the two receipts and two issues during the month of November.

Date	Code	DR £	CR £
6 November			
6 November			
14 November			
14 November			
22 November			
22 November			
27 November			
27 November			

161

ADDITIONAL DATA

The following information relates to direct labour costs incurred in producing product Z during November 2007.

Normal time hours worked	350 hours
Overtime at time and a half worked	60 hours
Overtime at double time worked	40 hours
Total hours worked	450 hours
Normal time hourly rate	£8 per hour

Task 1.3

Overtime premiums paid are included as part of direct labour cost.

Calculate the total cost of direct labour for product Z for the month of November 2007.

ADDITIONAL DATA

Breckville Dairies Ltd. has the following departments involved in one of the stages of production:

- Materials Mixing
- Product Packing
- Maintenance

The budgeted fixed overheads relating to the departments for the next quarter are:

	£	£
Insurance of machinery		33,600
Rent and rates		91,200
Indirect labour costs:		
Materials Mixing	35,750	
Product Packing	87,450	
Maintenance	12,250	
Total		135,450
Total fixed overheads		260,250

The following information is also available:

Department	Net book value of fixed assets £'000	Square metres occupied	Number of employees
Materials mixing	360	550	7
Product packing	180	400	24
Maintenance	60	50	3
Total	600	1,000	34

Fixed overheads are allocated or apportioned to the departments on the most appropriate basis. The total maintenance overheads are then reapportioned to the two production departments. 60% of the Maintenance department's time is spent maintaining equipment in the Materials mixing department.

Task 1.4

Use the following table to allocate or apportion the fixed overheads between the production departments, using the most appropriate basis.

Fixed overhead	Basis of allocation or apportionment	Total cost £	Materials Mixing £	Product Packing £	Maintenance £
Insurance of machinery		33,600			
Rent and rates		91,200			
Indirect labour costs		135,450			
Maintenance					
Totals		260,250			

practice exam 5 – unit 6

ADDITIONAL DATA

The Materials Mixing department is highly automated, and operates with expensive machinery. The Product Packing department, on the other hand, is highly labour intensive.

The following budgeted information relates to next quarter:

	Materials Mixing	Product Packing
Number of machine hours	3,940	2,840
Number of labour hours	3,200	10.920

Task 1.5

Using your calculations in Task 1.4 and the information above, calculate the budgeted fixed overhead absorption rates (recovery rates) for the next quarter using the most appropriate bases of absorption for:

a) the Materials Mixing department
b) the Product Packing department

Note. You should round your answers to whole pounds.

ADDITIONAL DATA

The following information relates to product R during the month of October 2007.

	£	Units
Direct materials cost per unit	12.20	
Direct labour cost per unit	27.80	
Total variable overheads cost	20,000	
Total fixed overheads cost	50,000	
Number of units sold		800
Number of units produced		1,000

Note. There were no opening stocks.

Task 1.6

a) Calculate the cost per unit of product R under:

i) Variable (marginal) costing

ii) Full absorption costing

b) State how much the difference in the closing stock valuation and the reported profit for October would be under the two costing principles.

practice exam 5 – unit 6

SECTION 2 (Suggested time allowance: 95 minutes)

ADDITIONAL DATA

The company has produced three forecasts of activity levels for the next quarter for product S. The original budget was to produce only 1,000 units, but production levels of 1,200 units and 1,500 units are also feasible.

Task 2.1

a) Complete the table below, in order to estimate the production cost per unit of S at the three different activity levels.

Units made	1,000	1,200	1,500
Costs	£	£	£
Variable costs:			
▪ direct materials	3,000		
▪ direct labour	7,000		
▪ overheads	6,000		
Fixed costs:			
▪ indirect labour	9,800		
▪ overheads	19,000		
Total cost	44,800		
Cost per unit	44.80		

b) Identify THREE factors that are relevant to predicting how the cost per unit of S would change if sales and production could be increased to 10,000 units per quarter.

i) _____

_____

_____

ii) _____

_____

_____

iii) _____
_____
_____

ADDITIONAL DATA

Product S will be sold for £40.00/unit at all three feasible activity levels of 1,000; 1,200; and 1,500 units.

Task 2.2

a) Calculate the budgeted breakeven sales, in units, for product S.

_____

_____

_____

_____

_____

_____

b) Complete the table below to calculate:

   i) the margin of safety (in units) at each of the three feasible activity levels, by comparing the level of sales forecast with the break-even level

   ii) the margin of safety as a percentage for each of the three activity levels.

Forecast sales (units)	1,000	1,200	1,500
Break-even sales (units)			
Margin of safety (units)			
Margin of safety (%)			

practice exam 5 – unit 6

c) Explain the significance of your calculation of the percentage margin of safety for each of the three feasible activity levels.

    i)   1,000 units

    ii)   1,200 units

    iii)   1,500 units

practice exam 5 – unit 6

ADDITIONAL DATA

The company produces product T within a single production process. During the month of October 2007 the input into the process was 1,200 litres at a cost of £12,000. There were no opening or closing stocks and all output was fully completed.

The table below shows the actual process results for the month:

Input (litres)	Output (litres)	Normal loss (litres)	Abnormal loss (litres)	Abnormal gains (litres)	Scrap value of all losses (£ per litre)
1,200	1,000	200	0	0	£5

Task 2.3

a) Calculate the cost per litre of output.

b) Complete the entries in the product T process account below.

Description	Litres	Unit cost (£)	Total cost (£)	Description	Litres	Unit cost (£)	Total cost (£)
Input to process				Normal loss			
				Output from process			

171

practice exam 5 – unit 6

ADDITIONAL DATA

The company has two products, V and W, that need the same machine mixing process. The number of available machine hours, however, for this particular mixing machine is limited to only 3,000 during the next quarter.

The following information is available:

Product	V	W
Selling price/unit (£)	30	40
Marginal cost/unit (£)	20	25
Machine hours required/unit	2	5
Demand (forecast sales next quarter)	1,000	1,500
Total fixed costs for both products	£9,000	

Task 2.4

Using the above information, complete the table below to recommend how many units of products V and W should be made in order to maximise profits, taking account of the machine hours available.

Product	V	W	Total
Contribution/unit (£)			
Machine hours/unit			
Contribution/machine hour (£)			
Product ranking			
Machine hours available			
Machine hours allocated to: Product……. Product…….			
Units made			
Total contribution earned (£)			
Less: fixed costs (£)			
Profit/loss made (£)			

172

ADDITIONAL DATA

The company is considering investing in a new mixing machine that will cost £1.5million and which will reduce operating costs. The following information is relevant to this decision.

- The payback period would be 3.6 years. The company's policy is for projects to pay back within 4 years.

- The net present value is £200,000 negative.

- The internal rate of return is 12%. The company's cost of capital is 15%

Task 2.5

Based on the information given above, write a BRIEF report to the Chief Accountant in which you advise on the basis of EACH of the three criteria above whether the proposed investment should be made. Make an overall accept/reject recommendation.

REPORT	
To:	Subject:
From:	Date:

This page is for the continuation of your report. You may not need all of it.

AAT

SAMPLE SIMULATION
UNIT 6

QUALITY CANDLES LTD

This is the AAT's Sample Simulation for Unit 6. Its purpose is to give you an idea of what an AAT simulation looks like. It is not intended as a definitive guide to the tasks you may be required to perform.

The suggested time allowance for this Assessment is four hours. Up to 30 minutes' extra time may be permitted in an AAT simulation. Breaks in assessment may be allowed in the AAT simulation, but it must normally be completed in one day.

Calculators may be used but no reference material is permitted.

AAT sample simulation – unit 6

COVERAGE OF PERFORMANCE CRITERIA AND RANGE STATEMENTS

All performance criteria are covered in this simulation.

Element	PC Coverage
6.1	**Record and analyse information relating to direct costs and revenues**
A	Identify direct costs in accordance with the organisation's costing procedures.
B	Record and analyse information relating to direct costs.
C	Calculate direct costs in accordance with the organisation's policies and procedures.
D	Check cost information for stock against usage and stock control practices.
E	Resolve or refer queries to the appropriate person.
6.2	**Record and analyse information relating to the allocation, apportionment and absorption of overhead costs**
A	Identify overhead costs in accordance with the organisation's procedures.
B	Attribute overhead costs to production and service cost centres in accordance with agreed bases of allocation and apportionment.
C	Calculate overhead absorption rates in accordance with agreed bases of absorption.
D	Record and analyse information relating to overhead costs in accordance with the organisation's procedures.
E	Make adjustments for under and over recovered overhead costs in accordance with established procedures.
F	Review methods of allocation, apportionment and absorption at regular intervals in discussions with senior staff, and ensure agreed changes to methods are implemented.
G	Consult staff working in operational departments to resolve any queries in overhead cost data.
6.3	**Prepare and evaluate estimates of costs and revenues**
A	Identify information relevant to estimating current and future revenues and costs.
B	Prepare estimates of future income and costs.
C	Calculate the effects of variations in capacity on product costs.
D	Analyse critical factors affecting costs and revenues using appropriate accounting techniques and draw clear conclusions from the analysis.
E	State any assumptions used when evaluating future costs and revenues.
F	Identify and evaluate options and solutions for their contribution to organisational goals.
G	Present recommendations to appropriate people in a clear and concise way and supported by a clear rationale.

Any missing range statements should be assessed separately.

PART ONE

INSTRUCTIONS

This simulation is designed to let you show your ability to record and evaluate costs and revenues.

The simulation is designed to be attempted in two parts. You are allowed four hours in total to complete your work. You should spend:

- two hours on the tasks in Part 1, covering Elements 6.1 and 6.2;
- two hours on the tasks in Part 2, covering Element 6.3.

The simulation contains a large volume of data which you will need in order to complete the tasks. The information you require is provided in the sequence in which you will need to deal with it. However you are advised to look quickly through all of the material before you begin. This will help you to familiarise yourself with the situation and the information available.

Write your answers in the Answer Booklet provided on pages 193–212. If you need more paper for your answers, ask the person in charge.

You should write your answers in blue or black ink, not pencil. You may use correcting fluid, but in moderation. You should cross out your errors neatly and clearly.

Your work must be accurate, so check your work carefully before handing it in.

Coverage of performance criteria and range statements

It is not always possible to cover all performance criteria and range statements in a single simulation. Any performance criteria and range statements not covered must be assessed by other means by the assessor before a candidate can be considered competent.

Performance criteria and range statement coverage for this simulation is shown on page 176.

THE SITUATION

Your name is Bobby Forster and you work as the Accounts Assistant for Quality Candles Limited. The company manufactures candles of all kinds, including hand made candles. The candles are sold to wholesalers, to retailers, and direct to the public through the company's mail order division.

The manufacturing operations

The manufacturing operations involve three production cost centres and two service cost centres.

Production cost centres	Service cost centres
Manufacturing	Stores
Painting and finishing	Maintenance
Packing	

The time period covered by this simulation

The company's year end is 31 December. This simulation is concerned with activities during the quarter ending 31 December 2007, and with planning activities for the year ending 31 December 2008.

AAT sample simulation – unit 6

THE TASKS TO BE COMPLETED (PART ONE)

Element 6.1 (one hour)

1. Refer to the stores record card on page 195 of the Answer Booklet.

    - Complete this stores record card using the information from the materials documentation on pages 195 and 196 of the Answer Booklet and page 181 of this book. You will need to identify and apply the stock valuation method in use and you are advised that VAT is not entered in the cost accounting records.

    - Show the volume and value of the stock at the close of the week ending 10 October 2007. Any returns from production cost centres to stores are valued at the price of the most recent batch issued from stores.

2. Refer to the materials requisition note and materials returned note on page 196 of the Answer Booklet.

    - Complete the column headed 'Cost office use only' on each of the two documents.

3. Refer to your completed stores record card on page 195 of the Answer Booklet.

    - Prepare a memo for the general manager, drawing attention to any unusual issues concerning the stock levels for this item during the week. Your memo should highlight the issues, point out any possible consequences, and suggest any action that might be taken to prevent the unusual situations occurring. Use the blank memo form on page 197 of the Answer Booklet.

4. Refer to the internal policy document on page 182 of this book and the piecework operation card on page 198 of the Answer Booklet.

    - Complete the piecework operation card using the information provided. You will need to do the following:

        - Calculate the piecework payment for each day.
        - Calculate any bonus payable for the day.
        - Calculate the total wages payable for the day.
        - Complete the analysis of total wages payable for the week.

5. Refer to the piecework operation card on page 198 of the Answer Booklet.

    - Identify any possible discrepancy in the activity data and write a memo to the supervisor, Roy Hart, explaining clearly what you think the discrepancy might be. Use the blank memo form on page 199 of the Answer Booklet.

AAT sample simulation – unit 6

Element 6.2 (one hour)

6. Refer to the memo on page 183 of this book.

    ■ Perform the production overhead allocation and apportionment exercise using the analysis sheet on page 200 of the Answer Booklet. You will see that the task has already been started in respect of indirect labour. The data that you have gathered is on pages 183 and 184 of this booklet.

7. Refer to the first memo on page 185 of this book.

    ■ Calculate the production overhead absorption rates for 2008. You will need to make use of the following:

    – The blank working paper on page 201 of the Answer Booklet;

    – The data on pages 183 and 184 of this book;

    – Your results for the total production department overhead for 2008 on page 200 of the Answer Booklet.

    All absorption rates should be calculated to the nearest penny.

8. Refer to the second memo on page 185 of this book.

    ■ Re-calculate the total production overhead for each production department, reversing the order of apportionment of the service department overheads. Use the working paper on page 202 of the Answer Booklet. You will need to do the following:

    – Transfer your figures for total department overhead for all five departments from your overhead analysis sheet on page 200 of the Answer Booklet.

    – Re-apportion the service department overheads, apportioning the stores costs first to the other four departments on the basis of the number of material requisitions. Then re-apportion the total overhead of the maintenance department to the three production departments, on the basis of maintenance hours.

    Perform all calculations to the nearest £000.

9. ■ Review your results from Task 8 and write a memo to the general manager. In your memo you should:

    – comment on the effect of the change in method;

    – explain whether you think it is necessary to instigate a change in the method of re-apportionment of service department costs.

    Use the blank memo form on page 203 of the Answer Booklet.

10. Refer to the memo and the production overhead data on page 186 of this book.

    ■ Complete the journal entry form on page 204 of the Answer Booklet.

    ■ Write a memo to the production manager detailing any queries concerning the data and suggesting possible causes of any discrepancies you have identified. Use the blank memo form on page 205 of the Answer Booklet.

180

SALES INVOICE
Threadshop Limited
25 Lyme Street, Taunton TA2 4RP

Invoice to:
Quality Candles Limited
2 Norman Lane
Winterbury
RT5 8UT

VAT Registration: 254 1781 26
Date/tax point: 9 October 2007
Invoice numvber: T543
Your order: 47346

Description of goods/services	Total (£)
Candlewick thread, 200 metre rolls 80 rolls @ £2.38	190.40
Goods total VAT @ 17.5%	190.40 33.32
Total due	223.72

Checked against GRN number: 427
Date received: 9 October 2007
Signed: J Jones

Terms: net 30 days

INTERNAL POLICY DOCUMENT

Document no: 18
Subject: Wages
Issued: August 2007

Piecework scheme

A piecework scheme is to be introduced into the manufacturing department in order to reward efficient and productive operatives.

A piecework rate per batch of £0.50 will be paid for each batch of accepted output produced during a day.

In addition a bonus will be paid of 4 per cent of the piecework payment for any day on which the number of batches rejected by Quality Control is less than 5 per cent of the total number of batches produced.

A guaranteed daily wage of £50 is payable if the piecework payment + bonus amounts to less than £50 in any day.

Analysis of wages

Piecework payments and guaranteed daily wages paid will be treated as direct wages costs.

Bonus payments will be treated as indirect wages costs.

Discrepancies on piecework operation cards

The company wishes to pay wages and report labour rates promptly. Therefore employees will initially be paid for the total wages calculated according to the data contained on the weekly piecework operation card.

Any discrepancies on operation cards will be referred to the supervisor. Any alterations to wages will be agreed with the employee before adjustment is made to the next wage payment.

INTERNAL MEMO

To: Bobby Forster, Accounts Assistant
From: General Manager
Subject: Budgeted production costs for 2008
Date: 28 October 2007

As you know we have begun our budgetary planning exercise for 2008.

I understand that you have been working on the analysis of budgeted production costs. Could you please pull together all the information you have gathered and carry out the allocation and apportionment exercise for production overhead costs for 2008.

Thanks. Then we will have the necessary information that we need to calculate the pre-determined overhead absorption rates for 2008.

Data for production overhead analysis for 2008

1. Summary of budgeted production costs for 2008

	£000
Direct materials	200
Indirect materials	40
Direct labour	420
Indirect labour:	
Manufacturing department	22
Painting and finishing department	14
Packing department	11
Stores	35
Maintenance	16
Rent and rates	105
Protective clothing	31
Power	40
Insurance	24
Heat and light	35
Depreciation	48
Other production overheads	15
Total budgeted production costs	1,056

2. Other data

	Manufact-uring	Painting/finishing	Packing	Stores	Mainten-ance
Direct materials cost (£000)	150	25	25	–	–
Floor area (000 sq metres)	30	10	16	8	6
Power usage (%)	50	10	30	5	5
Net book value of equipment (£000)	220	80	120	40	20
Maintenance hours (000)	7	4	3	1	–
Materials requisitions (000)	18	10	9	–	11
Direct labour hours (000)	20	28	10	–	–
Machine hours (000)	200	14	90	–	–

3. Company procedures for the allocation and apportionment of production overheads

- 30 per cent of the total indirect materials cost is apportioned to stores and 30 per cent to maintenance. The remaining 40 per cent is apportioned to the production departments according to the direct materials cost.

- Rent and rates and heating and lighting costs are apportioned according to the floor area occupied by each department.

- The cost of protective clothing is allocated to the manufacturing department.

- Power costs are apportioned according to the power usage in each department.

- Insurance and depreciation costs are apportioned according to the net book value of equipment in each department.

- Other production overheads are apportioned equally to the production departments.

- The total cost of the maintenance department is apportioned to the other four departments according to the number of maintenance hours.

- After a charge has been received from the maintenance department, the total cost of the stores department is apportioned to the three production departments according to the number of material requisitions.

- All calculations are rounded to the nearest £000.

INTERNAL MEMO

To: Bobby Forster, Accounts Assistant
From: General Manager
Subject: Pre-determined overhead absorption rates
Date: 28 October 2007

Many thanks for all your hard work on the overhead analysis.

Could you please now use the results of your analysis to calculate overhead absorption rates for the three production departments for 2008. We have decided that the most appropriate bases of absorption will be as follows:

- Manufacturing department: machine hour rate;
- Painting and finishing department: labour hour rate;
- Packing department: machine hour rate.

Thanks for your help.

INTERNAL MEMO

To: Bobby Forster, Accounts Assistant
From: General Manager
Subject: Re-apportionment of service department costs
Date: 4 November 2007

I have been giving some thought to the method that we use to re-apportion the service department costs to the production departments.

As you know, at present it is our policy to apportion the maintenance costs to all cost centres before we re-apportion the total stores costs to the production cost centres.

I would like to see the effect of altering the order of re-apportionment of service department costs. Could you please rework the figures so that we can review the results?

Let me have the results and your views as soon as possible, please.

INTERNAL MEMO

To: Bobby Forster, Accounts Assistant
From: General Manager
Subject: Overhead absorption for October 2007
Date: 8 November 2007

As you know it is company policy to accumulate the under or over-absorbed production overhead each month in an account maintained for this purpose.

The production overhead data for October 2007 has now been finalised.

Could you please complete the journal entry for the absorption of production overhead into the work in progress accounts and transfer any under or over absorption for the month. Complete the entries using the data provided, but please let the production manager know if you have any queries concerning the data.

Summary of production overhead data for October 2007

	£
Actual production overhead incurred	15,800
Production overhead to be absorbed into work in progress	
Manufacturing department	18,500
Painting and finishing department	7,400
Packing department	8,300

PART TWO

INSTRUCTIONS

This simulation is designed to let you show your ability to record and evaluate costs and revenues.

The simulation is designed to be attempted in two parts. You should already have completed the tasks in Part 1 and you should ensure that you have your answers to those tasks with you.

You are allowed four hours in total to complete your work.

- Two hours for the tasks in Part 1, covering Elements 6.1 and 6.2;
- Two hours for the tasks in Part 2, covering Element 6.3.

The simulation contains a large volume of data which you will need in order to complete the tasks. The information you require is provided in the sequence in which you will need to deal with it. However you are advised to look quickly through all of the material before you begin. This will help you to familiarise yourself with the situation and the information available.

Write your answers in the Answer Booklet provided on pages 193 to 212. If you need more paper for your answers, ask the person in charge.

You should write your answers in blue or black ink, not pencil.

You may use correcting fluid, but in moderation. You should cross out your errors neatly and clearly.

Your work must be accurate, so check your work carefully before handing it in.

AAT sample simulation – unit 6

THE SITUATION

Your name is Bobby Forster and you work as the Accounts Assistant for Quality Candles Limited. The company manufactures candles of all kinds, including hand made candles. The candles are sold to wholesalers, to retailers, and direct to the public through the company's mail order division.

The manufacturing operations

The manufacturing operations involve three production cost centres and two service cost centres.

Production cost centres	Service cost centres
Manufacturing	Stores
Painting and finishing	Maintenance
Packing	

The time period covered by this simulation

The company's year end is 31 December. This simulation is concerned with activities during the quarter ending 31 December 2007, and with planning activities for the year ending 31 December 2008.

THE TASKS TO BE COMPLETED (PART TWO)

Element 6.3 (two hours)

11. Refer to the memo on page 190 of this book and prepare the necessary information in response to the general manager's query. You will need to do the following.

    - Use the data on page 190 of this book and the working paper on page 206 of the Answer Booklet to identify the cost and revenue behaviour patterns to be used in your projections.

    - Use your identified cost and revenue behaviour patterns to complete the planned profit projection on page 207 of the Answer Booklet. There is space for your workings at the bottom of that page.

12. Refer to the first memo on page 191 of this book and answer the general manager's queries. You will need to do the following.

    (i) Use your identified cost and revenue behaviour patterns, adjusted for the change in materials cost, to prepare a revised planned profit statement for December. Complete the profit statement on page 208 of the Answer Booklet. There is space for your workings at the bottom of that page.

    (ii) Calculate the breakeven point in terms of the number of cases to be sold in December if the bulk discount is accepted. Use the blank working paper on page 209 of the Answer Booklet and round your answer up to the nearest number of whole cases. Also use the same working paper to calculate the margin of safety. Express your answer as a percentage of the increased planned activity for December.

    (iii) Prepare a memo to the general manager evaluating the results of your calculations. Your memo should contain the following:

    - Your comments on the resulting profit, breakeven point and margin of safety;
    - A statement of any assumptions you have used in evaluating the proposal.

    Use the blank memo form on page 210 of the Answer Booklet.

13. Refer to the second memo on page 191 of this book and do the following:

    (i) Use the working paper on page 211 of the Answer Booklet to calculate the payback period and the net present value of the proposed investment. Ignore inflation and perform all monetary calculations to the nearest £.

    (ii) Write a memo to the General Manager evaluating the proposal from a financial viewpoint and stating any assumptions you have made in your analysis. Use the blank memo form on page 212 of the Answer Booklet.

INTERNAL MEMO

To: Bobby Forster, Accounts Assistant
From: General Manager
Subject: Mail order division: revised plan for December 2007
Date: 9 November 2007

Could you please prepare the revised cost and revenue plan for the mail order division for December.

The plan is to sell 6,800 cases of candles and we will base our projections on the cost and revenue behaviour patterns experienced during August to October.

Thanks for your help.

Quality Candles Limited: mail order division

Actual results for August to October 2007

	August	September	October
Number of cases sold	7,000	6,200	5,900
	£	£	£
Candles cost	9,100	8,060	7,670
Packing materials cost	5,250	4,650	4,425
Packing labour cost	2,100	1,860	1,770
Packing overhead cost	5,400	5,240	5,180
Other overhead cost	2,500	*3,000	2,500
Total costs	24,350	22,810	21,545
Sales revenue	28,000	24,800	23,600
Profit	3,650	1,990	2,055

* Other overhead cost was £500 higher than usual during September owing to an unexpected machine breakdown which necessitated the hire of a packing machine to maintain production. This event will not recur in the future.

INTERNAL MEMO

To: Bobby Forster, Accounts Assistant
From: General Manager
Subject: Mail order division: bulk discounts for December 2007
Date: 10 November 2007

Many thanks for your splendid work on the cost and revenue projections for December.

We are looking for opportunities to increase profit and we have just heard that we can obtain a bulk discount for packing materials in December if we increase our activity level to 7,600 cases for the month. This will mean that packing material unit costs will reduce by 20 per cent.

Could you please recalculate the profit projection for December if we decide to increase activity to take advantage of the discount.

Also, please calculate the breakeven point in terms of the number of cases to be sold in December if we make this change. I would also like to have a note of the margin of safety we will have.

Please let me have the results of your calculations and your comments on the outcome as soon as you can.

INTERNAL MEMO

To: Bobby Forster, Accounts Assistant
From: General Manager
Subject: Purchase of delivery vehicles for mail order division
Date: 12 November 2007

We are considering the purchase and operation of our own fleet of delivery vehicles at the end of this year.

The distribution manager informs me that we will be able to cancel our current delivery contract and as a result we will enjoy cash savings of £34,800 each year from 2007 onwards, after taking account of the vehicle operating costs.

The vehicles will cost us £90,000 and will have a resale value of £5,000 when they are sold at the end of 2010.

Can you please appraise this proposal from a financial viewpoint? I need to know the payback period and the net present value at our usual discount rate of 12 per cent. As you know our minimum required payback period for all capital projects is three years.

Please let me have the results as soon as possible.

AAT

SAMPLE SIMULATION
UNIT 6

QUALITY CANDLES LTD

ANSWER BOOKLET

PART 1

Task 1

Sample calculations: working paper
Reversing the order of service department re-apportionments

Production overhead item	Total £000	Manufacturing £000	Painting/finishing £000	Packing £000	Stores £000	Maintenance £000
Total department overheads (from Task 6)	436	183	57	80	71	45
Apportion stores total	–	27	15	13	(71)	16
Apportion maintenance total	–	31	17	13	–	(61)
Total production dept overheads	436	241	89	106		

Tasks 1 and 2

MATERIALS REQUISITION

Department: Manufacturing
Document no: 252
Date: 08/10/2007

Code no	Description	Quantity	Cost office use only Value of issue (£)
CW728	Candlewick thread 200m rolls	40	

Received by: .... Signature: ....

MATERIALS RETURNED

Department: Manufacturing
Document no: 75
Date: 10/10/2007

Code no	Description	Quantity	Cost office use only Value of issue (£)
CW728	Candlewick thread 200m rolls	3	

Received by: .... Signature: ....

Task 3

MEMO

To:
From:
Subject:
Date:

Task 4

QUALITY CANDLES LIMITED
PIECEWORK OPERATION CARD

Operative name: __Mary Roberts__ Department: __Manufacturing__

Clock number: __R27__

Week beginning: __6 October 2007__

Activity	Monday	Tuesday	Wednesday	Thursday	Friday
Batches produced	120	102	34	202	115
Batches rejected	5	7	4	11	5
Batches accepted					
Rate per batch	£ 0.50	£ 0.50	£ 0.50	£ 0.50	£ 0.50
Piecework payment	£	£	£	£	£
Bonus payable	£	£	£	£	£
Total payable for day*	£	£	£	£	£

Total wages payable for week:
£

Direct wages

Indirect wages

Total wages

* Guaranteed daily wage of £50 is payable if piecework payment plus bonus amounts less than £50

Supervisor's signature: _A Peters_

Task 5

INTERNAL MEMO

To:
From:
Subject:
Date:

Task 6

Production overhead analysis sheet for 2008

Production overhead item	Total £000	Manufacturing £000	Painting/finishing £000	Packing £000	Stores £000	Maintenance £000
Indirect labour	98	22	14	11	35	16
Total department overheads						
Apportion maintenance total	—					( )
Apportion stores total	—				( )	
Total production dept overheads						

Task 7

Working paper

Calculation of production overhead absorption rates for 2008

Manufacturing department

Painting and finishing department

Packing department

Task 8

Sample calculations: working paper
Reversing the order of service department re-apportionments

Production overhead item	Total £000	Manufacturing £000	Painting/finishing £000	Packing £000	Stores £000	Maintenance £000
Total department overheads (from task 6)						
Apportion stores total	—				( )	
Apportion maintenance total	—				—	( )
Total production dept overheads						

202

Task 9

INTERNAL MEMO

To:
From:
Subject:
Date:

Task 10

Journal entry for production overheads

October 2007

Entries for overhead absorbed during the month

	Debit (£)	Credit (£)
Work in progress: manufacturing dept		
Work in progress: painting and finishing dept		
Work in progress: packing dept		
Production overhead control		

Entries for overhead under-/over-absorbed during the month

	Debit (£)	Credit (£)
Overhead over-/under-absorbed (P+L)		
Production overhead control		

Task 10 (continued)

INTERNAL MEMO

To:
From:
Subject:
Date:

PART 2

Task 11

Workings for determination of revenue and cost behaviour patterns

---

Sales revenue

Candles cost

Packing materials cost

Packing labour cost

Packing overhead cost

Other overheads cost

Task 11 (continued)

Quality Candles Limited: mail order division

Planned results for December 2007

December

Number of cases to be sold

£

Candles cost

Packing materials cost

Packing labour cost

Packing overhead cost

Other overheads cost

Total costs

Sales revenue

Profit

Space for workings

Task 12 (i)

Quality Candles Limited: mail order division

Planned results for December 2007: increased activity

	December
Number of cases to be sold	7,600
	£
Candles cost	
Packing materials cost	
Packing labour cost	
Packing overhead cost	
Other overheads cost	
Total costs	
Sales revenue	
Profit	

Space for workings

Task 12 (ii)

Quality Candles Limited: mail order division

Planned results for December 2007: increased activity

Calculation of breakeven point and margin of safety: working paper

Task 12 (iii)

INTERNAL MEMO

To:
From:
Subject:
Date:

Task 13 (i)

Working paper for the financial appraisal of purchase of delivery vehicles

Year	Cashflow £	Discount factor @ 12%	Present value £
2007	_____	1.000	_____
2008	_____	0.893	_____
2009	_____	0.797	_____
2010	_____	0.712	_____
2011	_____	0.636	_____

Net present value _____

Working space for calculation of payback period

Task 13 (ii)

INTERNAL MEMO

To:
From:
Subject:
Date:

PRACTICE SIMULATION
UNIT 6

HIGH HEAT LTD

practice simulation – unit 6

COVERAGE OF PERFORMANCE CRITERIA AND RANGE STATEMENTS

All performance criteria are covered in this simulation.

Element	PC Coverage
6.1	**Record and analyse information relating to direct costs and revenues**
A	Identify direct costs in accordance with the organisation's costing procedures.
B	Record and analyse information relating to direct costs.
C	Calculate direct costs in accordance with the organisation's policies and procedures.
D	Check cost information for stock against usage and stock control practices.
E	Resolve or refer queries to the appropriate person.
6.2	**Record and analyse information relating to the allocation, apportionment and absorption of overhead costs**
A	Identify overhead costs in accordance with the organisation's procedures.
B	Attribute overhead costs to production and service cost centres in accordance with agreed bases of allocation and apportionment.
C	Calculate overhead absorption rates in accordance with agreed bases of absorption.
D	Record and analyse information relating to overhead costs in accordance with the organisation's procedures.
E	Make adjustments for under and over recovered overhead costs in accordance with established procedures.
F	Review methods of allocation, apportionment and absorption at regular intervals in discussions with senior staff, and ensure agreed changes to methods are implemented.
G	Consult staff working in operational departments to resolve any queries in overhead cost data.
6.3	**Prepare and evaluate estimates of costs and revenues**
A	Identify information relevant to estimating current and future revenues and costs.
B	Prepare estimates of future income and costs.
C	Calculate the effects of variations in capacity on product costs.
D	Analyse critical factors affecting costs and revenues using appropriate accounting techniques and draw clear conclusions from the analysis.
E	State any assumptions used when evaluating future costs and revenues.
F	Identify and evaluate options and solutions for their contribution to organisational goals.
G	Present recommendations to appropriate people in a clear and concise way and supported by a clear rationale.

Any missing range statements should be assessed separately.

practice simulation – unit 6

DATA AND TASKS

This simulation is designed to let you show your ability to record and evaluate costs and revenues.

This simulation is divided into 13 tasks. You are advised to look through the whole simulation first to gain a general appreciation of your tasks.

The situation is provided below. The tasks to be completed are set out on pages 216 to 219.

Your answers should be set out in the Answer Booklet using the documents and working papers provided. You may require additional pages.

You are allowed a total of **four hours** to complete your work.

A high level of accuracy is required. Check your work carefully.

Correcting fluid may be used, but it should be used in moderation. Errors should be crossed out neatly and clearly. You should write in blue or black ink, not pencil.

THE SITUATION

You work as the Management Accounts Assistant for High Heat Limited. The company manufactures oven ranges for use in restaurants and other mass catering establishments. It employs about 75 people at its factory in Andover.

Cost centres

The production cost centres in High Heat Limited are a Machine Shop (incorporating raw materials stores) and an Assembly Shop.

The company also operates two service cost centres: a Testing Centre and a Staff Amenity Centre (including a canteen and a small gym).

The people involved in this simulation

Yourself	Management Accounts Assistant
Malcolm Harrison	Machine Shop Manager
Lynn Tilling	Assembly Shop Manager
Pamela Robinson	Purchasing Clerk
Karim Huq	Purchasing Manager
Ismay Ratliff	Production Director

The time period covered by this simulation

In this simulation you will be dealing with transactions and activities that occur in October and November 2007. You will also be preparing budget and forecast data for 2008 and evaluating information that relates to a four year planning horizon. At the end of this period of time the company plans to be operating from three sites, providing other types of kitchen appliance and consultancy services in addition to its current products. You perform the first task on 2 November 2007.

215

practice simulation – unit 6

THE TASKS TO BE COMPLETED

PART ONE – Record and analyse information relating to direct costs and revenues

Task 1

Refer to the extract of accounting information on page 220 of this booklet in relation to the production and sale of the Oven 900 model.

You are required to calculate the contribution to fixed costs made by the Oven 900 line in October on page 235 of the Answer Booklet.

Task 2

Refer to the stock record (stock card) for hi-grade filters on page 236 of the Answer Booklet and the documentation relating to receipts and issues of this part to the Assembly Shop on pages 220–222 of this booklet.

You are required to complete the stock record as far as the information available will allow, showing clearly the month end balance in units and value. Note that all issues are currently priced using the FIFO stock valuation method.

Task 3

You are required to:

a) check whether the company's stock control practices have been followed correctly for hi-grade filters during October

b) draft a memo to the Production Director, Ismay Ratliff, setting out your conclusions about stock control and purchasing practice, and suggesting actions which may address any problems. Use the memo form on page 237 of the Answer Booklet.

practice simulation – unit 6

Task 4

You are required to:

a) refer to the memo about stock valuation from the Production Director, Ismay Ratliff, on page 223 of this booklet

b) complete the stock records on page 239 of the Answer Booklet using the AVCO method

c) draft a memo in reply to her queries on page 238 of the Answer Booklet

Task 5

Refer to the Time Sheets for Sanjeev Patel and Jacob Ellis on page 240 and 241 of the Answer Booklet and the extract from the Payroll Guide on page 224 of this booklet.

You are required to:

a) complete the total columns on the time sheets
b) complete the analysis of hours sections of the time sheets
c) complete the analysis of gross pay sections of the time sheets.

Task 6

Draft a memo to Malcolm Harrison, the Machine Shop Manager, setting out any discrepancies in Jacob Ellis's time sheet and asking for help in identifying the reason for it. Use the blank memo form on page 242 of the Answer Booklet.

PART TWO – Record and analyse information relating to the allocation, apportionment and absorption of overhead costs

Task 7

Refer to the memo about production overhead absorption rates for 2008 from Ismay Ratliff, the Production Director, dated 5 November on page 223 of this booklet.

On page 243 of the Answer Booklet complete the calculation of under-/over-absorption of production overheads, and indicate clearly whether the under-/over-absorbed amount is to be debited or credited in the profit and loss account.

217

practice simulation – unit 6

Task 8

Refer to the memo about production overhead absorption rates for 2008 from Ismay Ratliff, the Production Director dated 12 November on page 225 of this booklet and the data on page 226 of this booklet.

You are required to:

a) at the top of the memo on page 244 of the Answer Booklet, calculate a single factory-wide production overhead absorption rate per direct labour hour for 2008

b) complete the memo to the Production Director, explaining why the change in absorption methods would be a good idea.

Task 9

Refer to the memo about production overhead absorption rates for 2008 from Ismay Ratliff, the Production Director, dated 19 November on page 227 of this booklet.

You are required to using the overhead analysis sheets on pages 245 and 246 of the Answer Booklet, calculate the production overhead absorption rates (to two decimal places) as requested, using first the step down method and then the direct method for apportioning primary allocations to the production areas.

PART THREE – Prepare and evaluate estimates of costs and revenues

Task 10

Refer to the memo about new sites and products from Ismay Ratliff, the Production Director, dated 25 November on page 228 of this booklet.

You are required to:

a) on page 247 of the Answer Booklet, calculate the payback period and the net present value of the project

b) on page 248 of the Answer Booklet, prepare a memo to the Production Director by detailing your results and commenting on the proposal. State any assumptions that you have made in your calculations.

Task 11

Refer to the memo about producing large size dishwashers from Ismay Ratliff, the Production Director, dated 27 November on page 229 of this booklet. Refer also to the data on page 229 of this booklet concerning the proposal.

You are required to:

a) on page 249 of the Answer Booklet, use the information concerning selling prices to determine the projected sales volume for the large-size dishwashers

b) on page 249 of the Answer Booklet, use the unit cost estimates to analyse the dishwashers's cost behaviour patterns and to determine the projected costs for your calculated sales volume

c) complete the projected costs and revenues statement on page 250 of the Answer Booklet

Task 12

Refer to the memo about further analysis of the dishwasher product from Ismay Ratliff, the Production Director, dated 29 November on page 230 of this booklet.

You are required to:

a) on page 257 of the Answer Booklet, to carry out the calculations requested by the Production Director in relation to further analysis of the dishwasher. Calculate all figures to the nearest whole number

b) prepare a memo to the Production Director detailing your results and commenting on the proposal. You should also explain any assumptions that you have made in your calculations concerning the proposals. Use the blank memo form on page 252 of the Answer Booklet.

Task 13

Refer to the memo about new products at the new sites from Ismay Ratliff, the Production Director, dated 30 November on page 231 of this booklet.

You are required on page 253 of the Answer Booklet, to carry out the calculations requested by the Production Director in relation to the two new products. Calculate all figures to the nearest whole number.

practice simulation – unit 6

Oven 900 – extract of accounting information

Ledger account balances as at 31 October 2007

Ledger code	Account name	£	Debit or credit
S900	Sales Oven 900	78,530	Credit
M901	Material 1 issued to Oven 900 production	10,540	Debit
M902	Material 2 issued to Oven 900 production	5,960	Debit
M903	Material 3 issued to Oven 900 production	15,635	Debit
L900	Gross wages of direct labour on Oven 900 production	24,680	Debit
L901	Employer's NIC and pension on Oven 900 production	3,520	Debit
V900	Expenses of Oven 900 production	1,970	Debit

Stock of Oven 900s (at marginal cost)

	£
As at 1 October 2007	13,850
As at 31 October 2007	16,830

PURCHASE ORDER

HIGH HEAT LTD
Grundell Trading Estate,
Andover,
Hants SO9 7DF

Order number: 8094802

Date: 10 October 2007

Order placed by: Pamela Robinson

To: Power Filters
Wallop Industrial Estate
Andover

Order checked by: Karim Huq

Quantity	Ref. no.	Description	Unit price £	Total value £
75	FF783	Hi-grade filters	16.70	1,252.50

VAT at 17.5% is to be added where applicable. Price includes delivery to above address.

PURCHASE ORDER

HIGH HEAT LTD
Grundell Trading Estate,
Andover,
Hants SO9 7DF

To: Power Filters
Wallop Industrial Estate
Andover

Order number: 8097506

Date: 27 October 2007

Order placed by: Pamela Robinson

Order checked by:

Quantity	Ref. no.	Description	Unit price £	Total value £
80	FF783	Hi-grade filters	17.10	1,368.00

VAT at 17.5% is to be added where applicable. Price includes delivery to above address.

GOODS RECEIVED NOTE

HIGH HEAT LIMITD

Supplier: Power Filters

Number: 05791283
Order ref: 8094802

Date: 12 October 2007

Quantity	Material code number	Description
75	FF783	Hi-grade filters

Received and checked by: Malcolm Harrison

GOODS RECEIVED NOTE

HIGH HEAT LIMITD

Supplier: Power Filters

Number: 05792004
Order ref: 8097506

Date: 29 October 2007

Quantity	Material code number	Description
80	FF783	Hi-grade filters

MATERIALS REQUISITION

Area: Assembly Shop **Requisition number:** 165745 **Date:** 15 October 2007

Quantity	Code number	Description	Notes
60	FF783	Hi-grade filters	

Manager signature *Lynn Tilling*

MATERIALS REQUISITION

Area: Assembly Shop **Requisition number:** 166102 **Date:** 31 October 2007

Quantity	Code number	Description	Notes
90	FF783	Hi-grade filters	

Manager signature *Lynn Tilling*

practice simulation – unit 6

MEMORANDUM

To: Management Accounts Assistant
From: Ismay Ratliff, Production Director
Subject: Stock valuation October 2007
Date: 3 November 2007

Raw materials stock valuation

The company auditors have been talking to me about alternative methods of identifying the costs of raw materials that we use in our production. They have suggested we look at the Average Cost method (AVCO).

Please prepare example stock records for hi-grade filters for October 2007, using this alternative, so I can assess the impact of the Average Cost methods on valuation.

Part-finished goods valuation

We have also discussed the valuation of part-finished goods in our year-end accounts. Usually we aim to complete all items in the factory as at the year-end, 31 December, in advance of our two-week closure for Christmas and New Year. This year, however, I anticipate that we will have 40 Oven 678s in the Assembly Shop, 100% complete as to materials and machining but only 60% complete as to labour. The costs of a single Oven 678 are as follows:

	£
Materials	565.00
Labour	890.00
Expenses (variable overheads absorbed on machine hour basis)	200.00
	1,655.00

Please calculate the value for part-finished goods that we should show in our accounts.

Finished goods valuation

We have always valued finished goods at their marginal cost of production in the year-end financial accounts, although we use full absorption for management accounting purposes. The auditors have suggested that we should consider moving to a full absorption basis in the financial accounts as well. Please give me your views as to whether this is likely to increase or decrease the value of finished goods stock, and the effect this will have on profit.

HIGH HEAT LTD

Date   1 January 2007   **For year to:** 31 December 2007
Subject: Wages payments
Labour rates: Factory employees

Employee grade	£ per basic hour
A	10.00
B	8.50
C	7.00

All full-time employees are contracted to work 7.5 hours per day for a five day week. All employees get 5 weeks' annual leave, plus bank holidays.

All authorised holiday, sick and training time is paid at the employee's basic hourly rate.

Any hours worked in excess of the full-time equivalent of 7.5 per day, as indicated on the authorised Time Sheet, are to be paid as overtime at a rate of time and a half.

Productivity bonuses may be paid at the discretion of Managers, countersigned by the relevant Manager on the Time Sheet. Productivity bonuses are expressed in hours and paid at double time.

Analysis of wages

The following are to be treated as direct labour costs:

- payment for time spent on direct tasks
- the basic pay for overtime hours spent on direct tasks

The following are to be treated as indirect labour costs:

- overtime premium payments
- bonus payments
- idle time payments
- holiday pay
- sick pay
- payment for time spent on training

Discrepancies on Time Sheets

Employees will initially be paid for the hours attendance shown at the bottom of their Time Sheet at their basic rate.

Employees know that it is a serious matter if a Time Sheet is submitted to payroll without due authorisation and/or which is incorrect. For this reason, overtime rates and all bonus hours will not be paid if the Time Sheet contains a discrepancy. If it has not been authorised no payment can be made until it is so authorised.

MEMORANDUM

To: Management Accounts Assistant
From: Ismay Ratliff, Production Director
Subject: Absorption of production overheads for October 2007
Date: 5 November 2007

I would like you to complete the calculations for absorption of production overheads for October 2006. Here are the data you need:

- Actual production overhead expenditure   £68,750
- Total number of machine hours   4,590
- Absorption rate used for 2007   £13 per machine hour

Under or over-absorbed production overhead is written off to the profit and loss account each month.

Please let me know if you have any queries concerning the data.

MEMORANDUM

To: Management Accounts Assistant
From: Ismay Ratliff, Production Director
Subject: Production overhead absorption rates for 2008
Date: 12 November 2007

We need to get on with calculating the production overhead absorption rate for next year's budget.

As you know we currently use one absorption rate per machine hour for both production departments. I would like you to calculate this single rate for next year and include it in a memo to me.

In our monthly management meeting, the Assembly Shop Manager Lynn Tilling suggested that we should use a separate absorption rate for each of the two production departments: a machine hour rate in the Machine Shop and a direct labour hour rate in the Assembly Shop. I'm afraid to say I am not too sure what this means. In a memo, can you please explain what she meant: why should we change our absorption methods and why are the rates suggested by Ms Tilling likely to be the best in our circumstances?

Thanks for your help.

BUDGETED DATA FOR 2007

1) **Budgeted production costs**

	£	£
Direct production materials	2,163,000	
Direct labour	1,625,800	
Total budgeted direct cost		3,788,800
Budgeted production overheads:		
Indirect labour: production departments	406,600	
Managers' salaries		
Machine Shop	41,000	
Assembly Shop	41,000	
Testing Centre costs	124,800	
Staff Amenity Centre costs	70,500	
Machinery & equipment depreciation	25,200	
Rent, rates and power costs	101,300	
Other production overheads	44,600	
Total budgeted production overheads		855,000
Total budgeted production cost		4,643,800

2) **Other budget data**

	Machine shop	Assembly shop	Testing Centre	Staff Amenity Centre	Total
Direct employees	25	40			65
Indirect employees (production)	1	1	6	3	11
Machine hours	41,500	11,100			52,600
Direct labour hours	35,100	85,900			121,000
Testing Centre hours			10,800		
Fixed assets: net book value	85,400	19,500	15,000	6,100	126,000
Floor area (m²)	1,800	3,000	840	360	6,000

practice simulation – unit 6

MEMORANDUM

To: Management Accounts Assistant
From: Ismay Ratliff, Production Director
Subject: Production overhead absorption rates for 2008
Date: 19 November 2007

Thank you for explaining why we should change our method of overhead absorption.

Please go ahead and calculate the two separate new production overhead absorption rates for 2008, using the following data as well as what you already have.

Bases of allocation and apportionment of production overhead under the new absorption methods

- Rent, rates and power costs are to be apportioned according to the floor area occupied by each cost centre.

- Other production overheads are to be apportioned equally to the two production cost centres.

- Primary cost allocations should be apportioned to production departments using the step down method.

- Testing Centre costs are to be allocated on the basis of 25% machine shop, 75% assembly shop.

- Staff Amenity Centre costs are to be apportioned according to the total number of direct and indirect employees in each area.

- Machinery and equipment depreciation will be allocated on the basis of net book value.

Alternative basis

As a matter of interest, I would like to know what difference would be made to the rates if we used the direct method of apportionment of primary allocated costs instead of the step down method. Please make these calculations as well therefore, applying the following rules:

- Testing Centre costs are to be allocated on the basis of 25% machine shop, 75% assembly shop.

- Staff Amenity Centre costs are to be apportioned according to the total number of direct and indirect employees in each area.

practice simulation – unit 6

MEMORANDUM

To: Management Accounts Assistant
From: Ismay Ratliff, Production Director
Subject: New sites and products
Date: 25 November 2007

HIGHLY CONFIDENTIAL

We are considering opening two new factories, one in Scotland and one in Wales. We expect that the move will allow us to expand our product and service range considerably.

The company's policy is to evaluate all capital projects over a four year planning horizon, and we need a maximum payback period of three years. Our cost of capital is 6 per cent.

We have forecast the following cash flows for the expansion.

Year	Cash flows £
0	(1,000,000)
1	250,000
2	350,000
3	500,000
4	650,000

Discount factors at 6%: 0.9434 (year 1); 0.8900 (year 2); 0.8396 (year 3); 0.7920 (year 4).

Please could you work out the payback period and the Net Present Value of the expansion, and let me have your evaluation of the proposal as soon as possible?

MEMORANDUM

To: Management Accounts Assistant
From: Ismay Ratliff, Production Director
Subject: Producing large size dishwashers
Date: 27 November 2007

We are currently working on producing a range of industrial dishwashers, to satisfy demand from our existing customer base, from January 2008. We need you to produce some projections of our profit for the first year of the new product's sales.

Our sales staff say they can sell 150 industrial dishwashers next year at a price of £2,300 per machine to our existing customers. However, as we have capacity to produce rather more than that, and want to sell them to our new clients as well as our old ones, we have decided we can price them lower than that. Our sales staff tell us that we can sell 5 more machines for every £75 reduction in price. We have therefore decided to price them at £2,000 per machine.

We have put together cost estimates for production at two different levels of output. Please prepare a profit projection for 2008, assuming that all sales will be made at a selling price of £2,000 per machine.

Large size industrial dishwasher: unit cost estimates for 2008 production

Production volume	150 machines	160 machines
	£	£
	per unit	per unit
Direct materials	880.00	880.00
Direct labour	412.00	412.00
Production overheads	364.00	355.00
Other overheads	50.00	46.88
Total cost	1,706.00	1,693.88

MEMORANDUM

To: Management Accounts Assistant
From: Ismay Ratliff, Production Director
Subject: Producing large size dishwashers, and other matters
Date: 29 November 2007

HIGHLY CONFIDENTIAL

Analysis of dishwasher product

Thank you for your work on the profits that we can make on producing and selling dishwashers.

While we are very happy that the range looks like it will be profitable, we are fairly conservative about risk, and are therefore concerned that there should be a margin of safety of at least 25% of projected sales volume.

Please could you do some further calculations to answer the following questions:

- What is the projected margin of safety at the £2,000 selling price?

- What is the P/V ratio (we usually need a ratio of at least 20%)?

- There is a fair amount of uncertainty surrounding the estimate of production overheads because, as you know, we will probably be opening new sites. What is the maximum percentage increase in production overheads that we could incur before the new product begins to incur losses?

Please let me have your answers, and any comments you have about the proposal, in a memo.

MEMORANDUM

To: Management Accounts Assistant
From: Ismay Ratliff, Production Director
Subject: New products at the new sites
Date: 30 November 2007

HIGHLY CONFIDENTIAL

Contracts required by Welsh consultancy

We are planning a new consultancy service from our Welsh site, which will incur fixed costs of £50,000 in the first year. Each contract we take on is projected to make a contribution of £2,000. Please calculate how many contracts a year we need to take on in order to generate the target profit for the service, which is £80,000.

Limiting factor on production of large electric woks in Scotland

We are planning to make large-scale electric woks at our new site in Scotland. We will have 2,000 hours of the required machine time available, and 4,500 hours of the required labour. Each wok requires 14 hours of machine time and 20 hours of labour. Please identify for me the limiting factor on production of woks, and the maximum number of woks that we can produce.

PRACTICE SIMULATION UNIT 6

HIGH HEAT LTD

ANSWER BOOKLET

Task 1

Oven 900 – contribution to fixed costs for October 2007

                                                              £   £

Sales
Less: cost of sales

Contribution to fixed costs

Task 2

STOCK RECORD (STOCK CARD)

Part description: Hi-grade filters
Code: FF783
Maximum purchase price: £17.00

Maximum quantity: 100
Minimum quantity: 20
Reorder level: 50
Reorder quantity: 75

Date	Receipts Quantity	Receipts Price £	Receipts Total £	Issues Quantity	Issues Price £	Issues Total £	Balance Quantity	Balance Price £	Balance Total £
1 Oct							20	16.30	326.00
2 Oct	75	16.50	1,237.50				20	16.30	326.00
							75	16.50	1,237.50
							95		1,563.50
8 Oct				20	16.30	326.00			
				30	16.50	495.00			
				50		821.00	45		742.50

236

Task 3

MEMORANDUM

To: Production Director
From: Management Accounts Assistant
Subject: Stock of hi-grade filters, October 2007
Date: 5 November 2007

Task 4

MEMORANDUM

To: Ismay Ratliff, Production Director
From: Management Accounts Assistant
Subject: Stock valuation October 2007
Date: 3 November 2007

Raw materials stock valuation

Part-finished goods valuation

Finished goods valuation

STOCK RECORD

Part description: Hi-grade filters
Code: FF783
Valuation basis: AVCO

Date	\multicolumn{3}{c}{Receipts}	\multicolumn{3}{c}{Issues}	\multicolumn{3}{c}{Balance}
	Quantity	Price £	Total £	Quantity	Price £	Total £	Quantity	Price £	Total £
1 Oct							20	16.30	326.00
2 Oct	75	16.50	1,237.50				20	16.30	326.00
							75	16.50	1,237.50
							95	16.46	1,563.50
8 Oct				50	16.46	823.00	45	16.46	740.70

practice simulation – unit 6 – answer booklet

Task 5

TIME SHEET						
Week ending 31/10/07							
Name Sanjeev Patel						
Area Machine shop			**Employee number**		M042	
Grade B						
Activity	MON	TUES	WED	THURS	FRI	TOTAL
Oven 900 machining	9		9			
Oven 778 machining		9		3		
Sick				4.5		
Training					7.5	
Hours attendance	9.0	9.0	9.0	7.5	7.5	
Bonus hours	0.5	0.5	0.5			
Employee's signature Sanjeev Patel							
Manager's signature Malcolm Harrison							
ANALYSIS OF HOURS						
Basic rate hours						
Overtime hours						
Bonus hours						
ANALYSIS OF GROSS PAY						
	Hours	Rate £	£	£		
Direct hours (25.5 + 4.5)						
Indirect hours						
Sick						
Training						
Overtime hours at premium						
Bonus hours						
Total indirect						
Gross pay						

240

practice simulation – unit 6 – answer booklet

TIME SHEET						
Week ending 31/10/07							
Name Jacob Ellis							
Area Machine shop			**Employee number** M042		
Grade C							
Activity	MON	TUES	WED	THURS	FRI	TOTAL
Oven 900 machining						
Hours attendance						
Bonus hours						
Employee's signature *Jacob Ellis*							
Manager's signature							
ANALYSIS OF HOURS							
Basic rate hours						
Overtime hours						
Bonus hours						
ANALYSIS OF GROSS PAY							
	Hours	Rate £	£	£		
Direct hours						
Indirect hours						
Sick						
Training						
Overtime hours						
Bonus hours						
Total indirect						
Gross pay						

Task 6

MEMORANDUM

To: Malcolm Harrison, Machine Shop Manager
From: Management Accounts Assistant
Subject: Discrepancy on Time Sheet for Jacob Ellis
Date: 2 November 2007

Task 7

Calculation of under-/over-absorption of production overheads

October 2007

Total number of machine hours worked _____

Pre-determined overhead absorption rate per machine hour, 2007 _____

Total production overhead absorbed, October 2007 _____

Actual production overhead incurred _____

Production overhead over/(under) absorbed, October 2007 _____

The amount of £ _____ has been over-/under-* absorbed and will be debited/credited* to the profit and loss account.

(*Delete as applicable.)

practice simulation – unit 6 – answer booklet

Task 8

MEMORANDUM

To: Production Director
From: Management Accounts Assistant
Subject: Production overhead absorption rates for 2008
Date: 14 November 2007

Calculation of single machine hour rate

Problems with the single rate

Task 9

OVERHEAD ANALYSIS SHEET: BUDGET 2008

Rate using step down method of apportionment.

Overhead expense item	Basis of allocation/ apportionment	Total £	Machine Shop £	Assembly Shop £	Testing Centre £	Staff Amenity Centre £
Primary allocations and apportionments						
Indirect labour						
Manager salaries						
Testing Centre costs						
Staff Amenity Centre costs						
Depreciation						
Rent, rates, etc.						
Other o'heads						
Total primary allocation						
Reapportion Staff Amenity Centre						
Re-apportion Testing Centre						
Total production cost centre overhead allocation						

SPACE FOR CALCULATION OF ABSORPTION RATES FOR EACH PRODUCTION DEPARTMENT USING STEP DOWN METHOD:

Machine Shop =

Assembly Shop =

practice simulation – unit 6 – answer booklet

Alternative rates using direct method of apportionment

Overhead expense item	Basis of allocation/ apportionment	Total £	Machine Shop £	Assembly Shop £	Testing Centre £	Staff Amenity Centre £
Total primary allocations						
Apportion Test Centre costs						
Apportion Staff Amendity Centre costs						
Total production cost centre overhead allocation						

**SPACE FOR CALCULATION OF ABSORPTION RATES
FOR EACH PRODUCTION DEPARTMENT USING DIRECT APPORTIONMENT:**

Machine Shop =

Assembly Shop =

Task 10

Working paper for calculation of payback period and net present value

Payback period

Net present value

MEMORANDUM

To: Production Director
From: Management Accounts Assistant
Subject: New sites and products
Date: 25 November 2007

HIGHLY CONFIDENTIAL

Task 11

Working paper to determine sales volume, cost behaviour patterns and projected costs and revenues

Projected sales volume

Analysis of cost behaviour

practice simulation – unit 6 – answer booklet

Projected costs and revenues for new product range next year

Output volume (machines)

	£	£
Sales revenue		
Projected costs		
Direct material		
Direct labour		
Production overhead		
Other overhead		
Total projected cost		
Projected annual profit		

Task 12

Working paper to calculate margin of safety, P/V ratio and maximum possible change in fixed production overheads

Margin of safety

Profit/volume (P/V) ratio

Possible change in fixed production overheads

MEMORANDUM

To: Production Director
From: Management Accounts Assistant
Subject: New large size dishwashers
Date: 29 November 2007

HIGHLY CONFIDENTIAL

I attach the calculations that I have made in response to your memo of today's date.

Analysis of dishwasher product

Task 13

MEMORANDUM

To: Production Director
From: Management Accounts Assistant
Subject: New products at the new sites
Date: 30 November 2007

HIGHLY CONFIDENTIAL

Contracts required by Welsh consultancy

Limiting factor on production of large electric woks in Scotland

AAT

SAMPLE SIMULATION
UNIT 7

HOMER LTD

COVERAGE OF PERFORMANCE CRITERIA AND RANGE STATEMENTS

All performance criteria are covered in this simulation.

Element	PC Coverage
7.1	**Prepare and present periodic performance reports**
A	Consolidate **information** derived from different units of the organisation into the appropriate form.
B	Reconcile **information** derived from different information systems within the organisation.
C	Compare results over time using an appropriate method that allows for changing price levels.
D	Account for transactions between separate units of the organisation in accordance with the organisation's procedures.
E	Calculate **ratios** and **performance indicators** in accordance with the organisation's procedures.
F	Prepare reports in the appropriate form and present them to management within the required timescales.
7.2	**Prepare reports and returns for outside agencies**
A	Identify, collate and present relevant information in accordance with the conventions and definitions used by outside agencies.
B	Ensure calculations of **ratios** and performance indicators are accurate.
C	Obtain authorisation for the despatch of completed **reports and returns** from the appropriate person.
D	Present **reports and returns** in accordance with outside agencies' requirements and deadlines.
7.3	**Prepare VAT returns**
A	Complete and submit VAT returns correctly, using data from the appropriate **recording systems**, within the statutory time limits.
B	Correctly identify and calculate relevant **inputs and outputs**.
C	Ensure submissions are made in accordance with current legislation.
D	Ensure guidance is sought from the VAT office when required, in a professional manner.

Any missing range statements should be assessed separately.

INSTRUCTIONS

This simulation is designed to let you show your ability to prepare reports and returns.

You should read the whole simulation before you start work, so that you are fully aware of what you will have to do.

You are allowed **three hours** to complete your work.

Write your answers in the Answer Booklet provided on pages 265–275. If you need more paper for your answers, ask the person in charge.

You should write your answers in blue or black ink, **not** pencil.

You may use correcting fluid, but in moderation. You should cross out your errors neatly and clearly.

Your work must be accurate, so check your work carefully before handing it in.

Coverage of performance criteria and range statements

It is not always possible to cover all performance criteria and range statements in a single simulation. Any performance criteria and range statements not covered must be assessed by other means by the assessor before a candidate can be considered competent.

Performance criteria and range statement coverage for this simulation is shown on page 256.

AAT sample simulation – unit 7

THE SITUATION

Your name is Amir Pindhi and you work as an Accounts Assistant for Homer Limited, Sestos Drive, Pantile Trading Estate CV32 1AW.

Homer Limited is a manufacturing company, producing a single product, the 'Bart'. The company's year end is 31 March.

Today's date is Monday 14 April 20X7.

Divisional structure of Homer Limited

All production activities are carried out in the Manufacturing division. This division transfers most of its output to the Sales Division, which sells the output to external customers.

The Manufacturing Division transfers finished output to the Sales division at full production cost, but without any mark-up for profit. The Manufacturing division also sells some of its finished output direct to external customers.

Accounting for VAT

Homer Limited is registered for VAT.

Sales of Barts to UK customers are subject to VAT at the standard rate of 17.5%.

The company also exports to other countries within the European Union (EU). Such exports qualify as zero-rated. The company does not export to countries outside the EU. The company does not import any goods or services.

The local VAT office for Homer Limited is at Bell House, 33 Lambert Road, Coventry CV12 8TR.

Application for bank loan

The company is about to seek a long-term loan from its bankers to finance expansion plans.

The bank has requested some financial information in support of this application, and one of your responsibilities will be to present this information in the form required by the bank.

Presenting your work

Unless you are told otherwise:

- all ratios and statistics should be computed and presented to two decimal places;
- monetary amounts should be computed and presented to the nearest penny.

THE TASKS TO BE COMPLETED

1. Refer to the table on page 261 of this book which analyses monthly sales achieved by each of the company's two divisions during the years ended 31 March 20X6 and 31 March 20X7.

   - Consolidate these figures to arrive at the monthly sales and cumulative sales for each month in the two year period. Note that this task relates only to sales made to external customers, not to transfers within the company from the Manufacturing division to the Sales division. You should set out your answer on the schedule on page 267 of the Answer Booklet.

2. Using the figures calculated in Task 1, plot a line graph on page 268 of the Answer Booklet. The graph should show the cumulative sales achieved month by month during the year ended 31 March 20X6 and, as a separate line, the cumulative sales achieved month by month during the year ended 31 March 20X7. As in Task 1, you are concerned only with the sales to external customers, not with internal transfers from Manufacturing to Sales.

3. On page 262 of this book you will find month-by-month values of an index appropriate to the industry in which Homer operates. The values given are stated by reference to a base figure of 100, which was the value of the index in the base period January 20X2.

   - Calculate the indexed value of the monthly sales to external customers, in March 20X7 terms, for each month's sales in the year ended 31 March 20X7. Your answer should be set out on page 269 of the Answer Booklet in accordance with the notes on that page.

4. Refer to the information on page 262 of this book.

   - Complete the loan application form on page 270 of the Answer Booklet.

   - Write a memo to the Accountant, Sonia Liesl, enclosing the form for her attention and approval prior to its submission to the bank. Use the blank memo form on page 271 of the Answer Booklet and date your memo 14 April 20X7.

5. Write a memo to Sonia Liesl, presenting the following statistics for her information, and very briefly suggesting a possible reason for the movement in each statistic's value since year ended 31 March 20X6. (The 20X6 values are given in brackets below.)

   - The gross profit percentage for year ended 31 March 20X7 (The percentage in year ended 31 March 20X6 was 43.15%).

   - The net profit percentage for year ended 31 March 20X7 (20X6: 7.84%).

   - The production cost per 'Bart' produced and sold in year ended 31 March 20X7 (20X6: £10.83).

   - The value of sales earned per employee in year ended 31 March 20X7 (20X6: £26,018.13).

   Use the memo form on page 272 of the Answer Booklet and date your memo 14 April 20X7.

AAT sample simulation – unit 7

6. Refer to the information on pages 262 and 263 of this book that relates to the company's VAT return for the quarter ended on 31 March 20X7.

- Complete the blank return on page 273 of the Answer Booklet. Note that the return is to be signed by the Accountant, Sonia Liesl, and that payment of any balance due to HMRC will be made by cheque.

7. Refer to the memo from Sonia Liesl on page 263 of this booklet.

- Draft a letter to HMRC (in the name of Sonia Liesl) asking for the required information. Use the letterhead on page 274 of the Answer Booklet.

8. Reply to Sonia Liesl's memo giving her the brief details she requests, and enclosing the draft letter prepared in Task 7 above. Use the blank memo form on page 275 of the Answer Booklet.

Monthly sales during the years ended 31 March 20X6 and 31 March 20X7

All figures in £000. All figures exclude VAT.

	Sales Division	Manufacturing Division		
	Total	To external customers	To Sales Division	Total
20X5/X6				
April	350	34	185	219
May	225	46	128	174
June	190	32	96	128
July	255	54	138	192
August	310	36	166	202
September	238	24	148	172
October	220	20	125	145
November	295	34	172	206
December	240	39	182	221
January	257	20	150	170
February	230	14	155	169
March	340	45	218	263
20X6/X7				
April	339	42	197	239
May	189	53	119	172
June	223	14	109	123
July	295	44	214	258
August	280	50	176	226
September	265	34	138	172
October	219	12	119	131
November	322	50	170	220
December	316	39	180	219
January	281	29	148	177
February	248	24	168	192
March	240	51	185	236

Industrial index: base = 100 (January 20X2)

20X6	April	123.8
	May	124.4
	June	124.9
	July	125.7
	August	126.3
	September	127.0
	October	127.5
	November	128.1
	December	128.9
20X7	January	129.6
	February	130.2
	March	131.0

Statistical information relating to year ended 31 March 20X7

Production cost of Barts produced and sold in the year	£2,190,000
Gross profit for the year	£1,470,000
Administration costs for the year	£580,000
Distribution costs for the year	£430,000
Total of all other costs for the year	£150,000
Net profit for the year before taxation	£310,000
Net profit for the previous year before taxation	£278,000
Total capital employed	£6,590,000
Number of Barts produced and sold in the year	199,000
Average number of employees in the year	143

The following details have been extracted from the company's daybooks. (All figures are exclusive of VAT.)

SALES DAY BOOK TOTALS
QUARTER ENDED 31 MARCH 20X7

	January £	February £	March £	Total £
UK sales: standard rated	282,862.57	245,871.89	269,088.11	797,822.57
EU sales: zero-rated	27,143.05	26,126.66	21,920.34	75,190.05
Total	310,005.62	271,998.55	291,008.45	873,012.62
VAT on UK sales	49,500.95	43,027.58	47,090.42	139,618.95

PURCHASES DAY BOOK TOTALS
QUARTER ENDED 31 MARCH 20X7

	January £	February £	March £	Total £
Purchases/expenses	186,007.66	163,265.69	171,295.45	520,568.80
VAT on purchases/expenses	32,551.34	28,571.50	29,976.70	91,099.54

A debt of £658, inclusive of VAT, was written off as bad in March 20X7. The related sale was made in June 20X6. Bad debt relief is now to be claimed.

MEMO

To: Amir Pindhi
From: Sonia Liesl
Subject: VAT on imports
Date: 11 April 20X7

As you may know, we have been in discussions with a supplier based in the Far East. We are considering importing certain components in future for use in our manufacturing activities.

Please could you remind me very briefly of the VAT implications if we decide to proceed with this. Please also draft a letter to HMRC, in my name, requesting relevant publications so that we can be sure we account for the VAT correctly.

Thanks for your help.

AAT

SAMPLE SIMULATION
UNIT 7

HOMER LTD

ANSWER BOOKLET

Task 1

Sales to external customers
Manufacturing and Sales divisions combined

	Monthly totals £'000	Cumulative total for the year £'000
20X5/X6		
April		
May		
June		
July		
August		
September		
October		
November		
December		
January		
February		
March		
20X6/X7		
April		
May		
June		
July		
August		
September		
October		
November		
December		
January		
February		
March		

Notes

1) In the first column, enter the monthly total of external sales achieved by the two divisions.
2) In the second column, enter the cumulative total of external sales in the accounting year.

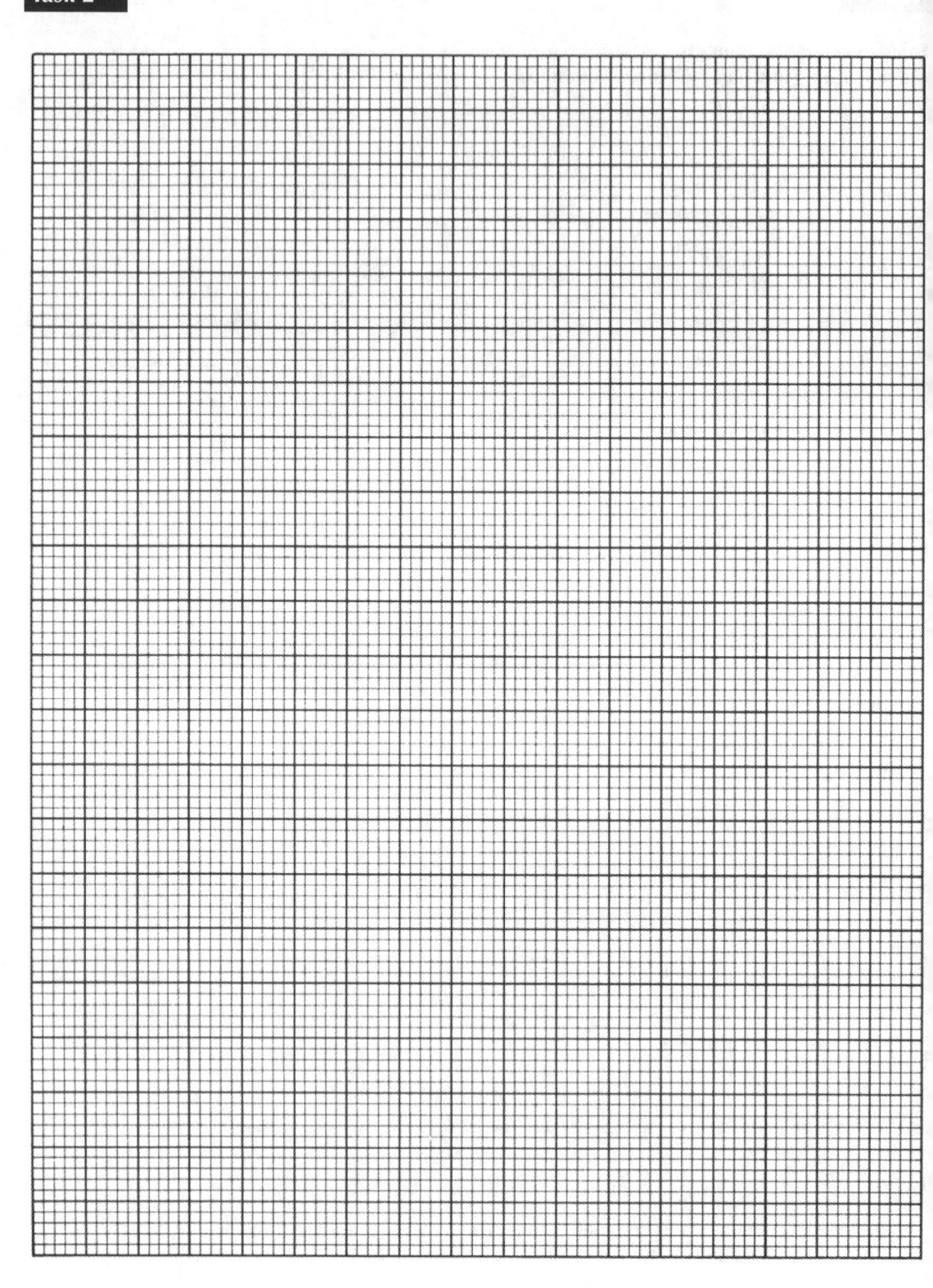

Task 2

Task 3

Indexed sales to external customers
Manufacturing and Sales divisions combined

	Unadjusted totals £'000	Index factor	Indexed totals £'000
20X6/X7			
April			
May			
June			
July			
August			
September			
October			
November			
December			
January			
February			
March			

Notes

1) In the first column, insert the monthly totals of external sales calculated in Task 1.
2) In the second column, insert the index factor required to convert to March 20X7 values.
3) In the third column, calculate the monthly sales in March 20X7 terms (to the nearest £1,000).

Task 4

LOAN APPLICATION (extract)

Name of applicant company _____

Latest year for which accounting information is available _____

Total sales revenue

In latest year for which accounts are available £ _____

In previous year £ _____

Percentage change (+/-) _____

Net profit after all expenses, before taxation

In latest year for which accounts are available £ _____

In previous year £ _____

Percentage change (+/-) _____

Gross profit margin (%) _____

Net profit margin (%) _____

Return on capital employed (%) _____

Notes

1) In the case of a company with a divisional structure, all figures should refer to the results of the company as a whole, not to individual divisions within the company.

2) Unless otherwise stated, all questions relate to the latest year for which accounting information is available.

3) Figures should be actual historical values, with no indexing for inflation.

4) Return on capital employed is defined as net profit for the year before taxation, divided by total capital employed.

Task 4 (continued)

MEMO

To:

From:

Subject:

Date:

Task 5

MEMO

To:

From:

Subject:

Date:

Task 6

Value Added Tax Return
For the period
01 01 X7 to 31 03 X7

For Official Use

Registration number: 625 7816 29

Period: 03 X7

You could be liable to a financial penalty if your completed return and all the VAT payable are not received by the due date.

Due date: 30.04.X7

HOMER LIMITED
SESTOS DRIVE
PANTILE TRADING ESTATE
CV32 1AW

For Official Use

If you have a general enquiry or need advice please call our National Advice Service on 0845 010 9000

ATTENTION

If this return and any tax due are not received by the due date you may be liable to a surcharge.

If you make supplies of goods to another EC Member State you are required to complete an EC Sales List (VAT 101).

Before you fill in this form please read the notes on the back and the VAT Leaflet "*Filling in your VAT return*" and "*Flat rate schemes for small businesses*", if you use the scheme. Fill in all boxes clearly in ink, and write 'none' where necessary. Don't put a dash or leave any box blank. If there are no pence write "00" in the pence column. Do not enter more than one amount in any box.

For official use			£	p
	VAT due in this period on sales and other outputs	1		
	VAT due in this period on acquisitions from other EC Member States	2		
	Total VAT due (the sum of boxes 1 and 2)	3		
	VAT reclaimed in this period on purchases and other inputs (including acquisitions from the EC)	4		
	Net VAT to be paid to Customs or reclaimed by you (Difference between boxes 3 and 4)	5		
	Total value of sales and all other outputs excluding any VAT. Include your box 8 figure	6		
	Total value of purchases and all other inputs excluding any VAT. Include your box 9 figure	7		
	Total value of all supplies of goods and related services, excluding any VAT, to other EC Member States	8		
	Total value of all acquisitions of goods and related services, excluding any VAT, from other EC Member States	9		

If you are enclosing a payment please tick this box.

DECLARATION: You, or someone on your behalf, must sign below.

I, _____ declare that the
(Full name of signatory in BLOCK LETTERS)
information given above is true and complete.

Signature _____ Date _____ 20 ___

A false declaration can result in prosecution.

Task 7

HOMER LIMITED
Sestos Drive, Pantile Trading Estate CV32 1AW
Telephone: 02467 881235

Registered office: Sestos Drive, Pantile Trading Estate CV32 1AW
Registered in England, number 2007814

Task 8

MEMO

To:
From:
Subject:
Date:

PRACTICE SIMULATION
UNIT 7

DONALD RATHERSON & CO

PERFORMANCE CRITERIA

The following performance criteria are covered in this practice simulation.

Element		PC Coverage
7.1		**Prepare and present periodic performance reports**
	A	Consolidate **information** derived from different units of the organisation into the appropriate form.
	B	Reconcile **information** derived from different information systems within the organisation.
	C	Compare results over time using an appropriate method that allows for changing price levels.
	D	Account for transactions between separate units of the organisation in accordance with the organisation's procedures.
	E	Calculate **ratios** and **performance indicators** in accordance with the organisation's procedures.
	F	Prepare reports in the appropriate form and present them to management within the required timescales.
7.2		**Prepare reports and returns for outside agencies**
	A	Identify, collate and present relevant information in accordance with the conventions and definitions used by outside agencies.
	B	Ensure calculations of **ratios** and performance indicators are accurate.
	C	Obtain authorisation for the despatch of completed **reports and returns** from the appropriate person.
	D	Present **reports and returns** in accordance with outside agencies' requirements and deadlines.
7.3		**Prepare VAT returns**
	A	Complete and submit VAT returns correctly, using data from the appropriate **recording systems**, within the statutory time limits.
	B	Correctly identify and calculate relevant **inputs and outputs**.
	C	Ensure submissions are made in accordance with current legislation.
	D	Ensure guidance is sought from the VAT office when required, in a professional manner.

Any missing range statements should be assessed separately.

practice simulation – unit 7

INSTRUCTIONS

This simulation is designed to test your ability to prepare reports and returns.

This simulation is divided into 10 tasks. You are advised to look through the whole simulation first to gain a general appreciation of your tasks.

The situation is provided below. The tasks to be completed are set out on pages 280–282.

Your answers should be set out in the Answer Booklet provided.

You are allowed three hours to complete your work.

A high level of accuracy is required. Check your work carefully before handing it in.

Correcting fluid may be used but it should be used in moderation. Errors should be crossed out neatly and clearly. You should write in blue or black ink, not pencil.

THE SITUATION

Introduction

Donald Ratherson & Co is a business which makes and sells equipment for professional decorators, such as ladders, internal scaffolding and paintguns. Its premises are in Ascot in Berkshire, with a showroom in London.

The business has three business units (plus an accounting and administration section).

- The Manufacturing Unit in Ascot buys in materials from suppliers and makes equipment, which is then transferred either to the Mail Order Unit or to the Showroom. In both cases items are transferred at full production cost, so there is no inter-departmental profit.

- The Mail Order Unit in Ascot buys in equipment for resale from outside suppliers and also sources them internally from the Manufacturing Unit. It then sells to customers who order by post, phone or internet.

- The Showroom operates from premises in London. It displays equipment bought in from outside and also sources internally from the Manufacturing Unit. Its customers tend to be large retailers who require specialist equipment and service in respect of large window displays in their shops.

You work as Deputy Accountant for the business. The people with whom you deal are as follows:

Ian Yates   Chief Accountant

Donald Ratherson   Owner

The simulation requires you to perform tasks relating to the previous full financial year ended 30 September 20X7. You also need to look at data relating to the month ending 31 October 20X7 and to complete the business's VAT return for the quarter ending on that date. Today's date is 12 November 20X7.

practice simulation – unit 7

Accounts and reports

In the business's accounting system, costs are attributed to the different business units as follows.

- Direct manufacturing costs, including raw materials, wages and expenses, to the Manufacturing Unit
- Direct mail order and showroom costs, including goods for resale, wages and expenses, to the Mail Order Unit and Showroom respectively
- Other overheads of the Ascot site, including all accounting and administration costs, to the three business units according to an agreed ratio

Each month and year the cost and revenue statements for each of the three Business Units are added together in a standard form to produce a consolidated statement of costs and revenue. The balances that exist between the Manufacturing Unit and the Mail Order Unit and the Showroom must be reconciled before this consolidated statement can be finalised.

The business is a member of the Institute of Decorators. Data from the statement of costs and revenue, plus other data, is provided to the Institute annually.

Accounting for VAT

Donald Ratherson & Co is registered for VAT. All sales to UK customers are standard-rated for VAT. Supplies to EU countries qualify as zero-rated. The company does not export to non-EU countries. It does not import any of its goods or services from outside the EU, nor does it make taxable acquisitions from EU countries.

The local VAT office for Donald Ratherson & Co is at Lyle House, Henry Road, Guildford GU8 5CM.

THE TASKS TO BE COMPLETED

Note that in all tasks monetary amounts are to be calculated to the nearest £, and ratios and percentages are to be calculated to two places of decimals.

Task 1

The company's owner, Donald Ratherson, feels that in the most recent year ending 30 September 20X7, the business was more profitable than he had expected, but he wonders how far inflation accounts for this and how far it was as a result of improved efficiency. Ian Yates has handed you details of the business's annual costs and revenues for the previous year ended 30 September 20X6, which are given on page 290 in the Answer Booklet. He has also identified some data, plus two indices that specifically relate to the full year's figures, which he has set out in a memo to you on page 283 in this booklet.

You are required to complete the table on page 290 in the Answer Booklet by re-stating the business's revenues and costs for the year ended 30 September 20X7 in line with Ian Yates's memo.

practice simulation – unit 7

Task 2

Use the data on pages 284 and 285 in this booklet to produce the consolidated costs and revenues statement for the business for the year ending 30 September 20X7, on page 291 in the Answer Booklet.

Task 3

Refer to the memo dated 11 November 20X7 from Ian Yates on page 286 in this booklet.

You are required to prepare a memo to Ian Yates providing the information requested. Use the blank memo form on page 292 in the Answer Booklet, the table on page 293 in the Answer Booklet, the time series graph on page 294 and the sheet of graph paper on page 295 in the Answer Booklet.

Task 4

For some years, Donald Ratherson & Co's most popular product has been the LadderPaint modular system. Data related to LadderPaint's production and sales is shown on page 287 in this booklet. For the year ended 30 September 20X7:

You are required to:

a) calculate the production cost per LadderPaint system transferred from the Manufacturing Unit

b) calculate the percentage of manufacturing costs represented by LadderPaint systems

c) calculate the sales value per unit of LadderPaint sold

d) calculate the gross profit margin per unit of LadderPaint

e) calculate the percentage of total Mail Order and Showroom revenue represented by LadderPaint sales in the year

f) complete the comparison of actual and budgeted manufacturing costs for LadderPaint and calculate the productivity ratio.

Set out your answers on page 296 in the Answer Booklet, where you will find comparative figures for 20X6.

Task 5

On page 297 in the Answer Booklet there is an extract from the standard form issued by the Institute of Decorators.

You are required to complete the standard form by inserting the relevant accounting figures, ratios and statistics required by the Institute.

281

practice simulation – unit 7

Task 6

You are required to send a memo to Ian Yates, enclosing the completed form and report, and requesting him to authorise them before despatch to the Institute. Use the blank memo form on page 298 in the Answer Booklet.

Task 7

Refer to the extracts from Business Unit cost and revenue statements for October 20X7, and the further data relating to transactions at the end of the month, on page 287 in this booklet.

You are required to prepare a reconciliation between the inter-unit balances using the format on page 299 in the Answer Booklet.

Task 8

Refer to the data on page 288 in this booklet.

You are required to:

a) complete the business's VAT control account on page 299 in the Answer Booklet.

b) complete the business's VAT return for the quarter ended 31 October 20X7 on page 300 in the Answer Booklet. You are not required to sign the VAT return.

Task 9

The Showroom of Donald Ratherson & Co sold some goods with a market value of £15,000 to a customer, GHA Stores plc, in February 20X7 on 30 days' credit. Donald Ratherson was informed yesterday that GHA Stores plc had ceased trading and the debt is irrecoverable. This is the first time that Donald Ratherson & Co has had a substantial bad debt.

You are required to write to the local VAT Office, seeking confirmation of your understanding of the steps that Donald Ratherson & Co needs to take in order to claim bad debt relief for the VAT element of this debt, and the timescale in which the steps should be taken so that relief is obtained as soon as possible. Use page 301 in the Answer Booklet.

Task 10

Donald Ratherson has been talking to his personal accountant and has realised that there are a few issues to do with VAT with which he is unfamiliar. His personal accountant began to put a checklist of points together for Donald, but this is still incomplete.

You are required to complete the checklist for Donald on pages 302 and 303 in the Answer Booklet.

Data for Task 1

MEMO

To: Deputy Accountant
From: Ian Yates
Subject: Trends affecting Donald Ratherson & Co's performance
Date: 11 November 20X7

I have identified the following specific factors that have affected our performance over the year from 1 October 20X6 to 30 September 20X7:

- Showroom prices to customers have risen by 8% on average, but Mail Order prices have only risen by 4%.

- In the Manufacturing Unit, raw materials prices have risen by 3% on average.

- The prices paid by Mail Order and Showroom for goods for resale have risen 2% on average

- Wage rates in the Manufacturing Unit and the Mail Order Unit rose by 5%

- Wage rates in the Showroom rose by 7%

- Expenses in the Mail Order Unit and Showroom rose by 3% on average

- Expenses in the Manufacturing Unit rose on average by 4%

- Overheads of the Ascot site, including accounting and administration costs, have been on average 5% higher.

I also attach some relevant indices from the Institute of Decorators relating to our business.

Institute of Decorators

Indices for manufacturers of decorating equipment

Years ending in	Revenue	Gross profit
20X3	100.0	100
20X4	104.2	103.9
20X5	108.3	107.8
20X6	109.7	108.1
20X7	111.5	109.6

practice simulation – unit 7

Data for Task 2

Cost statement: Manufacturing Unit

Year ended 30 September 20X7

	£
Raw materials	
Opening stock	14,016
Purchases	134,352
Total actual fixed overheads	148,368
Closing stock	(20,736)
Cost of raw materials used in year	127,632
Wages	178,685
Expenses	19,145
Transfer cost to Mail Order Unit and Showroom (= production cost)	325,462
Allocated costs of Ascot site, including accounting and administration costs (65%)	60,125
Total Manufacturing Unit costs	385,587
Average number of employees	12

Cost and revenue statement: Mail Order Unit

	£	£
Sales		1,146,354
Goods for resale		
Opening stock	24,130	
Purchases	289,645	
Closing stock	(21,717)	
	292,058	
Transfer cost of goods for resale from Manufacturing Unit	260,369	
Cost of goods sold in year		(552,427)
Mail Order Unit gross profit		593,927
Wages		(165,728)
Expenses		(55,242)
Allocated costs of Ascot site, including accounting and administration costs (20%)		(18,500)
Mail Order Unit net profit		354,457
Average number of employees		11

Cost and revenue statement: Showroom

Year ended 30 September 20X7

	£	£
Sales		1,092,240
Goods for resale	37,620	
Opening stock	228,840	
Purchases	(41,382)	
	225,078	
Transfer cost of goods for resale from Manufacturing Unit	65,093	
Cost of goods sold in year		290,171
Showroom gross profit		802,069
Wages		(144,000)
Expenses		(57,600)
Allocated costs of Ascot site, including accounting and administration costs (15%)		(13,875)
Showroom net profit		586,594
Average number of employees		8

practice simulation – unit 7

Data for Task 3

MEMO

To: Deputy Accountant
From: Ian Yates
Subject: Results for the year ended 30 September 20X7
Date: 11 November 20X7

I would like you to prepare a report for me, which I shall show to Donald Ratherson. Use the table that I have supplied to you.

Please set out in the table the consolidated figures for costs and revenues for the year ended 30 September 20X7 against the full comparable figures (inflation-adjusted) for the year ended 30 September 20X7 (ignore the figures adjusted using the Institute of Decorators indices). Set out the differences between the two sets of figures, both in monetary amount and in percentage terms, and a calculation of the gross profit margin, net profit margin and return on capital employed percentages for both years (I have included figures on average capital employed for both years in the table).

Please also construct a component bar chart for the 20X7 figures and the inflation-adjusted 20X6 figures, breaking down total sales revenue for the two periods into:

- net profit
- cost of sales
- wages
- expenses
- accounting and administration costs.

Finally, I attach the time series graph that we prepared this time last year, showing the total revenue and profit figures for the business since 20X1. Please complete the graph for the year ended 31 October 20X7, and then extend the trend line by eye to give me an idea of what sales and profit should be in the year ended 31 October 20X8. Enter your estimates of these two figures in the space provided beneath the graph.

Please include an accompanying introductory memo, highlighting the profitability ratios you have calculated, and referring to the table, the bar chart and the time series graph.

Data for Task 4

LadderPaint
Production and sales data for the year ended 30 September 20X7

	Units	£
Sales		
By Mail Order Unit	988	151,164
BY Showroom	762	116,586
		267,750
Production costs	1,750	
Metal		13,875
Resins		2,740
Cord		3,655
Paint		3,950
Packaging		1,265
		25,485
		77,760
Wages (8,750)		77,760
Expenses		11,520
		114,765

Notes. There were no opening or closing stocks of LadderPaint or the relevant raw materials in any unit.

Budgeted production for the year was 1,500 units, produced in 6,000 hours.

Data for Task 7

Cost statement extract: Manufacturing unit
Month ended 31 October 20X7

	£
Production cost of items transferred to Mail Order Unit and Showroom	27,122

Cost and revenue statement extract: Mail Order Unit
Month ended 31 October 20X7

	£
Transfer cost of goods for resale from Manufacturing Unit	15,985

Cost and revenue statement extract: Showroom
Month ended 31 October 20X7

	£
Transfer cost of goods for resale from Maufacturing Unit	10,644

On further investigation, it is found that some goods have been transferred from Manufacturing but have not been recorded in the other units. The production cost of the goods are as follows.

	£
Goods transferred to Mail Order Unit	107
Goods transferred to Showroom	386

Data for Task 8

Donald Ratherson & Co

Sales Day Book (SDB) summary August to October 20X7

	Aug £	Sept £	Oct £	Total £
UK: Standard-rated	185,463	186,795	189,674	561,932
Other EU: Zero-rated	10,856	9,745	8,796	29,397
VAT	32,456	32,689	33,193	98,338
Total	228,775	229,229	231,663	389,667

Donald Ratherson & Co

Purchases Day Book (PDB) summary August to October 20X7

	Aug £	Sept £	Oct £	Total £
Purchases	185,463	56,745	57,912	170,060
Expenses	7,355	7,496	8,001	22,852
VAT	13,673	9,115	7,596	30,384
Total	76,431	73,356	73,509	389,667

Donald Ratherson & Co

Cash Book (CB) summary August to October 20X7

	Aug £	Sept £	Oct £	Total £
Expenses	286	195	23	504
VAT	25	17	2	44
Total	331	212	25	548

PRACTICE SIMULATION
UNIT 7

DONALD RATHERSON & CO

ANSWER BOOKLET

practice simulation – unit 7 – answer booklet

Task 1

	Actual 20X6 £	Actual 20X6 £	Factor	Restated 20X6 £	Restated 20X6 £
Sales					
Mail Order		1,001,456	☐		☐
Showroom		924,763	☐		☐
		1,926,219			
Cost of sales					
Raw materials	125,896		☐		☐
Goods for resale					
Mail Order	281,546		☐		☐
Showroom	216,875		☐		☐
		(624,317)			
Gross profit		1,301,902			
Wages					
Manufacturing Unit	169,842		☐	☐	
Mail Order	155,246		☐	☐	
Showroom	139,000		☐	☐	
		(464,088)			
Expenses					
Manufacturing Unit	15,746		☐	☐	
Mail Order	52,463		☐	☐	
Showroom	55,126		☐	☐	
		(123,335)			
Costs of Ascot site, including accounting and admin		(89,750)	☐	☐	
Net profit		624,729			☐

Restatement using Institute of Decorators' indices

	20X6 £	Index factor	Adjusted 20X6 figure £
Total revenue	1,926,219	☐	☐
Total gross profit	1,301,902	☐	☐

Task 2

Donald Ratherson & Co
Consolidated statement of revenues and costs for the year ended 30 September 20X7

	£	£	£

Sales
Cost of sales
Raw materials
Opening stock
Purchases
Closing stock

Goods for resale
Opening stock
Purchases
Closing stock

Gross profit
Wages
Expenses
Costs of Ascot site, including
   accounting and administration
   costs
Net profit

Space for workings

Task 3

MEMO

To: Ian Yates
From: Deputy Accountant
Subject: Report on results for year ended 30 September 20X7
Date: 12 November 20X7

Task 3 (continued)

Donald Ratherson & Co
Report on the comparison of revenues and costs for the year end 31 October 20X7 with inflation-adjusted figures for 20X6

	20X7		Adjusted 20X6		Difference	
	£	£	£	£	£	%
Sales						
Mail Order						
Showroom		_____		_____		
Cost of sales						
Raw materials						
Goods for resale						
Mail Order						
Showroom	_____		_____			
		_____		_____		
Gross profit						
Wages						
Manufacturing Unit						
Mail Order						
Showroom	_____		_____			
Expenses						
Manufacturing Unit						
Mail Order						
Showroom	_____		_____			
Cost of Ascot site, including accounting and administration		_____		_____		
Net profit		======		======		
Average capital employed		12,650,000		12,000,000		

Workings

			%	%
Gross profit margin				
Net profit margin				
Return on capital employed				

Task 3

Time series 20X1–X8

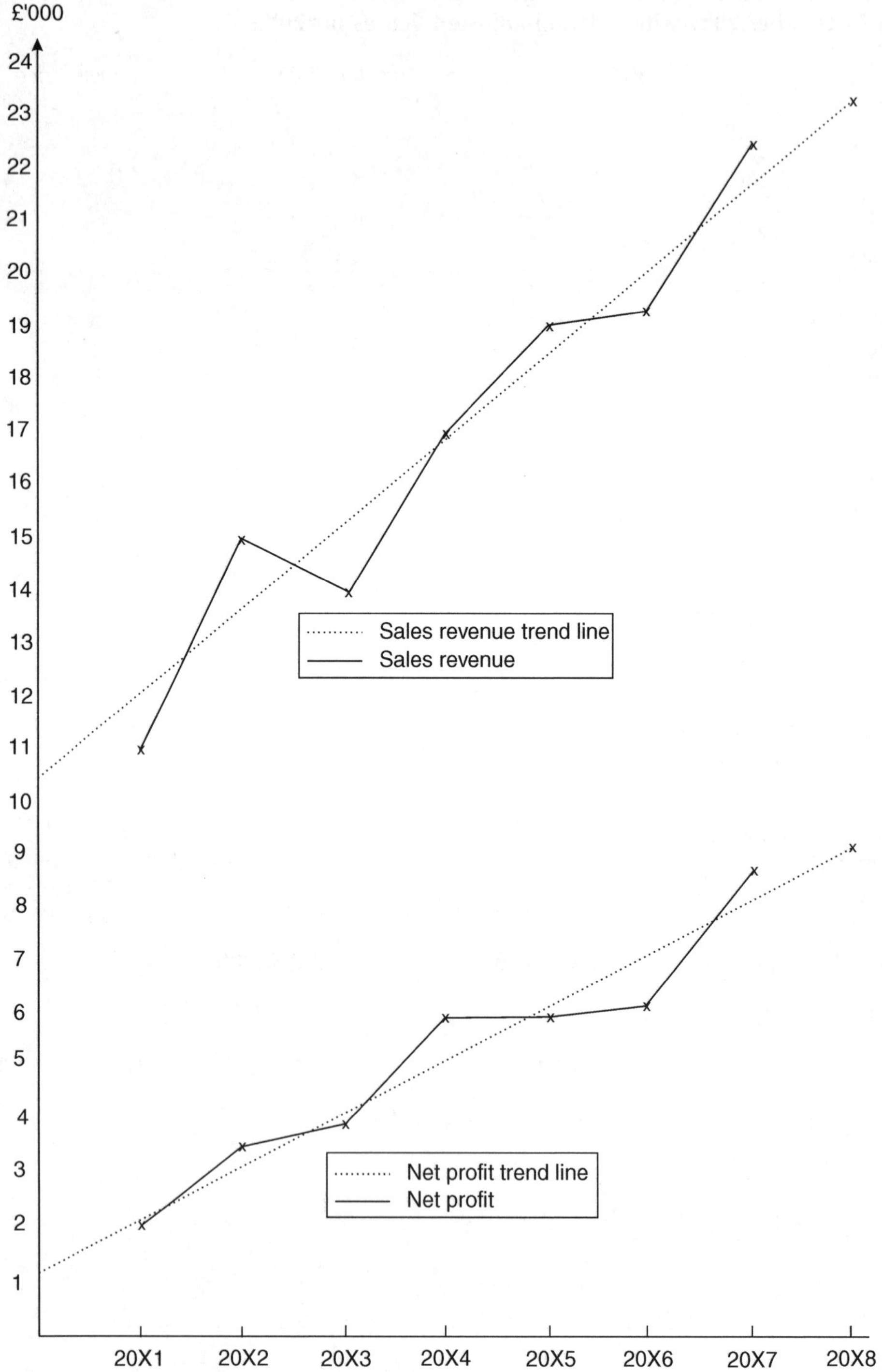

Forecast net profit for 20X7: £ ....

Forecast sales for 20X7: £ ....

Task 3 (continued)

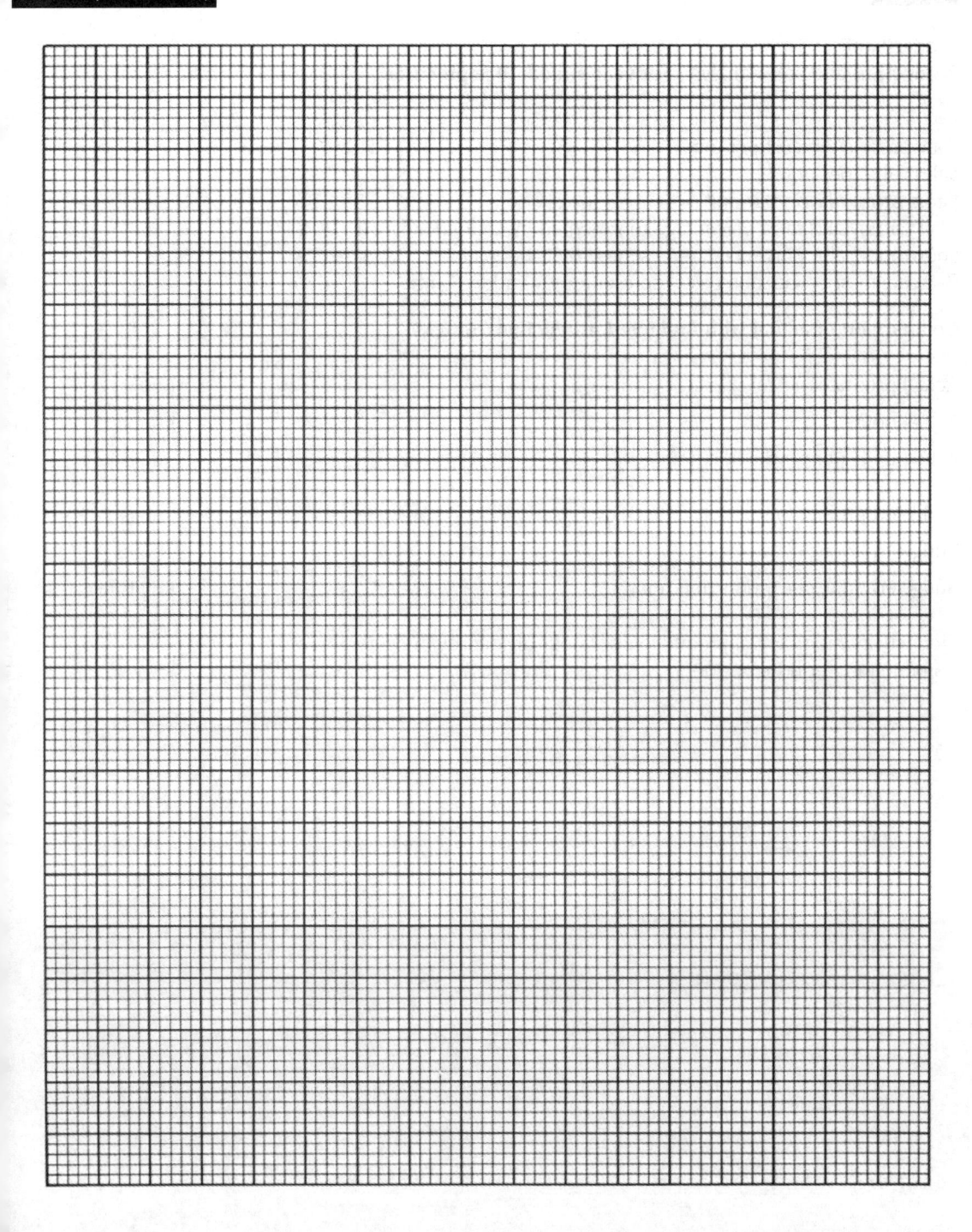

Task 4

LadderPaint
Production and sales analysis for year ended 30 September

	20X6	20X7	Workings
Total production cost per unit	£62.30	£	
Sales value per unit	£149.00	£	
Gross profit margin per unit	58.19%	%	
Mail Order Unit sales percentage represented by LadderPaint	15.20%	%	
Showroom sales percentage represented by LadderPaint	12.85%	%	
Percentage of production costs represented by LadderPaint	35.47%	%	

Comparison of actual with budgeted production 20X6/X7

Actual production   [_____] units

Actual hours   [_____] hours

Actual units per production hour   [_____] units/hr

Budgeted production   [_____] units

Budgeted hours   [_____] hours

Budgeted units per production hour   [_____] units/hr

Productivity ratio: actual production per hour divided by budgeted production per hour × 100%   [_____] %

practice simulation – unit 7 – answer booklet

Task 5

Institue of Decorators – standard form of return 20X7

Name of business: Donald Ratherson & Co

	Actual current year		Actual prior year	
Year ended	30 September 20X7		30 September 20X6	
Average number of employees	31		32	
	£	% of sales (1)	£	% of sales (1)
Sales		100		
Sales per employee				
Gross profit				
Net profit before taxation				
Average capital employed				
		%		%
Return on capital employed (2)				

	Inflation-adjusted prior year £
Prior year sales revenue adjusted for inflation using Institute index	
Prior year gross profit adjusted for inflation using Institute index	

		£	Comparison % of prior year actual figure
Current year actual sales exceed prior year actual sales by	Box 1		
Amount of increase accounted for by inflation (4)	Box 2		
Amount of increase in real terms	Box 1 – Box 2		
Current year actual gross profits exceed prior year's actual gross profits by	Box 3		
Amount of increase accounted for by inflation (4)	Box 4		
Amount of increase in real terms	Box 3 – Box 4		

Notes

1) All percentages are to be expressed to two decimal places

2) Return on capital employed is the net profit, divided by the average capital employed for the year, expressed as a percentage to two decimal places

3) All entries are to be based on figures for the business as a whole, excluding any transactions between divisions or business units within the business

4) Deduct actual results from inflation-adjusted results

Task 6

MEMO

To: Ian Yates
From: Deputy Accountant
Subject: Institute of Decorators' return and report
Date: 11 November 20X7

Task 7

Reconciliation of business units balances as at 31 October 20X7

	£	£

Mail Order Unit balance brought forward
Add: transfer from Manufacturing   _____
Closing Mail Order balance with Manufacturing
Showroom Unit balance brought forward
Add: transfer from Manufacturing   _____

Closing Showroom balance with Manufacturing   _____
Production cost of items transferred to Mail Order
   Unit and Showroom   ════════

Task 8

Donald Ratherson & Co

VAT Control Account

Administration/overheads

Date	Description	Debit £	Date	Description	Debit £
20X7			20X7		
31 Aug	Pay HMRC	49,654	1 Aug	B/d	49,654
		_____			_____
		══════			══════

practice simulation – unit 7 – answer booklet

Value Added Tax Return
For the period
to

For Official Use

Registration number

Period

You could be liable to a financial penalty if your completed return and all the VAT payable are not received by the due date.

Due date:

For Official Use

ATTENTION

If this return and any tax due are not received by the due date you may be liable to a surcharge.

If you make supplies of goods to another EC Member State you are required to complete an EC Sales List (VAT 101).

If you have a general enquiry or need advice please call our National Advice Service on 0845 010 9000

Before you fill in this form please read the notes on the back and the VAT Leaflet *"Filling in your VAT return"*.
Fill in all boxes clearly in ink, and write 'none' where necessary. Don't put a dash or leave any box blank. If there are no pence write "00" in the pence column. Do not enter more than one amount in any box.

			£	p
For official use	VAT due in this period on sales and other outputs	1		
	VAT due in this period on acquisitions from other EC Member States	2		
	Total VAT due (the sum of boxes 1 and 2)	3		
	VAT reclaimed in this period on purchases and other inputs (including acquisitions from the EC)	4		
	Net VAT to be paid to Customs or reclaimed by you (Difference between boxes 3 and 4)	5		
	Total value of sales and all other outputs excluding any VAT. Include your box 8 figure	6		00
	Total value of purchases and all other inputs excluding any VAT. Include your box 9 figure	7		00
	Total value of all supplies of goods and related services, excluding any VAT, to other EC Member States	8		00
	Total value of all acquisitions of goods and related services, excluding any VAT, from other EC Member States	9		00

If you are enclosing a payment please tick this box.

DECLARATION: You, or someone on your behalf, must sign below.

I,... declare that the
(Full name of signatory in BLOCK LETTERS)
information given above is true and complete.

Signature.. Date .... 20 ....

A false declaration can result in prosecution.

F

0196929   IB (October 2000)
VAT 100 (Half)

300

Task 9

DONALD RATHERSON & CO

Park Drive Trading Estate, Sunninghill Road, Ascot, Berks GU8 5ZD
Telephone: 01344 627896

practice simulation – unit 7 – answer booklet

Task 10

Checklist re VAT

Prepared for: Donald Ratherson

By: A N Accountant

1   The three types of supply for VAT purposes are: _____, _____ and _____ supplies.

2   A taxable person who makes only zero-rated outputs *can/cannot reclaim input tax on their purchases. (*Delete as applicable.)

3   In a month when the VAT registration limit is exceeded, a trader must notify HMRC within:

   _____

4   The effects of registration for VAT are that the trader:

   1   _____

   2   _____

   3   _____

5   A VAT invoice must show:

   information about the supplier: _____

   information about the invoice: _____

   information about the customer: _____

6   A less detailed VAT invoice can be issued where the total including VAT is less than £_____

7   The basic tax point for a VAT invoice is: _____

   _____

8   An earlier tax point than the basic tax point applies if: _____

   _____

9   To find out more detail about VAT without reference to the VAT Office one should refer to:

   _____

10   If we import raw materials from outside the EU we *must/need not pay input VAT on them. (*Delete as applicable.)

11   If we export goods to buyers outside the EU we must treat them as *standard rated/zero rated/exempt supplies. (*Delete as applicable.)

12   We would get automatic bad debt relief if we could be part of the _____ scheme, but our annual taxable turnover is too high.

13   We would only have to complete one VAT return per year if we were part of the _____ scheme, but our taxable turnover is too high.

302

practice simulation – unit 7 – answer booklet

14 In any dispute about VAT we would need to decide between:

1 _____

2 _____

3 _____

15 If we submit our VAT return late, HMRC will issue us with a _____

_____

You also asked me for some information on other matters:

16 The government body responsible for publishing government statistics is: _____

_____

17 An example of a regulatory body seeking a report or return is: _____

_____

18 Other types of outside organisation which may seek a report or return from us are:

1 _____

2 _____

3 _____

ANSWERS

answers to chapter 1: COSTING INFORMATION

1. Financial accounting is the recording of historical, or past, transactions of the business in order to be able to produce a set of financial statements in accordance with legal and accounting professional requirements. These financial statements are required by law for limited companies and are prepared for the use of those outside the business such as shareholders, lenders, customers and suppliers.

    Cost accounting is the recording of historical, or past, transactions of the business in order to provide useful information for the management of the business in order to carry out their functions of decision making, planning and control. The costing information can be presented in any manner which is useful to management as it is used solely by the management team within the business.

2. **Decision making** – many of the decisions that management will be required to make will be to do with production and sales of their products. Decisions will have to be made as to whether to produce a product in the first place – for this it will be necessary to know what the product is going to cost to make, what selling price can be set for it and therefore whether it is going to be profitable. Costing information will show the anticipated cost of the product and can also be used to set the selling price of the product if this is not dependent on market forces. In other instances management may have to make decisions about the levels of production for which they will need costs for different amounts of production. Management may also have to choose between products if there is competition for resources such as factory space or labour hours. Again detailed information about the costs of the products is required if an informed decision is to be made.

    Planning – once a decision has been taken to make a new product in the next period or to continue production of an existing one then a plan or budget will be drawn up. Budgets contain the details of the quantities and costs of production. They will include budgets for the quantity of materials required, the cost of those materials, the number of labour hours required, the cost of the labour and estimates of all the overheads of the business for the period.

    Control – control of costs is a vital element of management's role. One method of control is to compare the actual costs for a period to the budgeted costs for the same period. Any differences between actual cost and budgeted costs are known as variances and any significant variances should be investigated in order to determine their cause and to alter either the budgets or future operations in the light of the variances.

costing information – answers

3 a) The expenditure of a business can be classified as either capital expenditure or revenue expenditure. Capital expenditure is expenditure on the purchase of assets for long term use within the business, fixed assets. Revenue expenditure is all other expenditure of the business, the day to day purchases and running costs of the business.

b) Costs of a business can also be classified according to the function of the business that caused the cost. The main functions in manufacturing businesses are usually production, selling and distribution and administration. Costs will therefore be classified as production costs, selling and distribution costs or administration costs.

c) Costs can be classified according to their relationship with the product that a business makes or the unit of service that it provides. If the cost can be directly identified with a unit of production or service then it is known as a direct cost. All other costs which cannot be directly identified with the unit of production or service are known as indirect costs. When classifying costs in this manner it is usual to split the direct and indirect costs into three categories, materials, labour and expenses.

d) Some costs of a business will tend to alter as activity levels change while others will remain constant despite a change in activity levels. This is what is meant by analysing costs according to behaviour. If a cost remains constant irrespective of the level of activity then it is known as a fixed cost. If the cost varies directly with the level of activity then it is classified as a variable cost. Some costs have both a fixed and a variable element – this means that there is a fixed element that must be paid no matter what the level of activity and then there is a further element of the cost which will alter as activity levels alter. These costs are known as semi-variable costs. A further classification of cost is a step fixed cost. This is a cost that is fixed for a range of activity levels but outside this range will alter and then remain fixed for a further range of activity levels.

4

	Capital	Revenue
Purchase of a car for resale by a car dealer		✓
Purchase of a car for use by a salesman	✓	
Road tax payable on purchase of a car for use by a salesman		✓
Redecorating head office		✓
Installing new machinery	✓	
Cleaning of new machinery after initial use		✓

costing information – answers

5

	Production cost	Selling and distribution cost	Administration cost
Depreciation of salesmen's cars		✓	
Production manager's salary	✓		
Depreciation of machinery	✓		
Rent of office space			✓
Depreciation of delivery vans		✓	
CD-Roms for office computer			✓

6

	Direct cost	Indirect cost
Wages of factory supervisor		✓
Hire of plant for construction of a building by a building firm	✓	
Cleaning materials used in the factory		✓
Factory rent		✓
Wages of a trainee accountant in an accountancy firm	✓	
Cement used for construction of a building by a building firm	✓	

7
- a) Semi-variable cost
- b) Fixed cost
- c) Variable cost
- d) Fixed cost
- e) Step fixed cost

costing information – answers

8

	Units	Cost £
Highest level – June	145,000	424,000
Lowest level – April	110,000	340,000
Increase	35,000	84,000

Variable element of cost = $\dfrac{£84,000}{35,000 \text{ units}}$ = £2.40 per unit

	£
June production – variable costs (145,000 × £2.40)	348,000
Fixed costs (balancing figure)	76,000
Total production cost	424,000

9

	80,000 units £	130,000 units £	180,000 units £
Variable costs – production costs (£3.80 + 1.40 + 0.30 = £5.50)	440,000	715,000	990,000
Fixed cost – depreciation	30,000	30,000	30,000
Step fixed cost – rent	150,000	190,000	190,000
	620,000	935,000	1,210,000

10

a) Individual contracts
b) A passenger mile (or passenger kilometre)

11

	Total £	Prime cost £	Production expense £	Admin. expense £	Selling and distribution expense £
Wages of assembly employees	6,750	6,750			
Wages of stores employees	3,250		3,250		
Tyres for toy wheels	1,420	1,420			
Safety goggles for operators	810		810		
Job advert for new employees	84			84	
Depreciation of delivery vehicles	125				125
Depreciation of production machines	264		264		
Cost of trade exhibition	1,200				1,200
Computer stationery	130			130	
Course fee for AAT training	295			295	
Royalty for the design of wheel 1477	240	240			
	14,568	8,410	4,324	509	1,325

12 Cost behaviour patterns

a)

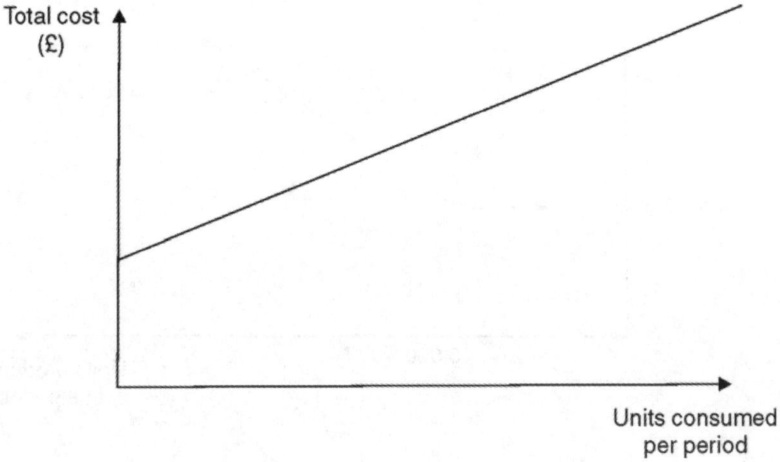
Total cost
(£)
Units consumed
per period

b)

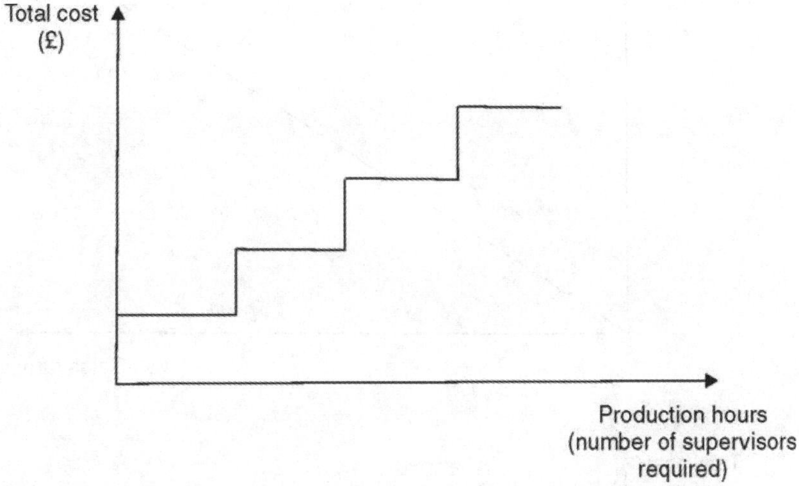
Total cost
(£)
Production hours
(number of supervisors
required)

costing information – answers

c)

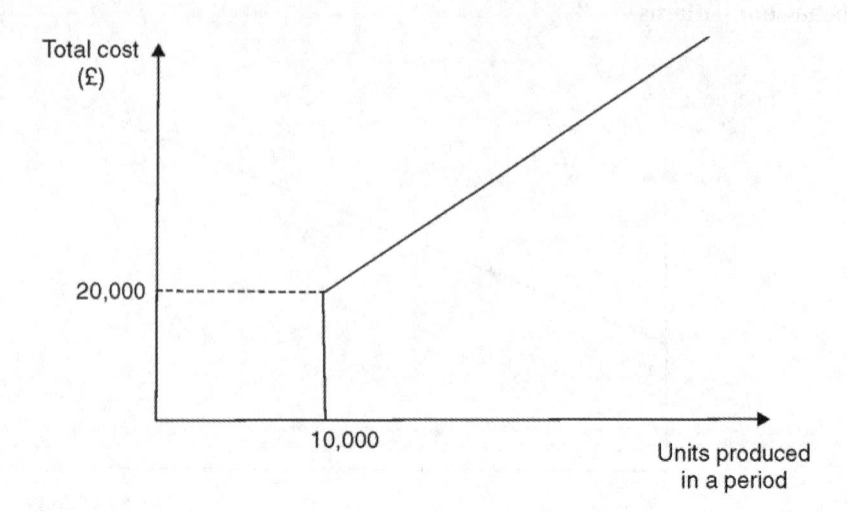

Total cost (£) vs Units produced in a period: horizontal at 20,000 up to 10,000 units, then rising linearly.

d)

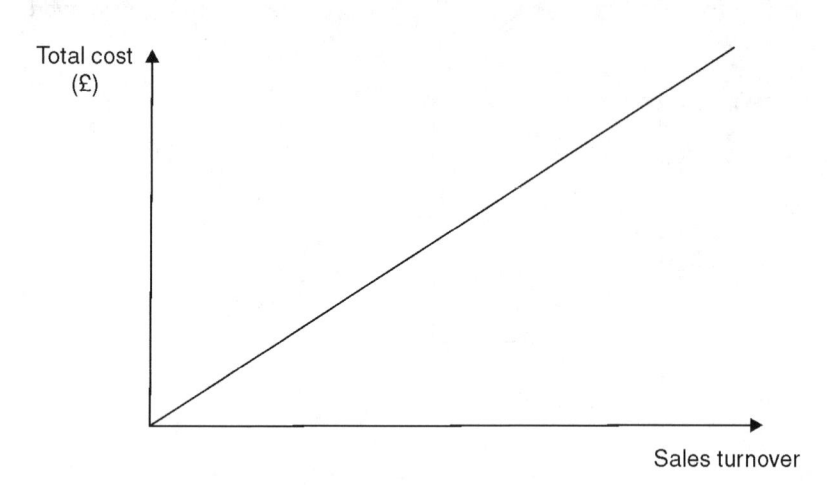

Total cost (£) vs Sales turnover: straight line from origin rising linearly.

e)

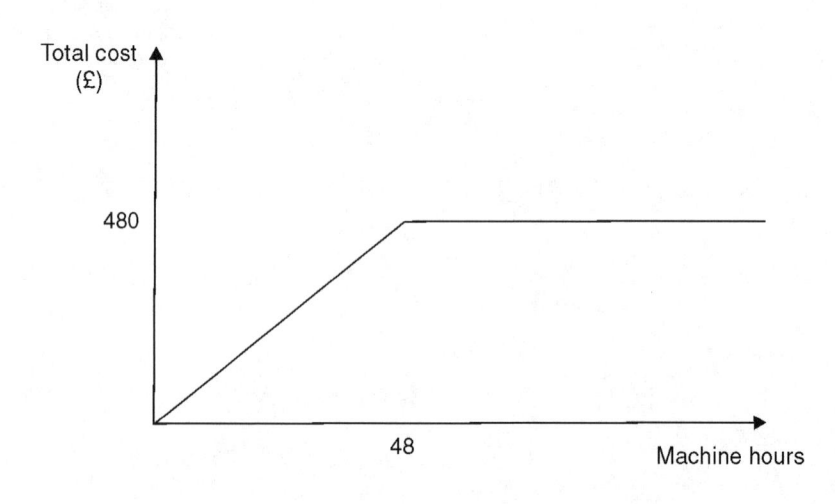

Total cost (£) vs Machine hours: rising linearly from origin to 480 at 48 machine hours, then horizontal at 480.

312

13

REPORT

To: Managing Director
From: Accounting Technician
Subject: Cost behaviour   **Date:** Today

The classification of costs by their behaviour

Costs may be classified in many different ways, but one of the most important ways from the point of view of managing a business is classification according to how costs change in response to changes in the level of activity. The main distinction is between **fixed costs** and **variable costs**.

Fixed costs are those that do not change whatever the level of activity. The cost of rental of a business premises is a common example: this is a constant amount (at least within a stated time period) that does not vary with the level of activity conducted on the premises. Other examples are business rates, salaries, buildings insurance and so on.

A sketch graph of a fixed cost would look like this.

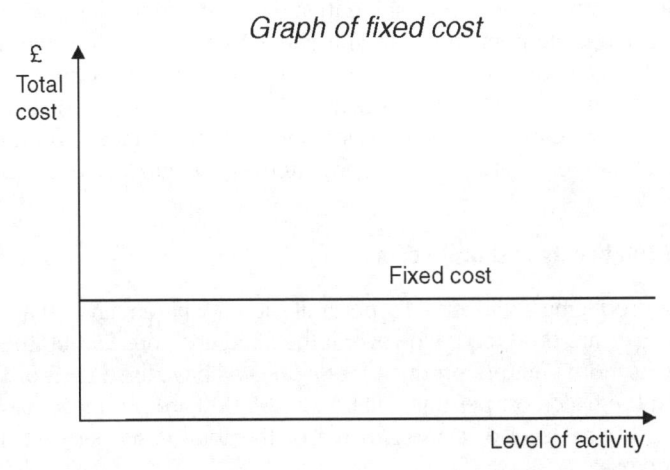

Graph of fixed cost

(£ Total cost on vertical axis; Level of activity on horizontal axis; horizontal line labelled "Fixed cost")

Variable costs, of course, are those that do vary with the level of activity: if a business produces two widgets, for example, it uses twice as many materials as it does for one widget. Similarly if it sells more goods, its sales administration costs like stationery and postage will vary proportionately.

A sketch graph of a variable cost would look like this.

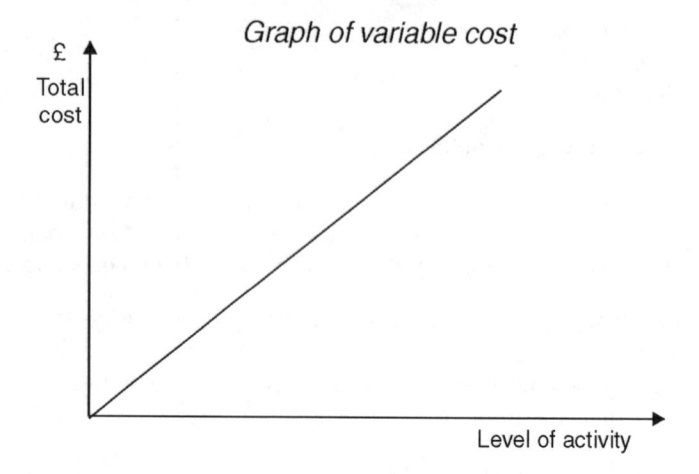

Graph of variable cost

(Graph: Total cost £ on y-axis, Level of activity on x-axis, showing a straight line rising from the origin.)

Many costs behave in a more complicated fashion than these simple models suggest. For example, a telephone bill has a **fixed element** (the standing charge) and a **variable element** (the cost of calls). These are called **mixed costs** (or semi-variable or semi-fixed costs). Other costs are stepped: that is, they are fixed within a certain level of activity but increase above or below that level at certain levels of activity. For example, if a second factory has to be rented to produce the required volume of output the cost of rent will double. Other patterns are exhibited when quantity discounts are available.

Cost behaviour and total costs and unit costs

If the variable cost of producing a widget is £5 per unit then it will remain at that cost per unit no matter how many widgets are produced. However if the fixed costs are £5,000 then the fixed cost per unit will decrease as more units are produced: one unit will have fixed costs of £5,000 per unit; if 2,500 are produced the fixed cost per unit will be £2; if 5,000 are produced fixed costs per unit will be only £1. Thus as the level of activity increases the total costs per unit (fixed costs plus variable costs) will decrease.

In sketch graph form this may be illustrated as follows.

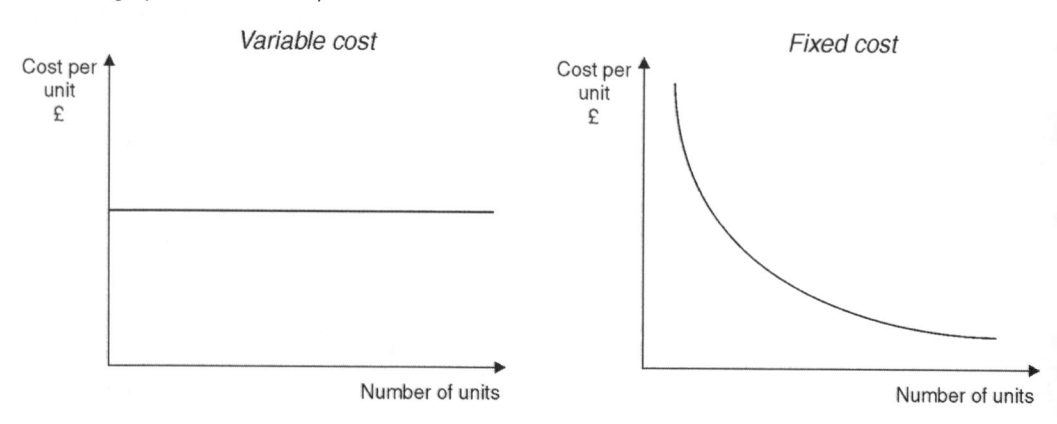

Variable cost

(Graph: Cost per unit £ on y-axis, Number of units on x-axis, showing a horizontal straight line.)

Fixed cost

(Graph: Cost per unit £ on y-axis, Number of units on x-axis, showing a curve decreasing hyperbolically.)

The importance of cost behaviour

The classification of costs according to behaviour serves a number of purposes, notably the following.

a) In **planning** it is necessary to know the cost that will be incurred at various possible levels of activity so that a level appropriate to the overall resources of the business may be chosen.

b) To **maintain control** of the business it is necessary to compare actual results achieved to those expected and this will require adjustments depending upon actual and expected levels of activity.

c) When **marginal costing** is used, for example for **decision making**, the distinction between fixed and variable costs is fundamental to this approach.

Signed: Accounting Technician

answers to chapter 2: MATERIALS COSTS

1 a) The three main categories of stock for a manufacturing business are **raw materials**, **work in progress** and **finished goods**

b) The internal document used to record the quantity of materials received from a supplier is known as a **goods received note**

c) The initial internal document that starts the purchasing process for materials is known as a **purchase requisition**

d) A **purchase order** is the document that is sent to a supplier to request the supply of materials

e) When materials are required from stores by the factory a **materials requisition** is filled out

f) A **purchase invoice** is the document received from a supplier of materials requesting payment

materials costs – answers

2

STOCK CARD

Description: 23 Electrical component EC23 **Bin No:** 413

Code No:

Receipts			Issues			Balance
Date	Reference	Quantity	Date	Reference	Quantity	Quantity
1 June						50
3 June	GRN0326	340				390
			5 June	MR0295	150	240
			10 June	MR0307	190	50
12 June	GRN0348	300				350
			20 June	MR0315	180	170
			25 June	MR0320	100	70
28 June	GRN0363	320				390

3

STORES LEDGER ACCOUNT

Stock item LRM

Code 8888

Date	Receipts Qty	Receipts Unit price £	£	Issues Qty	Issues Unit price £	£	Balance Qty	Balance Unit cost £	£
Op bal							100	2.00	200
3 Sept	400	2.10	840				500	2.08	1,040
4 Sept				200	2.08	416	300	2.08	624
9 Sept	300	2.12	636				600	2.10	1,260
11 Sept				400	2.10	840	200	2.10	420
18 Sept	100	2.40	240				300	2.20	660
20 Sept				100	2.20	220	200	2.20	440

Workings

With the weighted average cost method, a weighted average cost is calculated each time a new delivery is received. The weighting is provided by the number of units at each price brought into the calculation. The general formula is as follows:

$$\text{Average price per unit} = \frac{\text{Total value of existing stock} + \text{Total value of goods added to stock}}{\text{Units of existing stock} + \text{Units added to stock}}$$

materials costs – answers

4 a)

STORES LEDGER ACCOUNT

Stock item: XK2

Code: 041861

FIFO basis

Date	Receipts GRN	Qty	Unit price £	£	Issues Req No	Qty	Unit price £	£	Balance Qty	£
1 July									400	1,200.00
4 July					416	320	3.00	960	80	240.00
7 July	668	500	3.20	1,600					580	1,840.00
12 July					422	80	3.00	240		
						100	3.20	320	400	1,280.00
16 July					428	300	3.20	960	100	320.00
19 July	674	500	3.50	1,750					600	2,070.00
23 July					433	100	3.20	320		
28 July						130	3.50	455	370	1,295.00
					440	300	3.50	1,050	70	245.00

320

b)

STORES LEDGER ACCOUNT

Stock item: XK2

Code: 041861

LIFO basis

Date	Receipts				Issues				Balance	
	GRN	Qty	Unit price £	£	Req No	Qty	Unit price £	£	Qty	£
1 July									400	1,200.00
4 July					416	320	3.00	960	80	240.00
7 July	668	500	3.20	1,600					580	1,840.00
12 July					422	180	3.20	576	400	1,264.00
16 July					428	300	3.20	960	100	304.00
19 July	674	500	3.50	1,750					600	2,054.00
23 July					433	230	3.50	805	370	1,249.00
28 July					440	270	3.50	945		
						20	3.20	64	70	
						10	3.00	30		210.00

c)

STORES LEDGER ACCOUNT

Stock item: XK2

Code: 041861

AVCO basis

Date	Receipts				Issues				Balance	
	GRN	Qty	Unit price £	£	Req No	Qty	Unit price £	£	Qty	£
1 July									400	1,200.00
4 July					416	320	3.00	960	80	240.00
7 July	668	500	3.20	1,600					580	1,840.00
12 July					422	180	3.17	570	400	1,269.40
16 July					428	300	3.17	951	100	318.40
19 July	674	500	3.50	1,750					600	2,068.40
23 July					433	230	3.45	793	370	1,274.90
28 July					440	300	3.45	1,035	70	239.90

Workings

Calculation of weighted average price:

				£
4 July	80	@	3.00	240.00
7 July	500	@	3.20	1,600.00
	580		3.17	1,840.00
12 July	(180)	@	3.17	(570.60)
16 July	(300)	@	3.17	(951.00)
19 July	500	@	3.50	1,750.00
	600	@	3.45	2,068.40
23 July	(230)	@	3.45	(793.50)
28 July	(300)	@	3.45	(1,035.00)
	70	@	3.45	239.90

5 FIFO

		Units		Cost	Total cost £
1 July	Opening balance	220	@	5.60	1,232.00
3 July	Issue	(160)	@	5.60	(896.00)
		60			336.00
7 July	Purchase	300	@	6.00	1,800.00
		360			2,136.00
10 July	Issue	(60)	@	5.60	(336.00)
		(110)	@	6.00	(660.00)
		190			1,140.00
15 July	Issue	(100)	@	6.00	(600.00)
		90			540.00
20 July	Purchase	250	@	6.30	1,575.00
		340			2,115.00
24 July	Issue	(90)	@	6.00	(540.00)
		(110)	@	6.30	(693.00)
		140			882.00

a) Cost of issues (£896.00 + 336.00 + 660.00 + 600.00 + 540.00 + 693.00) = £3,725.00

b) Closing stock value = £882.00

LIFO

		Units		Cost	Total cost £
1 July	Opening balance	220	@	5.60	1,232.00
3 July	Issue	(160)	@	5.60	(896.00)
		60			336.00
7 July	Purchase	300	@	6.00	1,800.00
		360			2,136.00
10 July	Issue	(170)	@	6.00	(1,020.00)
		190			1,116.00
15 July	Issue	(100)	@	6.00	(600.00)
		90			516.00
20 July	Purchase	250	@	6.30	1,575.00
		340			2,091.00
24 July	Issue	(200)	@	6.30	(1,260.00)
		140			831.00

a) Cost of issues (£896.00 + 1,020.00 + 600.00 + 1,260.00) = £3,776.00

b) Closing stock value = £831.00

materials costs – answers

AVCO

		Units		Cost	Total cost £
1 July	Opening balance	220	@	5.60	1,232.00
3 July	Issue	(160)	@	5.60	(896.00)
		60			336.00
7 July	Purchase	300	@	6.00	1,800.00
		360		5.93	2,136.00
10 July	Issue	(170)	@	5.93	(1,008.10)
15 July	Issue	(100)	@	5.93	(593.00)
20 July	Purchase	250	@	6.30	1,575.00
		340		6.21	2,109.90
24 July	Issue	(200)	@	6.21	(1,242.00)
		140	@	6.21	867.90

a) Cost of issues (£896.00 + 1,008.10 + 593.00 + 1,242.00) = £3,739.10

b) Closing stock value = £867.90

6   The FIFO method of stock valuation makes the assumption that each time an issue is made from stock that this issue is of the earliest purchases which will often reflect the actual usage pattern as the oldest stocks will often be used first. This means that at the end of the period the closing stocks are valued at the most recent up-to-date prices. However this method also means that the cost of issues to production are made at varying different and possibly out-of-date prices – this in turn means that the profit shown, if prices are rising, will be higher than that under the LIFO method.

The LIFO method of stock valuation makes the assumption that each time an issue is made from stock that this issue is of the most recent purchases – effectively therefore the issue is being made from the top of the pile of stock which may reflect actual practice. Issues are therefore made at current up-to-date prices which means that managers are more aware of current prices as these are the ones that their department is being charged. However as with FIFO it does mean that the price being charged for issues is constantly changing. The closing stock under LIFO is valued at the earliest prices and therefore may be an extremely out of date figure. As issues are charged at current prices the profit shown under LIFO, if prices are rising, will be lower than that under FIFO and indeed this method is not recommended for use in the financial statements by SSAP 9.

7

Materials control account

	£		£
Opening stock	12,523	WIP	79,247
Creditors	83,469	Production overhead control	6,248
		Closing stock	10,497
	95,992		95,992

Work in progress control account

	£		£
Materials control	79,247		

Production overhead control account

	£		£
Materials control	6,248		

8 FIFO to LIFO

a) Changing from FIFO to LIFO during a period of rapidly rising prices would result in lower stock valuations.

b) Changing from FIFO to LIFO during a period of rapidly rising prices would result in higher costs of materials charged to production.

9 Protective gloves

Closing stock = Opening stock + purchases – issues
= 100 + 200 – 150 = 150 pairs

Value of closing stock = 150 pairs x £1.90 (purchase price on 7 November)
= £285

materials costs – answers

10 Wiggles plc

STORES RECORD CARD (STOCK CARD)

Material description: Paper

Code no: 1564A

		Receipts		Issues			Balance	
Date	Details	Sheets	£	Sheets	Unit price £	£	Sheets	£
	Opening stock						10,000	3,000
3 May	Purchase	4,000	1,600				14,000	4,600
6 May	Issue			7,000	0.33	2,310	7,000	2,290
12 May	Purchase	10,000	3,100				17,000	5,390
15 May	Issue			6,000	0.32	1,920	11,000	3,470
22 May	Issue			7,200	0.32	2,304	3,800	1,166
25 May	Purchase	10,000	3,200				13,800	4,366

11

STOCK RECORD CARD

Product: Motor oil

Centre: Servicing

	Receipts			Issues			Balance	
Date	Quantity	Cost per litre	Total cost	Quantity	Cost per litre	Total cost	Quantity	Total cost
	litres	£	£	litres	£	£	litres	£
B/f 1 May							2,100	2,100
4 May	2,400	1.20	2,880				4,500	4,980
8 May				3,300	2,400 x £1.20 900 x £1.00	3,780	1,200	1,200
10 May	3,000	1.10	3,300				4,200	4,500
11 May				3,200	3,000 x £1.10 200 x £1.00	3,500	1,000	1,000
17 May	5,000	1.00	5,000				6,000	6,000
18 May				5,400	5,000 x £1.00 400 x £1.00	5,400	600	600
23 May	6,400	0.95	6,080				7,000	6,680
24 May				4,420	4,420 x £0.95	4,199	2,580	2,481

Proof

600 litres @ £1.00 = £600
1,980 litres @ £0.95 = £1,881

Therefore, quantity of stock on 24 May = 600 litres + 1,980 litres = 2,580 litres at a value of £2,481 (£600 + £1,881).

answers to chapter 3:
LABOUR COSTS AND EXPENSES

1 a)
		£
	Basic pay 37 hours @ £6.80	251.60
	Overtime pay 6 hours @ £6.80 x 1.5	61.20
	Total gross pay	312.80

  b) Overtime payment   £61.20

  c) Overtime premium £6.80 x 0.5 x 6 hours   £20.40

2
	£
300 units @ £1.00	300.00
100 units @ £1.15	115.00
30 units @ £1.35	40.50
Total gross pay	455.50

3 a) Harry
	£
Product A £10.40 x 22	228.80
Product B £18.60 x 7	130.20
Total gross pay	359.00

  b) Stella
	£
Basic pay 35 hours @ £8.40	294.00
Overtime pay 8 hours @ £8.40 x 1 1/3	89.60
Total gross pay	383.60

  c) Yvette
	£
Basic salary £20,000/12	1,666.67
Bonus £20,000 x 5%	1,000.00
Total gross pay	2,666.67

labour costs and expenses – answers

4

Wages control account

	£		£
Bank	24,700	WIP	20,900
HMRC	6,200	Production overheads	12,400
Pension scheme	2,400		
	33,300		33,300

Work in progress control account

	£		£
Wages control	20,900		

Production overhead control account

	£		£
Wages control	12,400		

5

Freehold building = $\dfrac{£450,000 - 50,000}{40 \text{ years}}$

= £10,000

Machinery = $(£220,000 - 20,000) \times \dfrac{4,200}{32,000}$

= £26,250

Cars = $(£120,000 - 52,500) \times 25\%$

= £16,875

6

Work in progress control account

	£		£
Direct production costs	7,200		

Production overhead control account

	£		£
Indirect production costs	39,256		

labour costs and expenses – answers

7

Job no	Employee name	Number of hours	Rate £	Total cost £
N172	N Davies	2.25	6.60	14.85
	R Khan	1.00	6.80	6.80
				21.65
N174	J Pitman	6.00	10.00	60.00
M215	N Davies	2.00	6.60	13.20
	Y Chang	1.50	6.50	9.75
	R Khan	3.75	6.80	25.50
				48.45

8 a)   False.

   b)   True. Most expenses are the costs of other functions such as distribution, administration and finance.

   c)   False. Power to run machines is only a direct expense if the machine is dedicated to producing a particular product.

   d)   True.

331

answers to chapter 4:
OVERHEADS

1

	Total £	Assembly £	Finishing £	Stores £	Maintenance £
Indirect materials	18,700	16,500	2,200		
Indirect labour	22,800	7,500	6,200	4,500	4,600
Rent and rates	10,000	3,000	2,000	2,500	2,500
Heat and light	7,400	2,220	1,480	1,850	1,850
Supervisor's wages	9,880	5,720	4,160	–	–
Depreciation of machinery	8,400	5,250	1,750	525	875
	77,180	40,190	17,790	9,375	9,825
Stores		6,875	2,500	(9,375)	
Maintenance		5,731	4,094		(9,825)
		52,796	24,384	–	–

Workings

Rent and rates and light and heat are apportioned on the basis of floor area – assembly 30%, finishing 20%, stores and maintenance 25% each.

Supervisor's wages are apportioned on the basis of the supervisor's time in each department – 22:16

Depreciation is apportioned on the basis of net book value – 150:50:15:25

The stores overheads are then reapportioned on the basis of the number of materials requisitions and the maintenance overheads on the basis of the number of maintenance hours required.

overheads – answers

2

	Total £	A £	B £	Stores £	Canteen £
Indirect wages	75,700	7,800	4,700	21,200	42,000
Rent	24,000	9,600	6,400	3,200	4,800
Buildings insurance	2,000	800	533	267	400
Power	6,400	2,880	1,920	320	1,280
Heat and light	4,000	1,600	1,066	534	800
Supervisor's wages	10,000	10,000	–	–	–
Machinery depreciation	3,200	1,493	1,280	160	267
Machinery insurance	2,200	1,027	880	110	183
	127,500	35,200	16,779	25,791	49,730
Canteen		29,009	16,577	4,144	(49,730)
				29,935	
Stores		17,961	11,974	(29,935)	
		82,170	45,330	–	–

Workings

Rent, buildings insurance and heat and light are apportioned on the basis of floor area – 12:8:4:6

Power is apportioned using the percentages given.

Supervisor's wages are allocated directly to department A.

Machinery depreciation and insurance are apportioned on the basis of the net book value of the machinery – 140:120:15:25

Canteen costs are apportioned according to the number of staff that use it – 70:40:10

The stores costs are apportioned on the basis of the number of materials requisitions.

3

	Total £	Assembly £	Polishing £	Stores £	Maintenance £
	130,000	60,000	40,000	20,000	10,000
Stores		10,000	8,000	(20,000)	2,000
				–	12,000
Maintenance		7,200	4,800		(12,000)
	130,000	77,200	52,800	–	–

overheads – answers

4

a) Rate per unit

Cutting	Finishing
$\dfrac{58,600}{10,000}$	$\dfrac{42,400}{10,000}$
= £5.86 per unit	= £4.24 per unit

can be used where all products are of similar size and require a similar input in terms of time and resources of the departments

b) Rate per direct labour hour

$\dfrac{58,600}{4,000}$	$\dfrac{42,400}{24,000}$
= £14.65 per labour hour	= £1.77 per labour hour

most appropriate in labour intensive departments where most of the overhead relates to labour

c) Rate per machine hour

$\dfrac{58,600}{12,000}$	$\dfrac{42,400}{2,000}$
= £4.88 per machine hour	£21.20 per machine hour

most appropriate in a largely mechanised department where most of the overhead relates to machinery costs

5

a) $C = \dfrac{£125,000}{100,000}$

= £1.25 per machine hour

as C is a highly mechanised department most of the overhead will relate to the machinery therefore machine hours have been used to absorb the overhead.

$D = \dfrac{£180,000}{80,000}$

= £2.25 per direct labour hour

as D is a highly labour intensive department then most of the overhead will relate to the hours that are worked by the labour force therefore labour hours are used to absorb the overhead.

b) Product P – department C overhead   £1.25 x 5   =   £ 6.25
              department D overhead   £2.25 x 7   =   £15.75

overheads – answers

6 a) Overhead absorption rate = £5,400 / 1,200

= £4.50 per unit

Overhead incurred = £5,000
Overhead absorbed
1,000 units x £4.50 = £4,500

Under-absorbed overhead = £500 – a further expense in the P&L

b) Overhead absorption rate = £5,040 / 1,800

= £2.80 per direct labour hour

Overhead incurred = £5,100
Overhead absorbed
2,200 hours x £2.80 = £6,160

Over-absorbed overhead = £1,060 – a credit to the P&L

c) Overhead absorption rate = £320,000 / 80,000

= £4.00 per machine hour

Overhead incurred = £320,000
Overhead absorbed
82,000 x £4.00 = £328,000

Over-absorbed overhead = £8,000 – a credit to the P&L

overheads – answers

7 a)

Production overhead control account

	£		£
Creditors/cash – overheads incurred	5,000	WIP – overheads absorbed	4,500
		P&L – under-absorbed	500

b)

Production overhead control account

	£		£
Creditors/cash – overheads incurred	5,100	WIP – overheads absorbed	6,160
P&L – over-absorbed	1,060		
	6,160		6,160

c)

Production overhead control account

	£		£
Creditors/cash – overheads incurred	320,000	WIP – overheads absorbed	328,000
P&L – over-absorbed	8,000		
	328,000		

8 Overhead absorption rates are calculated as follows:

$$\text{Overhead absorption rate} = \frac{\text{Budgeted overheads}}{\text{Budgeted activity level}}$$

Using budgeted figures means that the actual overhead cost is unlikely to be the same as the overheads actually absorbed into production, as we are relying on two estimated figures (overheads and activity levels). These estimates are likely to differ from the actual values that are experienced during the period. Consequently, at the end of the period when the profit and loss account is drawn up, the profit figure will be wrong as the overhead charge will be the absorbed amount rather than the actual amount. The error in the profit figure will result from one of two possibilities.

a) If more overheads are absorbed than have actually been incurred, this is known as **over-absorption**.

b) If fewer overheads are absorbed than have actually been incurred, this is known as **under-absorption**.

The amount over- or under-absorbed is adjusted for in the profit and loss account after the production cost has been charged. Under-absorption means that too little overhead has been charged in the production cost, so a deduction is made from profit. Over-absorption means that too much overhead has been charged, so there is a compensating addition to profit.

overheads – answers

9 Machining department

	£
Overheads incurred	9,322
Overheads absorbed (£5 × 1,753)	8,765
Under-absorbed overhead	557

10 Happy Ltd

Actual fixed overheads for November	Basis	Total £	Warehouse £	Manufacturing £	Sales £	Administration £
Depreciation	Net book value	14,600	2,920	10,220	730	730
Rent	% floor space	48,000	9,600	31,200	2,400	4,800
Other property overheads	% floor space	12,800	2,560	8,320	640	1,280
Administration overheads	allocation	28,800	–	–	–	28,800
Staff costs	allocation	39,800	4,800	14,340	12,250	8,410
		144,000	19,880	64,080	16,020	44,020

answers to chapter 5: ABSORPTION COSTING AND MARGINAL COSTING

1 Trident Ltd

Marginal Costing Statement for March

	£	£
Sales revenue (4,000 × £40)		160,000
Variable costs		
Direct materials	25,000	
Direct labour	50,000	
Variable overheads	15,000	
Total variable costs		(90,000)
Total contribution for the period		70,000

The total contribution for the period is therefore £70,000. Fixed costs are treated as a period cost and are not included in the total contribution calculation.

2 a) **Absorption costing**

	£
Direct materials	12.00
Direct labour – cutting (2 × £7.40)	14.80
finishing	6.80
Variable overheads:	
Cutting ((£336,000/240,000) × 2)	2.80
Finishing (£132,000/120,000)	1.10
Fixed overheads:	
Cutting ((£144,000/240,000) × 2)	1.20
Finishing (£96,000/120,000)	0.80
	39.50

b) **Marginal costing**

	£
Direct materials	12.00
Direct labour – cutting (2 × £7.40)	14.80
finishing	6.80
Variable overheads:	
Cutting (£336,000/240,000 × 2)	2.80
Finishing (£132,000/120,000)	1.10
	37.50

absorption costing and marginal costing – answers

3 Cost per unit – absorption costing

		£
Direct materials	6.80	
Direct labour	3.60	
Variable costs (£32,400/24,000)		1.35
Fixed costs (£44,400/24,000)		1.85
		13.60

Cost per unit – marginal costing

	£
Direct materials	6.80
Direct labour	3.60
Variable costs (£32,400/24,000)	1.35
	11.75

a) Absorption costing – profit and loss account

	July £	July £	August £	August £
Sales (22,000 x £16)		352,000		
(25,000 x £16)				400,000
Less: cost of sales				
Opening stock (1,500 x £13.60)	20,400			
(3,500 x £13.60)			47,600	
Production (24,000 x £13.60)	326,400		326,400	
	346,800		374,000	
Less: closing stock (3,500 x £13.60)	(47,600)			
(2,500 x £13.60)			(34,000)	
		299,200		340,000
Profit		52,800		60,000

Marginal costing – profit and loss account

	July £	July £	August £	August £
Sales (22,000 x £16)		352,000		
(25,000 x £16)				400,000
Less: cost of sales				
Opening stock (1,500 x £11.75)	17,625			
(3,500 x £11.75)			41,125	
Production (24,000 x £11.75)	282,000		282,000	
	299,625		323,125	
Less: closing stock (3,500 x £11.75)	(41,125)			
(2,500 x £11.75)			(29,375)	
		258,500		293,750
Contribution		93,500		106,250
Fixed costs		44,400		44,400
		49,100		61,850

b) Reconciliation of profit figures

	July £	August £
Absorption cost profit	52,800	60,000
Increase in stock (3,500 – 1,500)		
x fixed c.p.u. 2,000 x £1.85	(3,700)	
Decrease in stock (3,500 – 2,500)		
x fixed c.p.u. 1,000 x £1.85		1,850
	49,100	61,850

4 Unit cost – absorption costing

	£
Direct materials	23.60
Direct labour (4 x £5.80)	23.20
Variable overheads (£88,000/8,000)	11.00
Fixed overheads (£51,200/8,000)	6.40
	64.20

Unit cost – marginal costing

	£
Direct materials	23.60
Direct labour (4 x £5.80)	23.20
Variable overheads (£88,000/8,000)	11.00
	57.80

a) Absorption costing – profit and loss account

	£	£
Sales (8,200 x £70)		574,000
Less: cost of sales		
Opening stock (840 x £64.20)	53,928	
Production cost (8,000 x £64.20)	513,600	
	567,528	
Less: closing stock (640 x £64.20)	41,088	
		526,440
Profit		47,560

Marginal costing – profit and loss account

	£	£
Sales (8,200 x £70)		574,000
Less: cost of sales		
Opening stock (840 x £57.80)	48,552	
Production cost (8,000 x £57.80)	462,400	
	510,952	
Less: closing stock (640 x £57.80)	36,992	
		473,960
Contribution		100,040
Less: fixed costs		51,200
Profit		48,840

b)

	£
Absorption costing profit	47,560
Decrease in stocks x fixed cost per unit (200 x £6.40)	1,280
Marginal costing profit	48,840

5   Absorption costing has the advantage of allowing managers to see whether the sales of their products are covering all of the production costs of those products. However, due to the different nature of fixed costs compared with variable costs, it is argued that contribution is a much more useful figure for management than a profit figure after production overheads have been apportioned. If fixed costs are included in the cost per unit then the unit cost will fall as activity levels increase simply due to the nature of the fixed cost not changing but being spread over more units of activity.

A further argument for the use of marginal costing rather than absorption costing for cost reporting purposes is to do with the profit differences and stock levels. Under absorption costing we have seen that it is possible to report a higher profit figure by increasing the closing stock levels. If a manager is assessed and possibly remunerated on the basis of the figure that he reports for profit then the profit can be manipulated by over producing and building up stock levels. Although this will increase absorption costing profit it may not be in the best interests of the organisation. This type of manipulation of profit cannot take place if marginal costing is used.

answers to chapter 6:
COSTING SYSTEMS

1. Batch costing is a form of costing that is similar to **job costing**, except that costs are collected for a **batch of items**. The cost unit is the **batch**. A cost per unit is calculated by **dividing the total batch cost by the number of units in the batch**.

2. **Costing methods**

    a) Job costing
    b) Batch costing
    c) Job costing

3. Job costing is an appropriate costing system in the type of business where the product that is produced is a 'one-off' job for a customer. Each individual job will tend to be different and have different materials, labour and expenses inputs. Therefore the costs of each individual job need to be specified.

4. **Job costing schedule**

	£
Direct materials	2,800.00
Direct labour	526.50
Overheads	234.90
Total costs	3,561.40
Profit (20% x 3,561.40)	712.28
	4,273.68
VAT	747.89
Total price	5,021.57

costing systems – answers

5

JOB NUMBER 2856

	Budget £	Actual £	Variance £
Direct materials			
■ wood	1,650.00	1,830.00	180.00 ADV
■ components	830.00	755.00	75.00 FAV
■ plastic	320.00	300.00	20.00 FAV
Direct labour			
■ Grade I - 30 hours	414.00	478.50	64.50 ADV
■ Grade III - 12 hours	132.00	77.00	55.00 FAV
Direct expenses			
■ hire of equipment	300.00	380.00	80.00 ADV
Overheads 42 x £4.60	193.20		
40 x £4.60		184.00	9.20 FAV
Total cost	3,839.20	4,004.50	165.30 ADV
Profit (3,839.20 x 25%)	959.80		
(4,799.00 – 4,004.50)		794.50	
	4,799.00	4,799.00	
VAT@ 17.5%	839.82	839.82	
Job cost	5,638.82	5,638.82	

6

Step 1 Calculate the number of normal loss units:
100,000 kg x 6% = 6,000 kg

Step 2 Calculate the expected output from the process:
100,000 kg – 6,000 kg = 94,000 kg

Step 3 Total the process costs:
£287,000 + 138,000 + 82,600 = £507,600

Step 4 Calculate the cost per unit of expected output:
$$\frac{£507,600}{94,000} = £5.40 \text{ per kg}$$

Process account

	kg	£		kg	£
Materials	100,000	287,000	Normal loss	6,000	–
Labour		138,000	Abnormal loss	2,000	10,800
Overheads		82,600	Output	92,000	496,800
	100,000	507,600		100,000	507,600

Process account

	kg	£		kg	£
Process account	2,000	10,800	Profit and loss	2,000	10,800

costing systems – answers

7 **Step 1** Calculate the number of normal loss units:
18,000 ltr x 5% = 900 ltr

Step 2 Calculate the expected output from the process:
18,000 ltr – 900 ltr = 17,100 ltr

Step 3 Total the process costs:
£35,800 + 7,200 + 11,720 = £54,720

Step 4 Calculate the cost per unit of expected output:

$$\frac{£54,720}{17,100} = £3.20 \text{ per litre}$$

Process account

	ltr	£		ltr	£
Materials	18,000	35,800	Normal loss	900	-
Labour		7,200	Output	17,500	56,000
Overheads		11,720			
Abnormal gain	400	1,280			
	18,400	56,000		18,400	56,000

Process account

	ltr	£		ltr	£
Profit and loss	400	1,280	Process account	400	1,280

345

answers to chapter 7:
COST BOOKKEEPING

1

Production overhead control account

	£		£
Overheads incurred	4,720	Overheads absorbed	
		1,400 × £3.20	4,480
	4,720	Under-absorbed overhead	240
			4,720

The under-absorbed overhead of £240 is debited to the profit and loss account as an additional cost.

2

Production overhead control account

	£		£
Overheads incurred	5,840	Overheads absorbed	
Over-absorbed overhead	223	940 × £6.45	6,063
	6,063		6,063

The over-absorbed overhead of £223 will be credited to the profit and loss account.

3

Materials control account

	£		£
Creditors	14,365	WIP control	11,632
		Closing stock	2,733
	14,365		14,365

Wages control account

	£		£
Gross wages (18,375 + 2,682)	21,057	WIP control	18,375
		Production overhead control	2,682
	21,057		21,057

cost bookkeeping – answers

Production overhead control account

	£		£
Wages control	2,682	Overhead absorbed – WIP	
Bank	6,243	1,530 × £5.20	7,956
		Under-absorbed overhead	969
	8,925		8,925

Work in progress control account

	£		£
Materials control	11,632	Finished goods	36,540
Wages control	18,375	Closing stock	1,423
Production overhead	7,956		
	37,963		37,963

4 a) & b)

Materials control account

	£		£
Opening stock	1,290	WIP control	6,620
Creditors	7,640	Administration overhead	990
		Closing stock	1,320
	8,930		8,930

Wages control account

	£		£
Gross wages (£5,430 + £1,460)	6,890	WIP control	5,430
		Production overhead control	1,460
	6,890		6,890

Production overhead control account

	£		£
Wages control	1,460	Overhead absorbed – WIP	
Cash	4,290	490 × £11.10	5,439
		Under-absorbed overhead (P&L)	311
	5,750		5,750

348

Work in progress control account

	£		£
Opening balance	1,540	Finished goods	12,200
Materials control	6,620	Closing balance	1,399
Production overhead	5,439		
	13,599		13,599

Finished goods control account

	£		£
Opening stock	1,830	P&L (bal fig)	12,380
WIP control	12,200	Closing stock	1,650
	14,030		14,030

Debtors control account

	£		£
Opening balance	7,200	Cash	6,800
Sales	14,700	Closing balance	15,100
	21,900		21,900

Creditors control account

	£		£
Cash	4,900	Opening balance	5,460
Closing balance	8,200	Materials	7,640
	13,100		13,100

Cash at bank account

	£		£
Opening balance	3,070	Creditors	4,900
Debtors	6,800	Production overheads	4,290
Closing balance	530	Administration overheads	1,210
	10,400		10,400

Administration overheads account

	£		£
Materials control	990	P&L	2,200
Cash	1,210		
	2,200		2,200

Sales account

	£		£
P&L	14,700	Debtors	14,700

c) **Profit and loss account for August**

	£
Sales	14,700
Cost of goods sold (finished goods)	(12,380)
Gross profit	2,320
Under-absorbed overhead	(311)
Administration overheads	(2,200)
Net loss	(191)

answers to chapter 8:
SHORT-TERM DECISION MAKING

1. Provided that the selling price and the variable costs remain constant then contribution per unit will also be constant no matter what the level of activity. However full production cost per unit will decrease as production levels increase as the fixed costs are spread over more units. Therefore the constant figure of contribution per unit is more useful in the decision making process.

2. a) Breakeven point $= \dfrac{£1,100,000}{£28-17}$

   $= 100,000$ units

   b) i) Margin of safety (units) = Budgeted sales – breakeven sales

   $= (115,000 - 100,000)$ units

   $= 15,000$ units

   ii) Margin of safety (% budgeted sales) $= \dfrac{115,000 - 100,000}{115,000} \times 100\%$

   $= 13\%$

3. Contribution per unit $= £(16 - 8) = £8$

   Contribution required to breakeven = fixed costs = £40,000

   Breakeven point $= \dfrac{\text{Fixed costs}}{\text{Contribution per unit}}$

   $= \dfrac{£40,000}{£8}$

   $= 5,000$ units

   Sales revenue at breakeven point = 5,000 units x £16 per unit
   = £80,000

short-term decision making – answers

4 Margin of safety = Budgeted sales volume – breakeven sales volume

Breakeven sales volume = $\dfrac{\text{Fixed costs}}{\text{Contribution per unit}}$

$= \dfrac{£110{,}000}{£55}$

= 2,000 units

Therefore, margin of safety (units) = 2,500 units – 2,000 units
= 500 units

Therefore, margin of safety (sales revenue) = margin of safety (units) x selling price per unit
= 500 units x £80
= £40,000

5 Target profit units = $\dfrac{£540{,}000 + 300{,}000}{£83 - 65}$

= 46,667 units

6 Profit volume ratio = $\dfrac{£40 - 28}{£40} \times 100\%$

= 30%

Target profit sales revenue = $\dfrac{£518{,}000 + 250{,}000}{0.3}$

= £2,560,000

7 Identify the limiting factor

Materials – at maximum demand

(4 x 20,000) + (5 x 25,000) + (3 x 8,000) = 229,000 kg

Labour hours – at maximum demand

(2 x 20,000) + (3 x 25,000) + (3 x 8,000) = 139,000 hours

Machine hours – at maximum demand

(4 x 20,000) + (3 x 25,000) + (2 x 8,000) = 171,000 hours

Therefore the only limiting factor is labour hours.

short-term decision making – answers

Contribution per labour hour

	R	S	T
Contribution	£11	£14	£19
Labour hours	2	3	3
Contribution per labour hour	£5.50	£4.67	£6.33
Ranking	2	3	1

Production plan

	Units	Labour hours used	Cumulative labour hours used
T	8,000	24,000	24,000
R	20,000	40,000	64,000
S (balance)	12,000	36,000	100,000
		100,000	

Contribution earned

	£
R (20,000 x £11)	220,000
S (12,000 x £14)	168,000
T (8,000 x £19)	152,000
	540,000

8

Sauce	Fudge	Butterscotch	Chocolate
	£	£	£
Selling price per bottle (W1)	2.00	2.00	1.00
Less: Unit variable costs			
Direct materials (W2)	0.20	0.25	0.10
Direct labour (W3)	0.60	0.50	0.25
Variable overheads (W4)	0.05	0.10	0.05
Contribution per bottle*	1.15	1.15	0.60
Profit volume ratio (%)**	57.5%	57.5%	60%

* Contribution = Selling price – Variable costs
** Profit volume ratio = x 100%

short-term decision making – answers

Workings

1. **Selling price per bottle**

    $$\text{Selling price per bottle} = \frac{\text{Total sales revenue}}{\text{Sales (bottles)}}$$

    Fudge sauce = $\frac{£1{,}000}{500}$ = £2 per bottle

    Butterscotch sauce = $\frac{£1{,}400}{700}$ = £2 per bottle

    Chocolate sauce = $\frac{£600}{600}$ = £1 per bottle

2. **Direct materials per bottle**

    $$\text{Direct materials per bottle} = \frac{\text{Total direct material costs}}{\text{Production volume (bottles)}}$$

    Fudge sauce = $\frac{£100}{500}$ = £0.20 per bottle

    Butterscotch sauce = $\frac{£175}{700}$ = £0.25 per bottle

    Chocolate sauce = $\frac{£60}{600}$ = £0.10 per bottle

3. **Direct labour cost per bottle**

    $$\text{Direct labour cost per bottle} = \frac{\text{Total direct labour costs}}{\text{Production volume (bottles)}}$$

    Fudge sauce = $\frac{£300}{500}$ = £0.60 per bottle

    Butterscotch sauce = $\frac{£350}{700}$ = £0.50 per bottle

    Chocolate sauce = $\frac{£150}{600}$ = £0.25 per bottle

4 Variable overheads per bottle

$$\text{Variable overheads per bottle} = \frac{\text{Total variable overhead costs}}{\text{Production volume (bottles)}}$$

Fudge sauce = $\frac{£25}{500}$ = £0.05 per bottle

Butterscotch sauce = $\frac{£70}{700}$ = £0.10 per bottle

Chocolate sauce = $\frac{£30}{600}$ = £0.05 per bottle

If the company only manufactures chocolate sauce, the sales revenue that it would need to earn each month to cover the fixed costs of £300 is:

$$\frac{\text{Fixed costs}}{\text{P/V ratio for chocolate sauce}} = \frac{£300}{60\%}$$

$$= \frac{£300}{60\%}$$

$$= £500$$

b) Therefore, the sales revenue required = £500 (which is 500 bottles of chocolate sauce at £1 each).

Alternatively, you could have calculated the breakeven point in volume terms ie the point at which fixed costs are covered.

$$\text{Breakeven point} = \frac{\text{Fixed costs}}{\text{Contribution per bottle of chocolate sauce}}$$

$$= \frac{£300}{£0.60} = 500 \text{ bottles}$$

Each bottle sells for £1, therefore sales revenue required to cover fixed costs = 500 x £1 = £500.

answers to chapter 9:
LONG-TERM DECISION MAKING

1. The time value of money is the principle that a sum of money received now is worth more than the same sum received at some time in the future due to the fact that this sum could be invested now to earn interest. This means that a sum of money receivable or payable at some time in the future is worth less than its face value now due to the interest that is lost on not investing. Therefore future cash flows must be discounted in order to determine their present value.

2. a) **Payback period**

	Cash inflows £	Cumulative cash inflows £
31 Dec 2009	15,000	15,000
31 Dec 2010	25,000	40,000
31 Dec 2011	35,000	75,000
31 Dec 2012	30,000	105,000

The payback period is 4 years if the cash flows are assumed to take place at the year end. Therefore the project should be rejected by the managers as it does not meet their payback criterion.

Even if the cash flows were assumed to occur evenly the payback period would still be more than three years.

b) **Net present value**

Year	Cash flow £	Discount factor @ 10%	Present value £
0	(95,000)	1.0000	(95,000)
1	15,000	0.9090	13,635
2	25,000	0.8264	20,660
3	35,000	0.7513	26,295
4	30,000	0.6830	20,490
5	30,000	0.6209	18,627
Net present value			4,707

As the project has a positive net present value then the managers should invest in the new plant and machinery as even after taking account of the time value of money the project shows a surplus.

c) In both calculations the cash flows have been assumed to occur at the end of the year.

357

long-term decision making – answers

d) The payback period investment criteria showed that the project should be rejected as the payback period method only considers the cash flows within the payback period limit. In fact in this case there are substantial cash flows later in this project's life. The net present value method takes account of all of the cash flows of the project and discounts each year's cash flows to take account of the time value of money. In this case the net present value is positive and therefore the investment is worthwhile even though it takes four years to payback the initial investment cost.

3 a) £24,000 x 0.8734   =   £20,9652

   b) £1,500 x 2.408   =   £3,603

   c) $\dfrac{£2,000}{0.06}$ =   £33,333

   d) £30,000 x 1.000   =   £30,000

4 **Net present value**

Year	Cash flow £	Discount factor @ 7%	Present value £
0	(84,000)	1.000	(84,000)
1	26,000	0.9346	24,300
2	30,000	0.8734	26,202
3	21,000	0.8163	17,142
4	14,000	0.7629	10,681
Net present value			(5,675)

On the basis of the net present value calculations, as the net present value of the business is negative, the directors should not purchase the sole trader's business.

5 a) **Net present value**

Year	Cash flow £	Discount factor @ 12%	Present value £
0	(355,000)	1.0000	(355,000)
1 (47 + 60)	107,000	0.8929	95,540
2 (55 + 60)	115,000	0.7972	91,678
3 (68 + 60)	128,000	0.7118	91,110
4 (53 + 60)	113,000	0.6355	71,811
5 (22 + 60)	82,000	0.5674	46,527
Net present value			41,666

Note that depreciation is not a cash flow and having been charged in arriving at the profit figure must be added back to find the cash inflow in each year.

b) It has been assumed that the profit is earned on the last day of each year.

c) The net present value of the investment is positive and on this basis the potential investment is worthwhile.

358

long-term decision making – answers

6   a)   **Net present value at 15%**

Year	Cash flow £	Discount factor @ 15%	Present value £
0	(180,000)	1.000	(180,000)
1	42,000	0.8696	36,523
2	50,000	0.7561	37,805
3	75,000	0.6575	49,312
4	80,000	0.5717	45,736
Net present value			(10,624)

At the cost of capital of 15% the project has a negative net present value, and should therefore be rejected.

b)   **Net present value at 10%**

Year	Cash flow £	Discount factor @ 10%	Present value £
0	(180,000)	1.0000	(180,000)
1	42,000	0.9090	38,178
2	50,000	0.8264	41,320
3	75,000	0.7513	56,347
4	80,000	0.6830	54,640
Net present value			10,485

If the project can be financed at 10%, it should be accepted as it has a positive NPV.

c)   The IRR is the discount rate or cost of capital at which the NPV of the project is zero. It tells a business the maximum discount rate at which the project is worthwhile.

7   **Confectioners Unlimited**

a) i)

	Year 2 £	Year 3 £	Year 4 £
Sales revenues	60,000	100,000	320,000
Variable costs	(30,000)	(50,000)	(160,000)
Net cash flows	30,000	50,000	160,000

	Net cash flows £	Cumulative cash flow £
Sales revenues	30,000	30,000
Variable costs	50,000	80,000
Net cash flows	50,000	240,000

The set-up costs of £160,000 are repaid at the end of year 4 (cash flows are received at the end of each year). The payback period is therefore 4 years.

long-term decision making – answers

ii)

	Year 1	Year 2	Year 3	Year 4	Year 5
	£'000	£'000	£'000	£'000	£'000
Set-up cost	(160)				
Sales revenue		60	100	320	100
Variable costs		(30)	(50)	(160)	(50)
Net cashflows	(160)	30	50	160	50
Present value factor	0.870	0.756	0.658	0.572	0.497
Present value*	(139.2)	22.68	32.90	91.52	24.85

*Present value = net cash flows × present value factor

Net present value (in £'000) = (139.2) + 22.68 + 32.90 + 91.52 + 24.85
= 32.75
= £32,750

b)

REPORT

To: Managing Director

From: Accounting Technician

Date: Today

Net present value

The financial effects of setting up a new ice-cream parlour have been appraised and the project has been found to have a net present value of £32,750. The project has a positive NPV at 15% and based on this, I would recommend that the project is accepted.

Internal rate of return

The company requires an annual rate of return of 15% on any new project and therefore a project such as this which has an IRR of 26% should be accepted.

(Based on the IRR alone, it is recommended that the company should accept any project which has an IRR greater than 15%.)

answers to chapter 10:
INTERNAL INFORMATION

1 a) The factory Supervisor will be concerned about the day to day operations of the factory employees. The type of information that he might require would include:

- schedules of production for each day/week in order to schedule the employees suitably
- details of employee's holidays in order to help to schedule the work
- details of absentees
- details of hours worked by each employee and in particular overtime hours
- whether production schedules are met
- requirements for any additional overtime

b) The Manufacturing Director will be concerned more about the costs and overall performance of the labour force. The type of information that he might require would include:

- summaries of hours worked in each period including overtime hours
- the breakdown of overtime hours into week day and weekend overtime
- whether production targets have been met
- total labour cost in each period
- all variances from budget for the labour force

c) The Managing Director will only really be concerned with any problem areas with the labour force. He will leave all other aspects to the factory supervisor and manufacturing director. The type of information that he might require would include:

- any significant labour variances from budget
- any excessive overtime worked
- any delays that have meant that production schedules have not been met

2 The general requirements for useful information are that it must be relevant, reliable, consistent and prompt. Each of these will be considered in turn.

Relevant – Information will be relevant if it is information that that particular person requires – not all personnel in the organisation will require the same amount of detailed information. The more junior management will require details about the day to day running of their part of the organisation but further up the management levels less detailed information will be required – the relevant information for higher levels of management will be overviews, summaries, variances and problem areas.

Reliable – In order to be useful information must be reliable – this means that it must be as accurate as possible. Some information is factual, such as the number of hours of overtime worked in a week – this must be correct. Other information may be more subjective, such as the possible reasons for more materials being used in a period than was budgeted for – however again this should be as accurate as is possible given the circumstances.

Consistent – Information that is provided within an organisation will tend to be provided on a regular basis, weekly, monthly, quarterly etc and this information will often be compared over time. It is therefore important that each time the information is provided that it is provided on a consistent basis – the same format and with the same bases for all calculations, otherwise a comparison of one period's information to that of another would not be of use.

Prompt – When management require internal information about their business then they require it in order to be able to make decisions and to plan and control the business. In order to be able to do this the information that they require must be up to date. If figures for production in the factory for a week are required they will normally be required early in the following week not two or three weeks later.

3   **Internal sources**

- Invoices
- Orders
- Delivery notes
- Job cards

4   **Cost accounting**

- Information about product costs and profitability
- Information about departmental costs and profitability
- Cost information to help with pricing decisions
- Budgets and standard costs
- Actual performance and variances between actual and budget
- Information to help with the evaluation of one-off decisions

5   The typical type of information that might be required by the partners of a firm of solicitors in order to be able to appraise the performance of the firm for the last month might include:

- chargeable hours of all levels of staff
- amounts billed to clients during the month
- amounts of overtime worked by staff
- levels of overheads for the month
- potential new clients gained in the month
- absentee/illness rates
- amounts billed per chargeable hour

6

	Abberville £	Bacup £	Calver £	Total £
Sales	137,489	195,374	104,328	437,191
Cost of sales	53,621	72,288	41,731	167,640
Gross profit	83,868	123,086	62,597	269,551
Expenses	33,373	37,121	22,952	93,446
Net profit	50,495	85,965	39,645	176,105

answers to chapter 11: PERFORMANCE MEASURES

1 Production and productivity

Production is the quantity or volume of output produced. It is the number of units produced, or the actual number of units produced converted into an equivalent number of 'standard hours of production'.

Productivity is the measure of the efficiency with which output has been produced.

2

	Quarter ending 30 June	Quarter ending 31 March
Cost per unit	$\dfrac{£567,900}{330,000} = £1.72$	$\dfrac{£580,400}{332,000} = £1.75$
Labour productivity	$\dfrac{330,000}{12,600 \text{ hours}} = 26.2$ units per hour	$\dfrac{332,000}{12,300} = 27$ units per hour
Productivity index	$\dfrac{330,000}{350,000} = 94.3\%$	$\dfrac{332,000}{320,000} = 103.8\%$

3 FACTORY

Cost per unit	$\dfrac{£557,800}{128,700}$	$= £4.33$ per unit
Labour productivity	$\dfrac{128,700}{39,400}$	$= 3.27$ units per hour
Labour productivity	$\dfrac{128,700}{280}$	$= 460$ units per employee
Productivity index	$\dfrac{128,700}{120,000}$	$= 107.3\%$

TELEPHONE SALES

Cost per order	$\dfrac{£14,560}{9,180}$	$= £1.59$ per order
Labour productivity	$\dfrac{9,180}{27}$	$= 340$ orders per person

performance measures – answers

4 Idle time is the time that the production workers are on the factory floor but are not actually producing the products of the organisation. Some idle time is necessary for Health and Safety reasons – workers must have time for coffee breaks, lunch breaks etc. This is known as unavoidable idle time as it is a necessary part of working life.

Other idle time however is a consequence of the manufacturing process. There may be bottlenecks in production which mean that some production workers are not able to work when they should. There may be machine breakdowns or a lack of materials that mean that there is no production to work on. The workers may have finished the assigned tasks for the day and no other task is available. This is all known as avoidable idle time as it is not strictly necessary although it is a practical aspect of factory life.

5

	Jan	Feb	Mar	Apr	May	June
Labour utilisation %	$\dfrac{2{,}100}{2{,}190}$	$\dfrac{2{,}050}{2{,}130}$	$\dfrac{2{,}220}{2{,}240}$	$\dfrac{2{,}200}{2{,}300}$	$\dfrac{2{,}310}{2{,}430}$	$\dfrac{2{,}250}{2{,}350}$
	95.9%	96.2%	99.1%	95.7%	95.1%	95.7%

6

	May	June	July
Fixed asset utilisation	$\dfrac{£360{,}000}{£210{,}000}$	$\dfrac{£402{,}000}{£190{,}000}$	$\dfrac{£398{,}000}{£200{,}000}$
	£1.71	£2.11	£1.99
Machinery utilisation	$\dfrac{£360{,}000}{28{,}000 \text{ hours}}$	$\dfrac{£402{,}000}{32{,}000 \text{ hours}}$	$\dfrac{£398{,}000}{31{,}000 \text{ hours}}$
	£12.86 per machine hour	£12.56 per machine hour	£12.84 per machine hour
Asset turnover	$\dfrac{£360{,}000}{£300{,}000}$	$\dfrac{£402{,}000}{£310{,}000}$	$\dfrac{£398{,}000}{£320{,}000}$
	£1.20	£1.30	£1.24

7 **Return on capital employed (ROCE)** also called return on investment, (ROI) is calculated as a percentage, as profit/capital employed × 100 and it shows how much profit has been made in relation to the amount of the resources invested.

performance measures – answers

8

	May	June	July
Gross profit margin	$\dfrac{530}{1{,}320}$	$\dfrac{570}{1{,}420}$	$\dfrac{530}{1{,}500}$
	40.2%	40.1%	35.3%
Net profit margin	$\dfrac{240}{1{,}320}$	$\dfrac{240}{1{,}420}$	$\dfrac{240}{1{,}500}$
	18.2%	16.9%	16.0%
ROCE	$\dfrac{240}{2{,}600}$	$\dfrac{240}{2{,}840}$	$\dfrac{240}{3{,}080}$
	9.2%	8.5%	7.8%

The gross profit margin has shown a significant decrease in July. The net profit margin decreased in June even though the gross profit margin was similar to that of May indicating an increase in expenses. The net profit margin again decreases in July largely due to the deteriorating gross profit margin.

The return on capital employed has decreased each month due to a combination of the gross and net profit margin decreases.

9

		May	June	July
a)	Cost per unit	$\dfrac{£416{,}000}{220{,}000}$	$\dfrac{£402{,}000}{215{,}000}$	$\dfrac{£403{,}000}{216{,}000}$
		1.89	£1.87	£1.87
b)	Labour productivity	$\dfrac{220{,}000}{1{,}400}$	$\dfrac{£215{,}000}{1{,}360}$	$\dfrac{216{,}000}{1{,}430}$
		157 per hour	158 per hour	151 per hour
c)	Productivity index	$\dfrac{220{,}000}{220{,}000}$	$\dfrac{215{,}000}{220{,}000}$	$\dfrac{216{,}000}{220{,}000}$
		100%	97.7%	98.2%
d)	Labour utilisation %	$\dfrac{1{,}400}{1{,}400}$	$\dfrac{1{,}360}{1{,}400}$	$\dfrac{1{,}430}{1{,}400}$
		100%	97.1%	102.1%

performance measures – answers

e)	Fixed asset utilisation	$\dfrac{£595{,}000}{£320{,}000}$	$\dfrac{£600{,}000}{£300{,}000}$	$\dfrac{£610{,}000}{340{,}000}$
		£1.86	£2.00	£1.79
f)	Asset turnover	$\dfrac{£595{,}000}{460{,}000}$	$\dfrac{£600{,}000}{£508{,}000}$	$\dfrac{£610{,}000}{£562{,}000}$
		£1.29	£1.18	£1.09
g)	Gross profit margin	$\dfrac{£179{,}000}{595{,}000}$	$\dfrac{£198{,}000}{£600{,}000}$	$\dfrac{£207{,}000}{£610{,}000}$
		30.1%	33.0%	33.9%
h)	Net profit margin	$\dfrac{£48{,}000}{£595{,}000}$	$\dfrac{£54{,}000}{600{,}000}$	$\dfrac{£58{,}000}{610{,}000}$
		8.1%	9.0%	9.5%
i)	ROCE	$\dfrac{£48{,}000}{460{,}000}$	$\dfrac{£54{,}000}{508{,}000}$	$\dfrac{£58{,}000}{562{,}000}$
		10.4%	10.6%	10.3%

There have been few major changes over the three-month period although perhaps the most notable is the increase in gross profit margin in June and July. This has led to an increased net profit margin in those months although no increase in return on capital employed.

On the whole the performance in June and July has not been as good as in May although one area of improvement is the decrease in the cost per unit in the last two months. However in July labour productivity decreased even though the labour utilisation level was good. However both fixed asset utilisation and asset turnover decreased contributing to the decrease in return on capital employed in July.

10 Net profit margin

$$\text{Net profit margin} = \dfrac{\text{Net profit}}{\text{Turnover}} \times 100$$

2008 $\dfrac{75{,}000}{600{,}000} \times 100 = 12.5\%$

2009 $\dfrac{80{,}000}{800{,}000} \times 100 = 10\%$

answers to chapter 12: WRITING A REPORT

1
- Title of the report
- Who the report is from and to
- Date
- Terms of reference
- Summary
- Main body of the report
- Conclusion
- Recommendations
- Appendix

2
REPORT

To: Sales Director
From: Accountant
Date: 19 August 20X7
Subject: Shop Profitability

Terms of reference

This report on the profitability of the shop for the last six months has been requested by the sales director. A number of performance measures for profitability have been calculated and are shown in the appendix to this report.

Summary

The performance measures indicate not only a substantial increase in sales over the first six months of the year but also a healthy increase in all areas of profitability.

Findings

The major change in the shop performance has been a 50% increase in turnover in the six month period from January to June 20X7. However this appears to have been achieved with an increase in profitability as well.

The gross profit margin has increased gradually each month from 40.9% in January to 45.2% in June. The net profit margin has also increased over the period from 14.8% to highs of 15.5% although there was a sharp decrease in March and April. This may have been due to costs incurred as part of the expansion such as advertising costs which then reverted to normal levels in later months.

The return on capital employed has largely followed the pattern of the net profit margin although over the period has shown a healthy increase from 9.4% to 10.6%. This increase has been helped by an increased asset turnover, or capital utilisation, which has leapt from 64 pence of sales per £1 of capital to 70 pence in June.

Conclusion

All profitability performance measures show a significant increase over the period combined with a large increase in turnover over the six months.

APPENDIX

Performance measures

	Jan	Feb	Mar	Apr	May	June
Gross profit margin	40.9%	42.0%	43.0%	43.6%	44.0%	45.2%
Net profit margin	14.8%	15.5%	14.0%	14.5%	15.5%	15.1%
Return on capital employed	9.4%	9.7%	9.0%	9.9%	10.7%	10.6%
Asset turnover	0.64	0.63	0.64	0.68	0.69	0.70

3

REPORT

To: Manufacturing Director
From: Accountant
Date: 20 July 20X7
Subject: Productivity of divisions

Terms of reference

This report on productivity in each of the three manufacturing divisions has been prepared for the manufacturing director. The findings of the report are based upon the performance measures shown in the appendix to this report.

Summary

There are no significant differences between the performance of the three divisions although on the whole the most productive division is Division B and the least productive Division A. The most concerning factor is probably the fact that both units produced and hours worked are below budget in all three divisions.

Findings

The cost per unit figures do not differ significantly between the three divisions although the range is £3.12 to £3.05 in Division C. If all three divisions could produce the products at a cost of £3.05 this would clearly help the profitability of the organisation as a whole.

The productivity per labour hour again shows no huge differences but only Division B has achieved the budgeted productivity of 30 units per labour hour.

The productivity index shows that all of the Divisions have produced less than the units that were budgeted for. In line with this the labour utilisation figures show that less hours were worked than were budgeted for. This may need to be investigated.

Of the three Divisions, Division B appears to have performed the best with a fairly low cost per unit together with budgeted productivity per hour and the best performance in terms of productivity index and labour utilisation. Division A appears to have performed less well than the other two divisions with all performance measures being lower.

Conclusion

There are no dramatic differences in the performance of the three divisions although on balance Division B appears to be the most productive and Division A the least.

APPENDIX

Performance measures

	Division A	Division B	Division C
Cost per unit	£3.12	£3.08	£3.05
Productivity per labour hour	28.6	30.0	28.8
Productivity index	88.9%	96.0%	90.9%
Labour utilisation	93.3%	96.0%	94.5%

answers to chapter 13: TABLES AND DIAGRAMS

1 **Significant digits**

   a) 2,197.28
   b) 2,197.3
   c) 2,197

2 **Decimal places**

   a) 38.178
   b) 38.18
   c) 38.2

3 An **independent variable** is a variable whose value affects the value of the dependent variable. On a graph, the **x axis** is used to represent the independent variable.

4 A **scattergraph** is a graph which is used to exhibit data, rather than equations which produce simple lines or curves, in order to compare the way in which the variables vary with each other.

5 a)

	A	B	C	D	E
1		June	July	August	September
2	Sales	48,700	50,200	45,600	46,800
3	Cost of sales	30,200	31,600	29,200	30,000
4	Gross profit	= B2 - B3	= C2 - C3	= D2 - D3	= E2 - E3
5	Expenses	12,200	12,500	11,400	11,700
6	Net profit	= B4 - B5	= C4 - C5	= D4 - D5	= E4 - E5
7	Capital	52,500	52,500	55,000	55,000
8	Gross profit %	=(B4/B2)*100	=(C4/C2)*100	=(D4/D2)*100	=(E4/E2)*100
9	Net profit %	=(B6/B2)*100	=(C6/C2)*100	=(D6/D2)*100	=(E6/E2)*100
10	ROCE	=(B6/B7)*100	=(C6/C7)*100	=(D6/D7)*100	=(E6/E7)*100
11	Asset turnover	=B2/B7	=C2/C7	=D4/D7	=E4/E7

tables and diagrams – answers

b)

	A	B	C	D	E
1		June	July	August	September
2	Sales	48,700	50,200	45,600	46,800
3	Cost of sales	30,200	31,600	29,200	30,000
4	Gross profit	18,500	18,600	16,400	16,800
5	Expenses	12,200	12,500	11,400	11,700
6	Net profit	6,300	6,100	5,000	5,100
7	Capital	52,500	52,500	55,000	55,000
8	Gross profit %	38.0	37.1	36.0	35.9
9	Net profit %	12.9	12.2	11.0	10.9
10	ROCE	12.0	11.6	9.1	9.3
11	Asset turnover	0.93	0.96	0.83	0.85

6

	A	B	C
1		Quarter ending 31/3	Quarter ending 30/6
2	Budgeted production	320,000	350,000
3	Actual production	332,000	330,000
4	Production cost	£580,400	£567,900
5	Hours worked	12,300	12,600
6	Cost per unit	=B4/B3	=C4/C3
7	Labour productivity	=B3/B5	=C3/C5
8	Productivity index	=(B3/B2)*100	=(C3/C2)*100

tables and diagrams – answers

7   MONTHLY SALES FIGURES

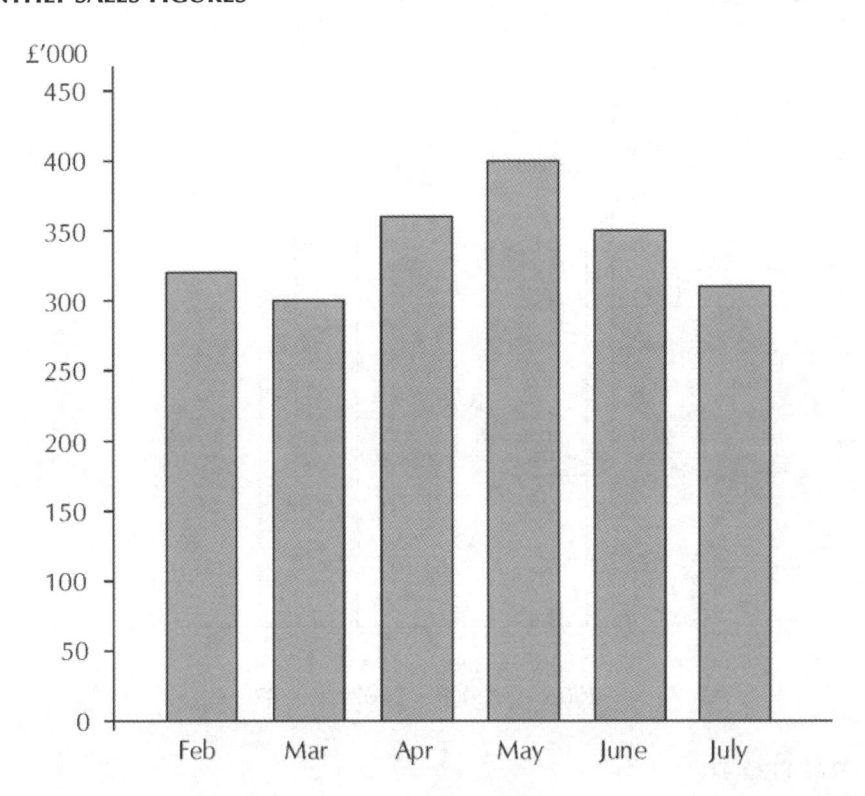

8   SALES, GROSS PROFIT, NET PROFIT

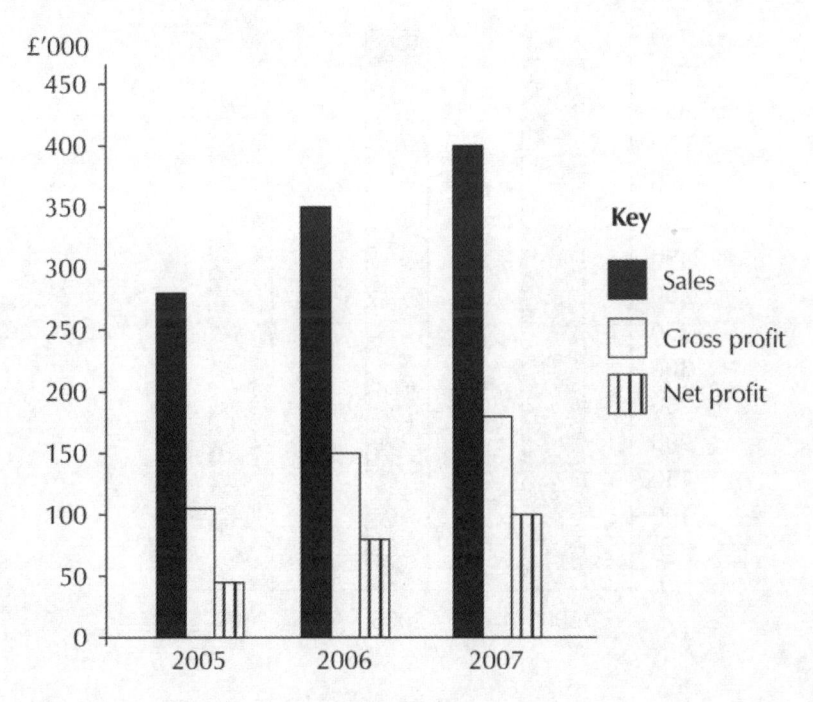

373

tables and diagrams – answers

9 DIVISIONAL SALES

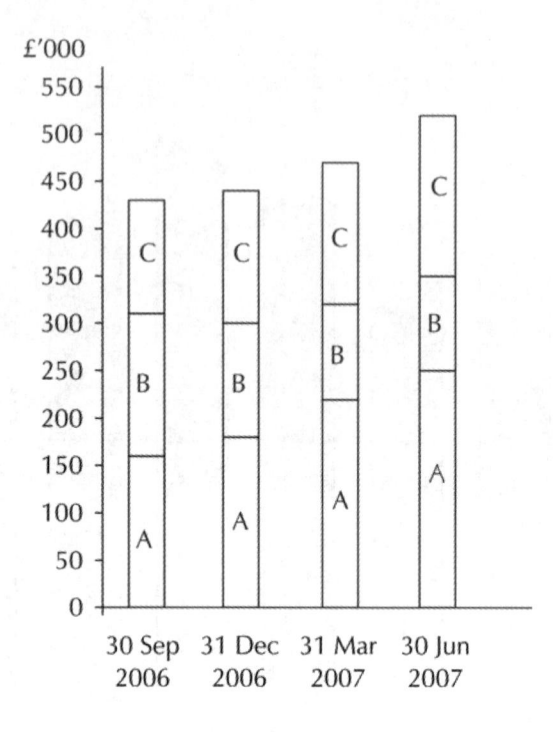

10 a) TOTAL PROFIT

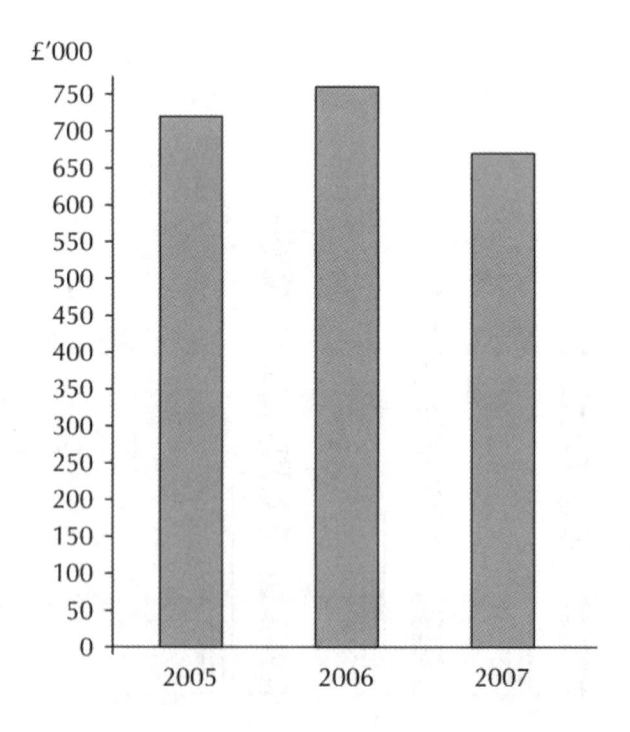

tables and diagrams – answers

b) **PROFIT BREAKDOWN**

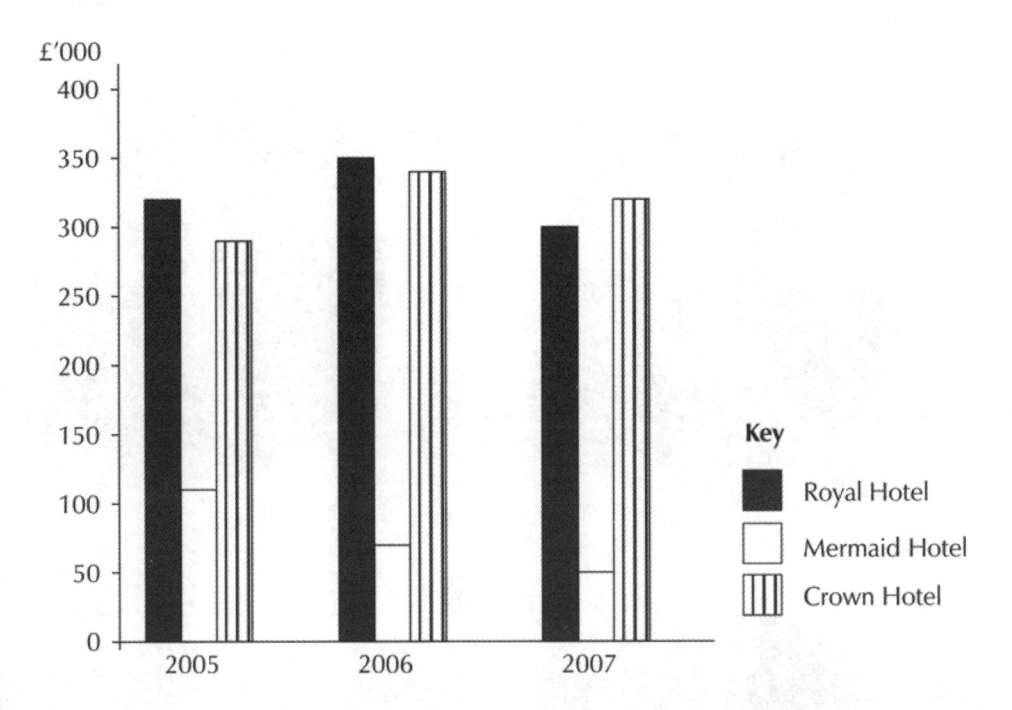

£'000

c) **PROFIT BREAKDOWN**

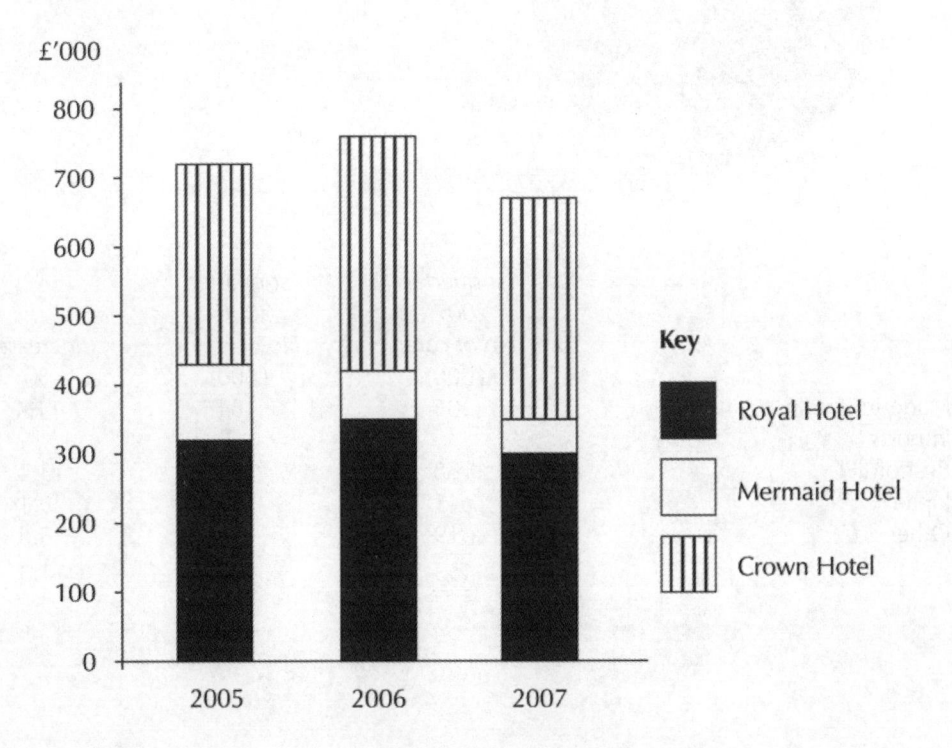

£'000

375

tables and diagrams – answers

11 TOTAL COSTS

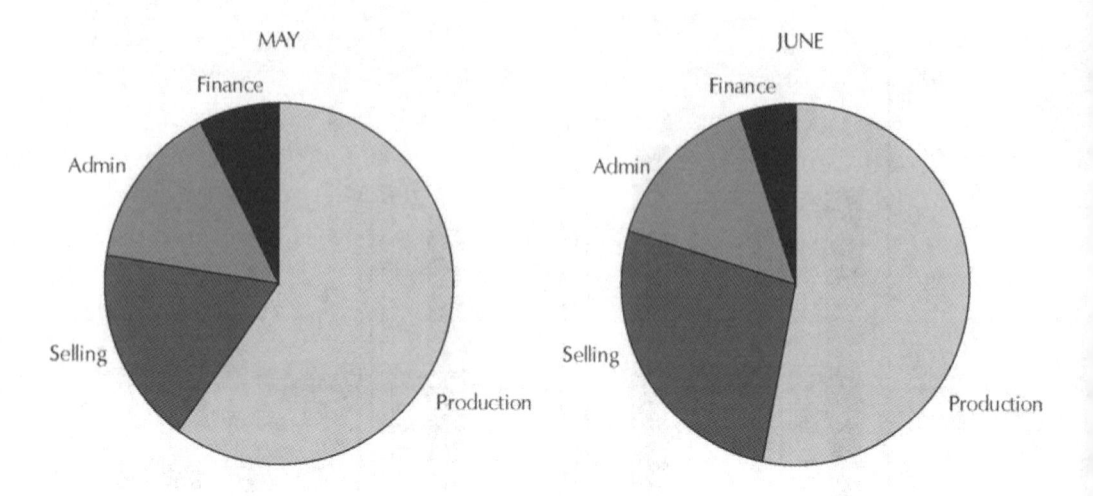

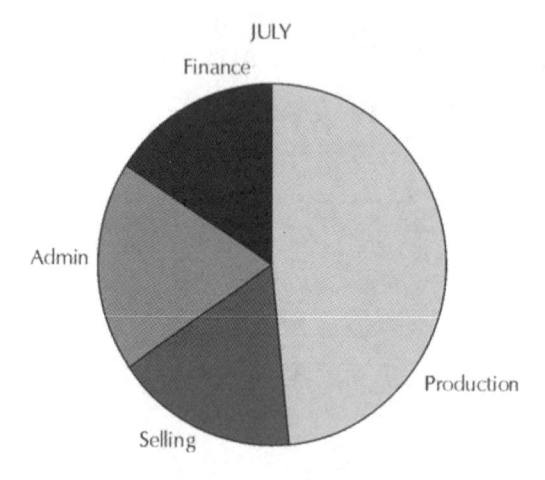

(Pie charts for MAY, JUNE, and JULY showing Finance, Admin, Selling, and Production costs)

12		1st quarter 2007 No of cars ('000)	1st quarter 2006 No of cars ('000)	Increase %
Made in Britain		205	184	11.4
Imports				
Rest of EU		188	166	13.3
Japan		41	39	5.1
Other		19	18	5.6
		453	407	11.3

376

13

a) AT Engineering Ltd

Sheet Metal Work Department
Wages for week ended 12 June

Operative	Total hours worked	Basic hourly rate £	Basic wages £	Hrs	Overtime premium One third £	Hrs	Double basic £	Total wages £
M	46	7.20	331.20	2	4.80	4	28.80	364.80
N	39	7.50	292.50	3	7.50			300.00
O	40	7.20	288.00					288.00
P	51	7.50	382.50	7	17.50	4	30.00	430.00
Q	52	8.40	436.80	8	22.40	4	33.60	492.80
R	34	7.20	244.80					244.80
	262		1,975.80		52.20		92.40	2,120.40

b) Weighted average wages cost $= \dfrac{£2{,}120.40}{262}$

= £8.09 per operative hour, to the nearest penny.

answers to chapter 14:
REPORTING FIGURES OVER TIME

1. a) **The mean**

    The arithmetic mean is the best known and most widely used average. The arithmetic mean of some data is the sum of the data, divided by the number of items in the data. It is widely used because it gives a convenient and readily understood indication of the general size of the data, it takes account of all items of data and it is suitable for further mathematical analysis. On the other hand, its value can be unduly influenced by a few very large or very small items of data.

    b) **The median**

    The median is the value of the middle member of a set of data, once the data have been arranged in either ascending or descending order. It is one sort of average and it has the following properties.

    - It is fairly easy to obtain.
    - It is not affected very much by extreme values.
    - It is not generally suitable for further statistical analysis.

    The median may be more useful than the arithmetic mean in certain circumstances, for instance when determining the average salary of the employees in a company. Since a few employees might have very high salaries, the arithmetic mean could be drawn upwards by these, out of the range of salaries earned by most employees. The mean would then not be representative. The median, however, would be the item in the middle of the ranking, which would be within the range of salaries earned by most employees.

    c) **Time series**

    A time series is simply a series of values recorded over time. Examples of a time series are:

    i) output at a factory each day for the last month
    ii) monthly sales over the last two years
    iii) the number of people employed by a company each year for the last 20 years

    Time series are often shown on a graph, with time always being the independent variable shown along the x axis, and the values at each time shown along the y axis.

    The features of a time series are normally taken to be:

    - a trend
    - cyclical variations
    - seasonal variations
    - random variations

379

reporting figures over time – answers

2 $\dfrac{159+62+55+86+104+168+192}{7} = \dfrac{826}{7}$

= **118 per day**

3

	£	3-month moving average £
July 2006	337,600	
August 2006	415,300	347,466.66
September 2006	289,500	323,733.33
October 2006	266,400	251,533.33
November 2006	198,700	241,233.33
December 2006	258,600	211,500.00
January 2007	177,200	211,700.00
February 2007	199,300	199,800.00
March 2007	222,900	226,100.00
April 2007	256,100	248,266.66
May 2007	265,800	295,866.66
June 2007	365,700	

4

Week	Costs £	4-week moving average £
1	128,500	
2	195,400	
		162,575
3	148,600	
		164,825
4	177,800	
		157,400
5	137,500	
		157,300
6	165,700	
		158,700
7	148,200	
		168,650
8	183,400	
		168,400
9	177,300	
		170,200
10	164,700	
		172,750
11	155,400	
		167,950
12	193,600	
		170,400
13	158,100	
		172,275
14	174,500	
		163,725
15	162,900	
16	159,400	

reporting figures over time – answers

5

	A	B	C	D
1	Week 1	128,500		
2				
3	Week 2	195,400		
4			=(B1+B3+B5+B7)/4	
5	Week 3	148,600		=(C4+C6)/2
6			=(B3+B5+B7+B9)/4	
7	Week 4	177,800		=(C6+C8)/2
8			=(B5+B7+B9+B11)/4	
9	Week 5	137,500		=(C8+C10)/2
10			=(B7+B9+B11+B13)/4	
11	Week 6	165,700		=(C10+C12)/2
12			=(B9+B11+B13+B15)/4	
13	Week 7	148,200		=(C12+C14)/2
14			=(B11+B13+B15+B17)/4	
15	Week 8	183,400		=(C14+C16)/2
16			=(B13+B15+B17+B19)/4	
17	Week 9	177,300		=(C16+C18)/2
18			=(B15+B17+B19+B21)/4	
19	Week 10	164,700		=(C18+C20)/2
20			=(B17+B19+B21+B23)/4	
21	Week 11	155,400		=(C20+C22)/2
22			=(B19+B21+B23+B25)/4	
23	Week 12	193,600		=(C22+C24)/2
24			=(B21+B23+B25+B27)/4	
25	Week 13	158,100		=(C24+C26)/2
26			=(B23+B25+B27+B29)/4	
27	Week 14	174,500		=(C26+C28)/2
28			=(B25+B27+B29+B31)/4	
29	Week 15	162,900		
30				
31	Week 16	159,400		

reporting figures over time – answers

6 a)

		3-month moving average
20X6	£	£
January	55,600	
February	52,700	54,800.00
March	56,100	55,200.00
April	56,800	57,066.67
May	58,300	58,533.33
June	60,500	59,233.33
July	58,900	59,533.33
August	59,200	59,800.00
September	61,300	60,866.67
October	62,100	62,266.67
November	63,400	62,733.33
December	62,700	62,466.67
20X7		
January	61,300	62,166.67
February	62,500	62,633.33
March	64,100	63,933.33
April	65,200	64,733.33
May	64,900	65,600.00
June	66,700	

reporting figures over time – answers

b) **MONTHLY SALES AND TREND**

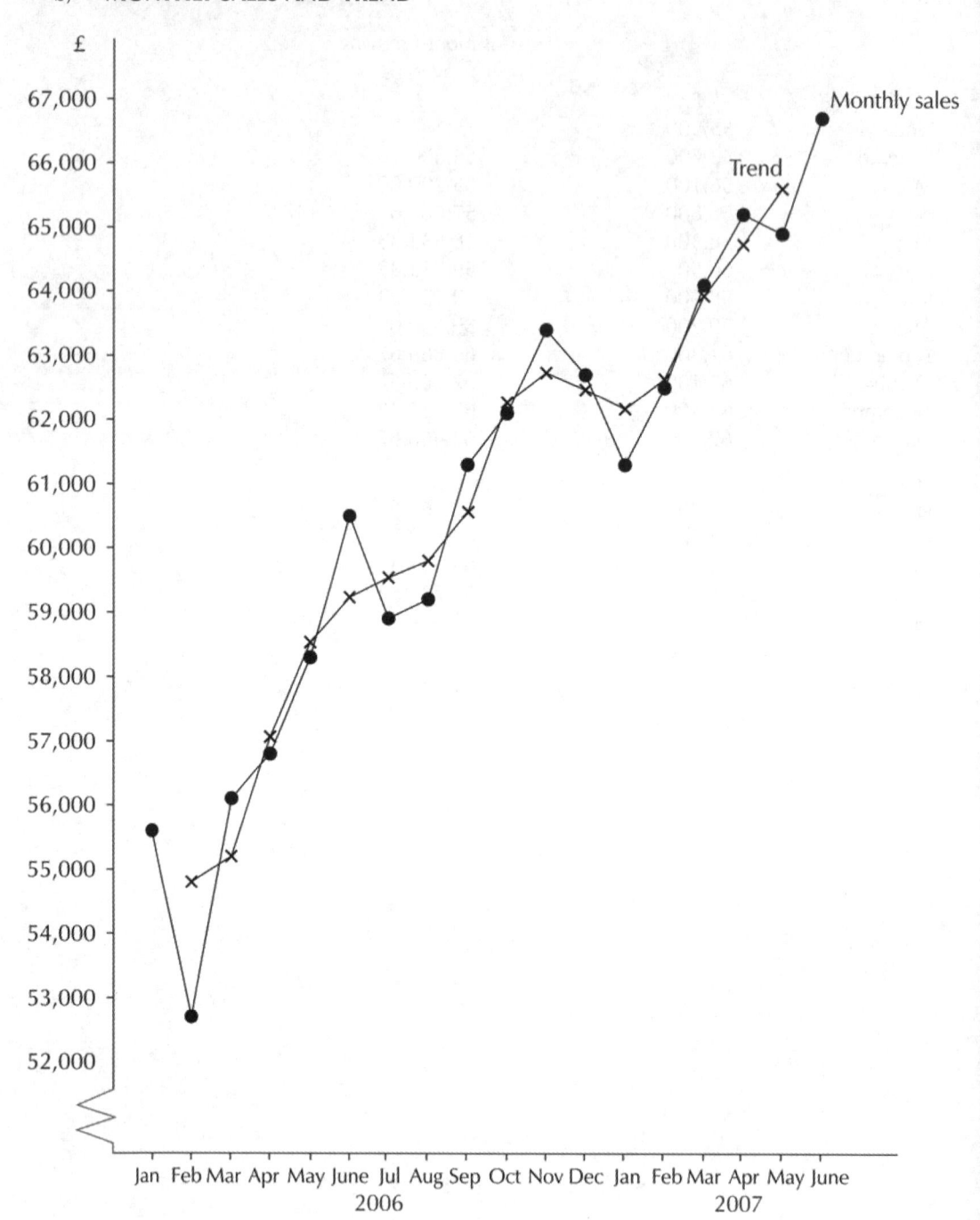

7   **Interpolation** is a method of estimating a figure within a range of figures already available. Therefore if the costs of production for a factory range from £126,700 for 30,000 units to £193,500 for 40,000 units then if an estimate were required for the production cost of 37,500 units this could be found from a graph of these costs by reading off the anticipated cost figure for 37,500 units.

    Extrapolation however is a method of estimating a figure that is outside the range of figures already available. Using the same production cost example, if an estimate was required for the production cost of 45,000 units then the graph line would have to be extended and the estimated cost figure read off from the extended graph.

8   A **price index** is an index which measures the change in the money value of a group of items over a period of time.

9

20X6	£		Index
August	527,500		100.00
September	513,400	513,400/527,500 x 100	97.33
October	556,700	556,700/527,500 x 100	105.54
November	523,400	523,400/527,500 x 100	99.22
December	582,300	582,300/527,500 x 100	110.39
20X7			
January	561,300	561,300/527,500 x 100	106.41
February	532,600	532,600/527,500 x 100	100.97
March	524,300	524,300/527,500 x 100	99.39
April	515,700	515,700/527,500 x 100	97.76
May	529,600	529,600/527,500 x 100	100.40
June	538,200	538,200/527,500 x 100	102.03

10 If £35,000 = 100%, then:

$$£42,000 = \frac{42,000}{35,000} \times 100\% = 120\%$$

$$£40,000 = \frac{40,000}{35,000} \times 100\% = 114\%$$

$$£45,000 = \frac{45,000}{35,000} \times 100\% = 129\%$$

$$£50,000 = \frac{50,000}{35,000} \times 100\% = 143\%$$

reporting figures over time – answers

The table showing sales for the last five years can now be completed, taking 2003 as the base year.

Year	Sales (£'000)	Index
2003	35	100
2004	42	120
2005	40	114
2006	45	129
2007	50	143

11 a) RPI adjusted sales

January		162,400
February	163,800 x 171.1/172.0	162,943
March	165,900 x 171.1/172.2	164,840
April	167,200 x 171.1/173.0	165,364
May	166,200 x 171.1/172.1	165,234
June	164,100 x 171.1/171.3	163,908
July	162,300 x 171.1/171.0	162,395
August	160,500 x 171.1/170.3	161,254

b) Index

January		100.0
February	162,943/162,400 x 100	100.3
March	164,840/162,400 x 100	101.5
April	165,364/162,400 x 100	101.8
May	165,234/162,400 x 100	101.7
June	163,908/162,400 x 100	100.9
July	162,395/162,400 x 100	100.0
August	161,254/162,400 x 100	99.3

c)

	A	B	C	D	E
1	January	162,400	171.1	=B1*(C1/C1)	=(D1/D1)*100
2	February	163,800	172.0	=B2*(C1/C2)	=(D2/D1)*100
3	March	165,900	172.2	=B3*(C1/C3)	=(D3/D1)*100
4	April	167,200	173.0	=B4*(C1/C4)	=(D4/D1)*100
5	May	166,200	172.1	=B5*(C1/C5)	=(D5/D1)*100
6	June	164,100	171.3	=B6*(C1/C6)	=(D6/D1)*100
7	July	162,300	171.0	=B7*(C1/C7)	=(D7/D1)*100
8	August	160,500	170.3	=B8*(C1/C8)	=(D8/D1)*100

reporting figures over time – answers

12

		2005	2006	2007
a)	Receipts per loaded coach km (£)	1.62	1.93	2.09
b)	Receipts per passenger km (pence)	5.70	6.20	6.40
c)	Passenger kms per loaded coach km (average coach load) (passengers)	28.50	31.20	32.70
d)	Total operating expenses per loaded coach km (£)	1.21	1.25	1.28

13 a)

	2005	2006	2007
Receipts per loaded coach km (2006 £)	1.74	2.01	2.09
Receipts per passenger km (2006 pence)	6.10	6.50	6.40
Total operating expenses per loaded coach km (2007 £)	1.30	1.30	1.28
Conversion factor	100.00	100.00	1.00
	93.20	96.10	

b) There was a real increase in fares per passenger kilometre in 2006; the slight decline in 2007 may partly reflect the impact of the new competitor. In spite of this new competition, real receipts per loaded coach kilometre increased by 20% between 2005 and 2007. There have been greater numbers travelling on each coach, in spite of the new competitor on the main routes: the average coach load has risen to 32.7 (approximately 70% of capacity, up 15% on 2005). Over the period, operating expenses per loaded coach kilometre have been contained, and indeed showed a drop of almost 2% in real terms in 2007. Profit, if measured as fares less operating expenses, has shown a substantial increase from £792,000 in 2005 (in money terms) to £1,613,000 in 2007.

answers to chapter 15: EXTERNAL REPORTING

1 The National Statistics 'themes' are:

- agriculture, fishing and forestry
- commerce, energy and industry
- compendia and reference
- crime and justice
- economy
- education and training
- health and care
- labour market
- natural and built environment
- population and migration
- social and welfare
- transport, travel and tourism
- other

BARDEN LOCAL DISTRICT COUNCIL
GRANT APPLICATION

PART 1 BUSINESS DETAILS

Business name ...... D. & G. Harper

Business address .... Harper House
.... East Park Road
.... Barden BD4 6GK

Business telephone ... 02185 3743

Business fax 02185 3264

Owner's name .... David and Gareth Harper

Email address .... dgh@dandgharper.co.uk

Type of business .... Curtain and blind manufacturer

PART 2 FINANCIAL DETAILS

2A TURNOVER AND PROFIT

Figures are to be provided for annual turnover and reported net profit for the last three complete financial years

Financial year ended:		UK turnover £	Export turnover £	Net profit £
Month	Year			
June	2005	378,690	10,580	74,110
June	2006	735,400	38,600	162,540
June	2007	882,400	48,340	204,770

2B WORKING CAPITAL

Figures are to be provided for working capital at the end of the most recent financial year.

Year ending: 30 June 2007

	£
Current assets	97,470
Minus: current liabilities	(42,170)
Working capital	55,300

2C FIXED ASSETS

Figures are to be provided for fixed asset totals at the end of the most recent financial year.

Year ending: 30 June 2007

	£
Land and buildings	184,500
Plant and machinery	190,400
Other	97,700
Total fixed assets	472,600

PART 3 NON FINANCIAL DETAILS

3A EMPLOYMENT DETAILS

Figures are to be provided for the number of employees for the last three financial years.

Financial year ended:		Number of full time employees	Number of part time employees
Month	Year		
June	2005	9	1
June	2006	14	3
June	2007	14	3

3B BUSINESS DETAILS

Date business started: ..1998...

Business type -   Sole trader   ☐

　　　　　　　　Partnership   ✓

　　　　　　　　Company   ☐

PART 4 GRANT APPLICATION

Indicate in the space provided the reasons for the grant application. If the grant application is processed further more detail will be requested at a later date.

..Grant application for £15,000 to help fund additional factory space and potential.....

..employment of 6 additional full time employees...

CHAMBER OF COMMERCE
ANNUAL ECONOMIC REVIEW

Please tick the appropriate box in answer to each question - all answers will be treated in the strictest confidence. All answers should be based upon the business performance for the last full financial year.

1   BUSINESS DETAILS

End of last full financial year:

Turnover range:

Up to £50,000	☐
£50,000 - £100,000	☐
£100,000 - £250,000	☐
£250,000 - £500,000	☑
£500,000 - £1,000,000	☐
Over £1,000,000	☐

Main business activity:

Engineering	☐	Health	☐
Construction	☑	Art and design	☐
Agriculture	☐	Transport	☐
Energy	☐	Tourism	☐
Retail	☐	Other (please state) ....
Education	☐	....

2 TURNOVER

Percentage of total turnover accounted for by export sales:

0%	✓	30% to 50%	☐
Up to 10%	☐	50% to 75%	☐
10% to 20%	☐	75% to 100%	☐
20% to 30%	☐		

Percentage increase/decrease in turnover compared to previous financial year:

Decrease Up to 20%	☐	Increase Up to 20%	☐
Decrease of 20% to 50%	☐	Increase of 20% to 50%	✓
Decrease of more than 50%	☐	Increase of more than 50%	☐

Percentage increase/decrease in net profit compared to previous financial year:

Decrease Up to 20%	☐	Increase Up to 20%	☐
Decrease of 20% to 50%	☐	Increase of 20% to 50%	✓
Decrease of more than 50%	☐	Increase of more than 50%	☐

3 BUSINESS CONFIDENCE

Do you consider that over the following 12 months:

Turnover	will increase	✓	Profitability	will increase	✓
	remain the same	☐		remain the same	☐
	decrease	☐		decrease	☐

answers to chapter 16:
VALUE ADDED TAX

1 a) From 1 May 2009 the VAT registration threshold is **£68,000**
    b) From 1 May 2009 the VAT deregistration limit is **£66,000** for taxable supplies
    c) VAT on purchases is known as **input** tax
    d) VAT on sales is known as **output** tax
    e) A VAT return is normally completed every **3** months

2 Standard rate of 17.5% (reduced to 15% until 31 December 2009)

   Reduced rate of 5%

   Zero rate 0%

3 a) £15,862.50 – as a business making exempt supplies cannot reclaim any input VAT
    b) £13,500.00 – as a business making zero-rated supplies can reclaim input VAT

4 If the business makes zero-rated supplies then it will not have to pay VAT over to HMRC but as a VAT registered business will be able to reclaim any input VAT suffered.

5 a) £16,685.00 – the VAT on cars for use in a business is not reclaimable

   b) £141.00 – the VAT on business entertaining is not reclaimable

6 a) 13 August 2009 – actual tax point
    b) 15 August 2009 – basic tax point
    c) 12 August 2009 – actual tax point
    d) 20 August 2009 – actual tax point

7 a) £25.69
    b) £34.65
    c) £33.95
    d) £43.90

value added tax – answers

8 a) VAT   £64.36
        Net of VAT   £367.80

   b) VAT   £39.13
        Net of VAT   £223.64

   c) VAT   £32.30
        Net of VAT   £184.60

   d) VAT   £46.19
        Net of VAT   £263.99

9
- The business name, address and VAT registration number
- The date of supply
- Description of goods/services
- For each applicable VAT rate the total including VAT and the VAT rate

10 All the invoices except d) look superficially plausible, but in fact d) is the only valid invoice. This shows the importance of attention to detail in applying VAT law.

   a) The invoice from Jupiter plc is invalid because the invoice number has been omitted.

   b) The invoice from Hillside Ltd is invalid because it does not show the supplier's address. In all other respects it meets the requirements for a valid VAT invoice.

   c) The invoice from Generous plc is invalid because the supplier's VAT registration number is not shown. Finally, the invoice is invalid because the applicable rates of VAT (17.5% and 0%) are not shown.

   d) The total value of the supply by Jewels & Co, including VAT, does not exceed £250, so a less detailed invoice is permissible.

   The invoice is valid, because it includes all the information which must be shown on a less detailed invoice.

answers to chapter 17:
VAT RECORDS

1   The errors in the previous period may be corrected through the VAT account (and on the VAT return) because the net error is £(700 + 800) = £1,500, which does not exceed the greater of £10,000 or 1% of turnover.

Standard rated purchases total £(9,950 + 5,792 + 8,168) = £23,910.

Standard rated sales total £(6,237 + 19,008 + 1,084) = £26,329.

PETER PERFECT
VAT ACCOUNT FOR THE VAT PERIOD FROM 1 JANUARY 2009 TO 31 MARCH 2009

VAT allowable	£	VAT payable	£
Input VAT allowable		Output VAT due	
£23,910 × 17.5%	4,184.25	£26,329 × 17.5%	4,607.58
Adjustment for credits		Adjustment for returned	
received (178 + 743) × 17.5%	(161.18)	sale £505 × 17.5%	(88.38)
Correction of error	800.00	Correction of error	(700.00)
	4,823.07		3,819.20
		Cash (receipt from	
		HM Revenue & Customs)	1,003.87
	4,823.07		4,823.07

2   The sale of plant (capital item) is excluded from the calculation of the partial exemption percentage.

Output VAT	£	£
£6,000,000 × 17.5%		1,050,000
		1,050,000
Input VAT		
Attributable to taxable supplies	600,000	
Unattributable £96,000 × 73% (see below)	70,080	
		670,080
Amount due to HM Revenue & Customs		379,920

The **partial exemption fraction** is $\dfrac{6,000+1,500-20}{6,000+1,500+2,800-20}$ = 0.727, rounded up to 73%.

397

VAT records – answers

3

VAT account

VAT deductible – input tax	£	VAT payable – output tax	£
Purchases day book	2,485.61	Sales day book	3,474.89
Cash payments book	624.78	Cash receipts book	993.57
EU acquisitions	925.47	EU acquisitions	925.47
	4,035.86		5,393.93
Less: credit notes received	210.68	Less: credit notes issued	441.46
Total VAT deductible	3,825.18	Total VAT payable	4,952.47
		Less: VAT deductible	3,825.18
		Due to HMRC	1,127.29

4

VAT account

VAT deductible – input tax	£	VAT payable – output tax	£
Purchases day book	4,668.14	Sales day book	6,275.78
Cash payments book	936.47	Cash receipts book	1,447.30
EU acquisitions	772.46	EU acquisitions	772.46
Bad debt relief	284.67		
Net overcharge for previous period (221.68 – 126.57)	95.11		
	6,756.85		8,495.54
Less: credit notes received	510.36	Less: credit notes issued	726.58
Total VAT deductible	6,246.49	Total VAT payable	7,768.96
		Less: VAT deductible	6,246.49
		Due to HMRC	1,522.47

Value Added Tax Return

For the period
01 04 09 to 30 06 09

For Official Use

Registration number: 234 4576 12

Period: 06 09

You could be liable to a financial penalty if your completed return and all the VAT payable are not received by the due date.

Due date: 31 July 2009

Waltzer Enterprises
Adam Industrial Park
Yarden
LR3 9GS

If you have a general enquiry or need advice please call our National Advice Service on 0845 010 9000

ATTENTION

If this return and any tax due are not received by the due date you may be liable to a surcharge.

If you make supplies of goods to another EC Member State you are required to complete an EC Sales List (VAT 101).

Before you fill in this form please read the notes on the back and the VAT Leaflet *"Filling in your VAT return"*.
Fill in all boxes clearly in ink, and write 'none' where necessary. Don't put a dash or leave any box blank. If there are no pence write "00" in the pence column. Do not enter more than one amount in any box.

Box	Description	£	p
1	VAT due in this period on sales and other outputs	10,177	80
2	VAT due in this period on acquisitions from other EC Member States	275	17
3	Total VAT due (the sum of boxes 1 and 2)	10,452	97
4	VAT reclaimed in this period on purchases and other inputs (including acquisitions from the EC)	6,163	12
5	Net VAT to be paid to Customs or reclaimed by you (Difference between boxes 3 and 4)	4,289	85
6	Total value of sales and all other outputs excluding any VAT. Include your box 8 figure	61,551	00
7	Total value of purchases and all other inputs excluding any VAT. Include your box 9 figure	37,729	00
8	Total value of all supplies of goods and related services, excluding any VAT, to other EC Member States	NONE	00
9	Total value of all acquisitions of goods and related services, excluding any VAT, from other EC Member States	1,572	00

If you are enclosing a payment please tick this box. ✓

DECLARATION: You, or someone on your behalf, must sign below.

I, ... declare that the
(Full name of signatory in BLOCK LETTERS)
information given above is true and complete.

Signature .... Date ....

A false declaration can result in prosecution.

VAT records – answers

Workings

			£
Box 1	Sales day book		10,082.76
	Cash receipts book		931.98
	Sales returns day book		(836.94)
			10,177.80
Box 4	Purchases day book – EU		275.17
	Purchases day book – UK		5,892.69
	Cash payments book		552.55
	Purchases returns day book		(557.29)
			6,163.12
Box 6	Sales day book – zero-rated		3,628.47
	Sales day book – standard rated		57,615.80
	Cash receipts book		5,325.65
	Sales returns day book – zero-rated		(236.34)
	Sales returns – standard rated		(4,782.57)
			61,551.01
Box 7	Purchases day book – EU		1,572.45
	Purchases day book – zero-rated		2,636.47
	Purchases day book – standard rated		33,672.57
	Cash payments book		3,157.46
	Purchases returns – zero-rated		(125.34)
	Purchases returns – standard rated		(3,184.57)
			37,729.04

6   If a net error of more than £10,000 and 1% of turnover is discovered then this cannot be adjusted for on the VAT return. Instead voluntary disclosure must be made to the local VAT Business Advice Centre using Form VAT 652 or in a letter.

7   If you have been registered for VAT for at least 12 months and the annual value of your taxable supplies, excluding VAT, is below £1,350,000 then you may be able to use the annual accounting scheme.

Under this scheme you make nine monthly direct debit payments based upon an estimate of the amount of VAT due. You must then prepare a VAT return for the year and send it in with the tenth balancing payment, by two months after the year end.

8   Because Zag plc makes some exempt supplies, not all the VAT on purchases can be recovered. The VAT on purchases which is not attributable to either taxable supplies or exempt supplies must be apportioned.

   a)   Box 1: VAT due on outputs

        The figure is £877,500 × 17.5% = £153,562.50

   b)   Box 2: VAT due on acquisitions

        None.

   c)   Box 3: sum of Boxes 1 and 2 = £153,562.50

   d)   Box 4: VAT reclaimed on inputs

        The figure is as follows.

        Apportionment percentage = (877,500 + 462,150)/(877,500 + 462,150 + 327,600) = 80.35%, rounded up to 81%.

	£
Tax on purchases attributable to taxable supplies £585,000 × 17.5%	102,375.00
Tax on unattributable purchases £468,000 × 17.5% × 81%	66,339.00
	168,714.00

        Zag plc will need to consider the standard method override if the above attribution differs substantially from one based on the use to which the inputs are put.

   e)   Box 5: net VAT to be paid or reclaimed

        The amount reclaimable is £(168,714 − 153,562.50) = £15,151.50.

Value Added Tax Return

For the period
01 04 09 to 30 06 09

For Official Use

Registration number: 483 8611 98
Period: 06 09

You could be liable to a financial penalty if your completed return and all the VAT payable are not received by the due date.

Due date: 31 July 2009

ZAG PLC
32 CASE STREET
ZEDTOWN
ZY4 3JN

If you have a general enquiry or need advice please call our National Advice Service on 0845 010 9000

ATTENTION

If this return and any tax due are not received by the due date you may be liable to a surcharge.

If you make supplies of goods to another EC Member State you are required to complete an EC Sales List (VAT 101).

Before you fill in this form please read the notes on the back and the VAT Leaflet "Filling in your VAT return". Fill in all boxes clearly in ink, and write 'none' where necessary. Don't put a dash or leave any box blank. If there are no pence write "00" in the pence column. Do not enter more than one amount in any box.

Box	Description	£	p
1	VAT due in this period on sales and other outputs	153,562	50
2	VAT due in this period on acquisitions from other EC Member States	NONE	
3	Total VAT due (the sum of boxes 1 and 2)	153,562	50
4	VAT reclaimed in this period on purchases and other inputs (including acquisitions from the EC)	168,714	00
5	Net VAT to be paid to Customs or reclaimed by you (Difference between boxes 3 and 4)	15,151	50
6	Total value of sales and all other outputs excluding any VAT. Include your box 8 figure		00
7	Total value of purchases and all other inputs excluding any VAT. Include your box 9 figure		00
8	Total value of all supplies of goods and related services, excluding any VAT, to other EC Member States		00
9	Total value of all acquisitions of goods and related services, excluding any VAT, from other EC Member States		00

If you are enclosing a payment please tick this box.

DECLARATION: You, or someone on your behalf, must sign below.

I, ... declare that the
(Full name of signatory in BLOCK LETTERS)
information given above is true and complete.

Signature .... Date ....

A false declaration can result in prosecution.

PRACTICE EXAM 1
UNIT 6

FLY 4 LESS PLC

SECTION 1

Task 1.1

a) and c)

Stock record card for aviation fuel

Date	Receipts Quantity Litres	Receipts Cost per Litre (£)	Receipts Total cost (£)	Issues Quantity Litres	Issues Cost per Litre (£)	Issues Total cost (£)	Balance Quantity Litres	Balance Total cost £
Balance as at 26 Nov							220,000	198,000
27 Nov (W1)	200,000	92.00	184,000				420,000	382,000
28 Nov (W1)				180,000	90.00	162,000	240,000	220,000
29 Nov (W2)	100,000	94.00	94,000				340,000	314,000
30 Nov (W3)				260,000	91.85*	238,800	80,000	75,200

Workings

W1 Receipts and issues per question

W2 Cost per litre = total cost/quantity = £94,000/100,000 = £0.94 per litre or 94.00 p per litre

W3

		£
Balance at 28 November	40,000 litres at £0.90 per litre =	36,000
	200,000 litres at £0.92 per litre =	184,000
		220,000
29 November	100,000 litres at £0.94 per litre =	94,000
Balance at 29 November		314,000

Using FIFO

Issue on 30 November	40,000 litres at £0.90 per litre =	36,000
	200,000 litres at £0.92 per litre =	184,000
	20,000 litres at £0.94 per litre =	18,800
	260,000 litres	238,800

Cost per litre = total cost/quantity = £238,800/260,000 = £0.9185 per litre or 91.85p per litre

b) The stock valuation method being used is FIFO (first in first out). The balance at 26 November was valued at £0.90 per litre (£198,000/220,000 litres) which was the same cost used for the issue of 180,000 litres on 28 November.

Task 1.2

Email

To: Chief Accountant
From: Accounting Technician
Subject: Aviation fuel stock policies
Date: 1 December 2008

a) Aviation fuel has been reordered in quantities between 100,000 and 200,000 litres which is in compliance with the stock control policy.

The stock control policy also requires a minimum of 150,000 litres of aviation fuel to be held. This policy has not been complied with as after the issue on 30 November there was only 80,000 litres remaining.

b) The economic order quantity (EOQ) aims to minimise stock costs. As order sizes increase then there will need to be fewer orders and hence ordering costs will decrease. However, as order sizes increase then higher average stock levels will be held. This will increase holding costs. The EOQ is the level at which the total of these costs is minimised.

Task 1.3

a) **The wages control account entries**

Wages control account

Debit	£	Credit	£
Bank (net wages/salaries)	10,000	Maintenance (direct labour)	7,000
HMRC (income tax and NIC)	2,000	Maintenance overheads	4,000
Pension contributions	1,000	Maintenance administration	2,000
	13,000		13,000

b) **Total payroll cost charged to the various cost accounts of the business**

Date	Code	DR	CR
30 November	6200	7,000	
30 November	8200		7,000
30 November	6400	4,000	
30 November	8200		4,000
30 November	6600	2,000	
30 November	8200		2,000

Task 1.4

	Basis of apportionment	Scheduled services £000	Charter flights £000	Aircraft maintenance and repairs £000	Fuel and parts store £000	General admin £000	Totals £000
Depreciation of aircraft	NBV of aircraft (W1)	21,840	14,560				36,400
Aviation fuel and other variable costs	Planned number of miles flown (W2)	23,210	18,990				42,200
Pilots' and aircrews' salaries	Allocated	5,240	4,709				9,959
Rent and rates and other premises costs	Floor space (W3)			6,300	3,780	2,520	12,600
Indirect labour	Allocated			9,600	3,200	7,800	20,600
Totals		50,300	38,259	15,900	6,980	10,320	121,759
Reapportion aircraft maintenance and repairs (W4)		9,540	6,360	(15,900)			
Reapportion fuel and parts store (W5)		3,839	3,141		(6,980)		
Reapportion general admin (W6)		5,160	5,160			(10,320)	
Total overheads to profit centres		68,839	52,920				121,759

practice exam 1 – unit 6 – answers

Workings

W1 Apportioned in ratio: 1,080,000 : 720,000

Scheduled services:	(1,080,000/1,800,000) x £36,400 =	£21,840
Charter flights:	(720,000/1,800,000) x £36,400 =	£14,560

W2 Apportioned in ratio: 215,600 : 176,400

Scheduled services:	(215,600/392,000) x £42,200 =	£23,210
Charter flights:	(176,400/392,000) x £42,200 =	£18,990

W3 Apportioned in ratio: 190,000 : 114,000 : 76,000

Aircraft maint & repairs:	(190,000/380,000) x £12,600 =	£6,300
Fuel and parts store:	(114,000/380,000) x £12,600 =	£3,780
General admin:	(76,000/380,000) x £12,600 =	£2,520

W4 Reapportion in ratio: 60% : 40%

Scheduled services:	60% x £15,900 =	£9,540
Charter flights:	40% x £15,900 =	£6,360

W5 Reapportion in ratio: 55% : 45%

Scheduled services:	55% x £6,980 =	£3,839
Charter flights:	45% x £6,980 =	£3,141

W6 Reapportion in ratio: 50% : 50% (equally)

Scheduled services and charter flights both:
50% x £10,320 = £5,160

Task 1.5

Overhead absorption rate per mile = total overheads of profit centre/planned number of miles

Scheduled services
Overhead absorption rate per mile: £68,839,000/215,600 planned miles = £319 per mile flown

Charter flights
Overhead absorption rate per mile: £52,920,000/176,400 planned miles = £300 per mile flown

Tutorial note: Credit would be given for correct calculation in Task 1.5 even using incorrect figures calculated in Task 1.4.

Task 1.6

a) Overhead absorbed = actual miles flown x overhead absorption rate per mile
= 6,890 x £300 = £2,067,000

b) Actual overhead incurred £2,079,000
Overhead absorbed £2,067,000

Therefore overhead is

Under-absorbed £12,000

c) The £12,000 will appear as a debit in the profit and loss account. Expenses will increase by £12,000 and profits decrease by £12,000.

practice exam 1 – unit 6 – answers

SECTION 2

Task 2.1

a)

Likely miles	5,000	6,000	7,000
	£000	£000	£000
Sales revenue (W1)	2,500	2,950	3,400
Variable/semi-variable costs:			
Aviation fuel (W2)	400	480	560
Landing and servicing fees (W3)	850	900	950
Other variable overheads (W4)	135	162	189
Fixed costs:			
Wages and salaries	420	420	420
Other fixed overheads	625	625	625
Total cost	2,430	2,587	2,744
Total profit	70	363	656
	£	£	£
Profit per mile flown (W5)	14.00	60.50	93.71

Tutorial note: Remember to round the profit per mile flown to the required two decimal places.

Workings

W1 Revenue per mile at 5,000 miles = £2,500,000/5,000 miles =   £500

Revenue at 6,000 miles = (£500 x 5,000) + ((£500 x 90%) x 1,000 miles) =   £2,950,000
Revenue at 7,000 miles = (£500 x 5,000) + ((£500 x 90%) x 2,000 miles) =   £3,400,000

W2 Aviation fuel is a variable cost

Cost per mile is at 5,000 miles = £400,000/5,000 miles =   £80

Cost at 6,000 miles = 6,000 miles @ £80 per mile =   £480,000
Cost at 7,000 miles = 7,000 miles @ £80 per mile =   £560,000

W3 Landing and servicing fees are a semi-variable cost

Cost at 6,000 miles = £600,000 + 6,000 miles @ £50 per mile =   £900,000
Cost at 7,000 miles = £600,000 + 7,000 miles @ £50 per mile =   £950,000

W4 Cost per mile at 5,000 miles = £135,000/5,000 miles =   £27

Cost at 6,000 miles = 6,000 miles @ £27 per mile =   £162,000
Cost at 7,000 miles = 7,000 miles @ £27 per mile =   £189,000

W5 Profit per mile flown = total profit/miles flown

Profit at 5,000 miles = £70,000/5,000 miles =   £14.00 per mile
Profit at 6,000 miles = £363,000/6,000 miles =   £60.50 per mile
Profit at 7,000 miles = £656,000/7,000 miles =   £93.71 per mile

b) i) Relevant costs are costs that are relevant for decision making. If a cost will change as a result of a decision it is seen to be a relevant cost. This contrasts with irrelevant costs which are those costs that will not change as a result of a decision. These costs can therefore be ignored when considering whether an action should be chosen.

ii) Variable costs and the variable element of the semi-variable costs are relevant costs. The fixed costs and the fixed element of the semi-variable costs are irrelvant in the short term.

Task 2.2

Calculation of required number of miles

Fixed costs (£000) (W1)	1,645
Target profit (£000)	60
	1,750
Sales revenue (£000)	2,500
Less variable costs (£000) (W2)	785
Contribution (£000)	1,715
Contribution per mile (£000)	343
Required number of miles to achieve target profit (W3)	4,971

Workings

W1 Landing and servicing fixed costs, wages and salaries and other fixed overheads

= 600 + 420 + 625 = £1,645

W2 Landing and servicing variable costs, aviation fuel and other variable costs

= 250 + 400 + 135 = £785

W3 Required number of miles to achieve target profit

= (Fixed costs + target profit)/contribution per mile

= 1,705,000/343 = 4,971 miles

practice exam 1 – unit 6 – answers

Task 2.3

Scheduled route	A	B	C	Total
Contribution per mile (£) (W1)	310	325	305	
Contribution per pilot hour (£'000) (W2)	124	100	152.5	
Route ranking	2	3	1	
Pilot hours available				124
Pilot hours allocated to each route	50	26	48	
Number of miles to fly in the route	20,000	8,000	24,000	
Total contribtuion earned (£'000) (W3)	6,200	2,600	7,320	16,120
Less: fixed costs (£'000)				3,300
Profit/loss made (£'000)				12,820

Tutorial note: Take care with where you put your decimal points when working with £'000. The Assessor for this paper noted that there were a number of candidates who calculated contribution to be a thousandth of the correct value!

Workings

W1 Contribution per mile = total contribution/total number of miles in the route

    A   Contribution per mile = 6,200,000/20,000 =   £310
    B   Contribution per mile = 5,200,000/16,000 =   £325
    C   Contribution per mile = 7,320,000/24,000 =   £305

W2 Contribution per pilot hour = total contribution/number of pilot hours required

    A   Contribution per pilot hour = 6,200,000/50 =   £124,000
    B   Contribution per pilot hour = 5,200,000/50 =   £100,000
    C   Contribution per pilot hour = 7,320,000/50 =   £152,500

W3 Total contribution earned

    A   48 hours at £152,500 per hour =   £7,320,000
    B   50 hours at £124,000 per hour =   £6,200,000
    C   124 hours - hours for C and A routes
          = 124 - 98 = 26 hours at £100,000 per hour =   £2,600,000

Task 2.4

Net present value of aircraft A

	Year 0 £ million	Year 1 £ million	Year 2 £ million	Year 3 £ million
Capital expenditure/disposal	(350)			50
Revenue		735	820	910
Operating costs		(455)	(495)	(574)
Net cash flows	(350)	280	325	386
PV factors	1.00000	0.86207	0.74316	0.64066
Discounted cash flows	(350)	241	242	247
Net present value	380			

Net present value of aircraft B

	Year 0 £ million	Year 1 £ million	Year 2 £ million	Year 3 £ million
Capital expenditure/disposal	(300)			35
Revenue		695	790	880
Operating costs		(460)	(515)	(565)
Net cash flows	(300)	235	275	350
PV factors	1.00000	0.86207	0.74316	0.64066
Discounted cash flows	(300)	203	204	224
Net present value	331			

Task 2.5

Report

To: The Chief Accountant
From: Accounting Technician
Subject: Replacement aircraft
Date: 1 December 2008

a) Aircraft A has a higher net present value and, therefore, other things being equal should be bought.

b) As the company's cost of capital increases, PV factors decrease. As PV factors decrease future cash flows decrease in value and the NPV falls. Thus increasing the company's cost of capital would make capital investments *less* viable.

c) Payback can be used to show how quickly the initial capital expeindutre costs can be recovered.

PRACTICE EXAM 2
UNIT 6

PREMIER LABELS LTD

ANSWERS

practice exam 2 – unit 6 – answers

SECTION 1

Task 1.1

a) Weighted Average Cost (AVCO) is being used for valuing issues to production.
b) Stock record card for plastic part AT3

Stock record card for plastic part AT3

Date	Receipts Quantity kgs	Receipts Cost per kg (£)	Receipts Total cost (£)	Issues Quantity kg	Issues Cost per kg (£)	Issues Total cost (£)	Balance Quantity kg	Balance Total cost £
Balance at 1 May							6,000	16,800
6 May	10,000	3.0000	30,000				16,000	46,800
17 May				7,000	2.9250	20,475	9,000 (W1)	26,325 (W1)
23 May	10,000	3.3525	33,525 (W2)				19,000 (W3)	59,850 (W4)
30 May				12,000	31,500 (W5)	37,800 (W6)	7,000 (W7)	22,050 (W7)

Workings

W1 16,000 kg – 7,000 kg = 9,000 kg at cost of £2.925 per kg = £26,325
W2 10,000 kg x £3.525 = £33,525
W3 10,000 kg + 9,000 kg = 19,000 kg
W4 £26,325 + £33,525 = £59,850
W5 Weighted average cost = £59,850 / 19,000 kg = £3.1500
W6 12,000 kg x £3.1500 = £37,800
W7 19,000 kg – 12,000 kg = 7,000 kg at cost of £3.1500 per kg = £22,050

Tutorial note: Ensure that the answer is to 4 decimal points as required in the question.

practice exam 2 – unit 6 – answers

Task 1.2

Email

To: AATStudent@Premier.net
From: ManagementAccountant@Premier.net
Subject: Compliance with stock control policy
Date: 16 June 2008

a) Our company's policy for part AT3 is that it should only be re-ordered when the stock balance falls to 4,000 kg and that the reorder quantity should be 8,000 kg. Both these elements of the stock control policy have not been complied with. Orders were delivered on 6 May and 23 May when we had 6,000 kgs and 9,000 kgs in stock respectively. Both orders were for 10,000 kgs.

b) The financial implication for the company of non compliance is that we will hold extra stock. There may be an associated cost for us, e.g. interest charges, stock handling costs and storage costs.

Task 1.3

a) The correct total cost of direct labour for the bottles is:

		£
Cost at normal rate	1,215 hours at £8 =	9,720
Cost at time and a half	180 hours at £4 =	720
Cost at double time	135 hours at £8 =	1,080
Total direct labour cost		11,520

Or:

Cost at normal rate:	900 hours at £8 =	£7,200
Cost at time and a half:	180 hours at £12 (£8 x 1.5) =	£2,160
Cost at double time:	135 hours at £16 (£8 x 1.5) =	£2,160
Total direct labour cost		£11,520

Tutorial note: The trainee has got the time and a half hours worked muddled with the double time hours worked.

b) The cost of direct labour per bottle = Total direct labour cost/number of bottles
= £11,520/57,600
= £0.20

417

Task 1.4

Overhead	Basis of allocation	Plastics moulding £	Labelling £	Stores £	Equipment maint £	Total £
Heat and lighting fixed cost	Equally (W1)	6,000	6,000	6,000	6,000	24,000
Heat and lighting variable cost	Floor area (W2)	19,200	10,800	4,800	1,200	36,000
Power for machinery	Per directions (W3)	19,600	8,400			28,000
Supervision	Direct labour costs (W4)	50,000	70,000			120,000
Stores wages	Allocated			72,000		72,000
Equipment maintenance salaries	Allocated				188,200	188,200
Depreciation of fixed assets	Apportioned - Net book value of fixed assets (W5)	48,000	24,000	9,000	3,000	84,000
Other overhead costs	Per directions (W6)	76,800	25,600	12,800	12,800	128,000
Total of primary apportion-ments		219,600	144,800	104,600	211,200	680,200
Reapportion equipment maintenance	Equal charges	70,400	70,400	70,400	(211,200)	
Reapportion stores	Material requisitions (W7)	130,200	44,800	(175,000)		
Total Production Department overheads		420,200	260,000			

Workings

W1 £24,000/4 = £6,000 each

W2 £36,000 in ratio 320:180:80:20

Plastic Mouldings	(320/ 600) x £36,000 = £19,200
Labelling	(180/ 600) x £36,000 = £10,800
Stores	(80/ 600) x £36,000 = £ 4,800
Equipment Maintenance	(20/ 600) x £36,000 = £ 1,200

W3 £28,000 in ratio 70:30

Plastic Mouldings	70% x £28,000 = £19,600
Labelling	30% x £28,000 = £ 8,400

W4 £120,000 in ratio 100:140

Plastic Mouldings	(100/240) x £120,000 = £50,000
Labelling	(140/240) x £120,000 = £70,000

W5 £84,000 in ratio 160:80:30:10

Plastic Mouldings	(160/ 280) x £84,000 = £48,000
Labelling	(80/ 280) x £84,000 = £24,000
Stores	(30/ 280) x £84,000 = £9,000
Equipment Maintenance	(30/ 280) x £84,000 = £3,000

W6 £128,000 in ratio 60:20:10:10

Plastic Mouldings	60% x £128,000 = £76,800
Labelling	20% x £128,000 = £25,600
Stores	10% x £128,000 = £12,800
Equipment Maintenance	10% x £128,000 = £12,800

W7 £175,000 in ratio 162, 750:56,000

Plastic Mouldings	(162,750/218,750) x £175,000 = £130,200
Labelling	(56,000/218,750) x £175,000 = £44,800

Task 1.5

a) **The Plastics Moulding department**

The budgeted overhead recovery (absorption) rates = Total production department overheads/budgeted machine hour

= £420,200/8,404 = £50 per machine hours

b) **The Labelling department**

The budgeted overhead recovery (absorption) rates = Total production department overheads/budgeted direct labour hours

= £260,000/16,250 = £16 per direct labour hour

practice exam 2 – unit 6 – answers

Task 1.6

a) The prime cost per batch of labelled pet food tins = Total prime costs/number of batches

Prime cost = Direct materials + Direct labour = £14,870 + £42,206 = £57,076

Therefore, prime cost per batch of labelled pet food tins = £57,076/15,020 = £3.80

b) The variable cost per batch of labelled pet food tins = total variable costs/number of batches

Variable cost = Prime cost materials + variable overheads = £57,076 + £48,064 = £105,140

Therefore, variable cost per batch of labelled pet food tins = £105,140/15,020 = £7.00

c) The full absorption cost per batch of labelled pet food tins = Full absorption costs/number of batches

Absorption cost = Variable costs + fixed overheads = £105,140 + £75,100 = £180,240

Therefore, full absorption cost per batch of labelled pet food tins = £180,240/15,020 = £12.00

SECTION 2

Task 2.1

a) Estimate of the production cost per unit at the different activity levels:

Cans made	50,000	60,000	70,000
Costs:	£	£	£
Variable costs: (W1)			W2
■ direct materials	5,250	6,300	7,350
■ direct labour	2,250	2,700	3,150
■ overheads	11,100	13,320	15,540
Fixed costs: (W2)			
■ indirect labour	9,200	9,200	9,200
■ overheads	15,600	15,600	15,600
Total cost	43,400	47,120	50,840
Cost per can (W3)	0.868	0.785	0.726

Workings

W1
	Variable costs per unit	Variable cost for 60,000 cans	Variable cost for 70,000 cans
Direct materials	5,250/50,000 = £0.105	£6,300	£7,350
Direct labour	2,250/50,000 = £0.045	£2,700	£3,150
Overheads	11,100/50,000 = £0.222	£13,320	£15,540

W2 Assume fixed costs do NOT vary as output increases from 50,000 to 70,000 units.

W3
	60,000 cans	70,000 cans
Cost per can	47,120/60,000 = 0.785	50,840/70,000 = 0.726

b) The cost per can decreases as the number of cans increases. This is because fixed costs do not increase as output increases from 50,000 to 70,000 cans. These fixed costs are, therefore, spread over a larger number of units and the effect of this is to decrease the cost per unit of the product.

c) If production volume for this product were to increase to 150,000 cans per period the effect on fixed costs, and cost per can, will depend on the behaviour of fixed costs.

If fixed costs do not change then costs per can will continue to fall. However, it is likely that fixed costs will increase as indirect labour and overheads will increase as output is more than doubled. The overall effect on costs per can will depend upon the relative size of these increases in fixed costs.

Task 2.2

The budgeted contribution per unit of A and B sold, and the company's budgeted profit for the year from these two products:

	A	B	Total
	(£)	(£)	(£)
Selling price per unit	1.50	1.20	
Less: variable costs per unit			
▪ direct materials	0.20	0.25	
▪ direct labour	0.12	0.14	
▪ variable overheads	0.15	0.19	
Contribution per unit	1.03	0.62	
Sales volume (units)	300,000	500,000	
Total contribution	309,000	310,000	619,000
Less: fixed costs			264,020
Budgeted profit or loss			354,980

Workings

W1   A   B

Selling price per unit
= Sales revenue/units
made and sold   £450,000/300,000 = £1.50   £600,000/500,000 = £1.20

W2 Variable costs per unit
= Variable cost/units made and sold

	A	B
Direct materials	£60,000/300,000 = £0.20	£125,000/500,000 = £0.25
Direct labour	£36,000/300,000 = £0.12	£70,000/500,000 = £0.14
Variable overheads	£45,000/300,000 = £0.15	£95,000/500,000 = £0.19

Tutorial note: Ensure that the answer is to 2 decimal points as required in the question.

Task 2.3

a)

Product	A	B
Fixed costs (£) (per question)	158,620	105,400
Unit contribution (£) (see above)	1.03	0.62
Breakeven sales (units) (W1)	154,000	170,000
Forecast sales (units)	250,000	400,000
Margin of safety (units)	96,000	230,000
Margin of safety (%) (W3)	38.40%	57.50%

Workings

W1   A   B

Breakeven sales
= Fixed costs/Unit contribution   £158,620/1.03   £105,400/0.62
                                              = 154,000   = 170,000

W2   Margin of safety (units)

= Forecast sales - Breakeven sales   250,000 - 154,000   400,000 - 170,000
                                                          = 96,000   = 230,000

W3   Margin of safety (%) = ((Forecast sales - Breakeven sales)/Forecast sales) x 100

For A,
Margin of safety (%) = ((250,000 - 154,000)/250,000) x 100 = 38.40%

For B,
Margin of safety (%) = ((400,000 - 170,000)/400,000) x 100 = 57.50%

b)   Product B has the better margin of safety.

Product B's sales can fall by 57.5% before it breaks even. Any greater fall than this will result in the company making a loss whereas Product A's sales can only drop by 38.4% before it starts to lose money.

practice exam 2 – unit 6 – answers

Task 2.4

The recommended number units of products A and B that should be made in order to maximise the profit that can be made taking account of the machine hours available:

	A	B	Total
Contribution/unit (£)	1.03	0.62	
Machine hours/unit	0.20	0.08	
Contribution/machine hour	5.15	7.75	
Product ranking	second	first	
Machine hours available			70,000
Machine hours allocated to:			
Product B		40,000	
Product A (balancing figure)	30,000		
Total contribution earned (£)	154,500	310,000	464,500
Less: fixed costs (£)			264,020
Profit/loss made (£)			200,480

Workings

W1 Machine hours per unit
    = Machine hours/number of units
    A: 60,000/300,000 = 0.20
    B: 40,000/500,000 = 0.08

W2 Contribution per machine hour
    = Total contribution/total machine hours
    A: £309,000/60,000 = £5.15
    B: £310,000/40,000 = £7.75

Task 2.5

a) **The net present value (NPV)**

	Year 0 £'000	Year 1 £'000	Year 2 £'000	Year 3 £'000
Capital expenditure/disposal	(600)			100
Sales income		900	1,350	750
Operating costs		(710)	(895)	(560)
Net cash flows	(600)	190	455	290
PV factors	1.000	0.9009	0.8116	0.7312
Discounted cash flows	(600)	171.17	369.28	212.05
Net present value	152.50			

424

b) **The payback period**

	Net cash flow £'000	Cumulative cash flow £'000
Year 0	(600)	(600)
Year 1	190	(410)
Year 2	455	45

Payback is in 1 and 410/455 years = 1.90 years (1 year and 329 days or 1 year and approx. 11 months)

Task 2.6

Report

To: The Management Accountant
From: AAT Trainee
Subject: Investment Appraisal
Date: DD/MM/YYYY

a) The project has a positive NPV of £152,500. As the project has a positive NPV it will increase the present value of the company and should, other things being equal, be undertaken.

The project has a payback period of 1.9 years. As this is within the three-year expected life of the project, it should be accepted.

b) Commercial factors that are relevant to this decision (any TWO from):

- The accuracy of the cash flow projections
- The risk involved in the project
- Other projects available
- The attitude of financial stakeholders to the project.

c) The internal rate of return (IRR) is the return from an investment, calculated to show the rate at which the present value of future cash flows from an investment is equal to the cost of the investment. Put another way, the internal rate of return for an investment is the discount rate that makes the present value of the investment's income stream total to zero. It is used to appraise capital investment projects. It can be seen as the maximum cost of capital that can be used to finance a project without reducing shareholder value, ie if a project has a IRR higher than the company's cost of capital then, other things being equal, the project should be accepted.

PRACTICE EXAM 3
UNIT 6

STOW SOLVENTS LTD

SECTION 1

Task 1.1

Parts a) and b) – stock record card for chemical RC976

	STOCK RECORD CARD FOR RC976									
	Receipts			Issues			Balance	
Date	Quantity Litres	Cost per Litre (£)	Total cost (£)	Quantity Litres	Cost per Litre (£)	Total cost (£)	Quantity Litres	Total cost £
Balance as of 1 Nov							8,000	3,200
5 Nov	4,000	0.52	2,080				12,000	5,280
12 Nov				5,000	0.40	2,000	7,000	3,080
18 Nov	4,000	0.55	2,200				11,000	5,280
28 Nov				6,000	0.48	2,880	5,000	2,400

c) Last in first out or LIFO is another method used for valuing stock issues.

d) A lower stock valuation would result if LIFO was used to value stocks.

Task 1.2

JOURNAL

Date	Code	DR (£)	CR (£)
5 November	1953	2,080	
5 November	0080		2,080
12 November	3265	2,200	
12 November	1953		2,200
18 November	1953	2,200	
18 November	0080		2,200
28 November	3341	2,880	
28 November	1953		2,880

Task 1.3

a) **Calculation of the total cost of direct labour for solvent S789 in November**

	£
Cost at normal rate (260 hours at £10/hr)	2,600
Cost at time and a half (40 hours at £15/hr)	600
Cost at double time (30 hours at £20/hr)	600
	3,800

b) **Calculation of the direct labour cost per unit of solvent S789 in November for equivalent finished production**

	Litres
Equivalent units produced (litres)	
Output to the next process	7,000
Closing work in progress (1,200 litres at 50%)	600
Total equivalent production	7,600

Direct labour cost per equivalent unit = total cost of direct labour (from 1.3 a)/total equivalent production

$$= \frac{£3,800}{7,600}$$

$$= £0.50$$

Task 1.4

Fixed overhead	Basis of apportionment	Chemical mixing £	Solvent bottling £	Maintenance £	Total cost £
Insurance of machinery	Net book value	30,240	15,120	5,040	50,400
Rent and rates	Floor space	75,240	54,720	6,840	136,800
Indirect labour costs	Allocated	53,625	131,175	18,375	203,175
Sub-total		159,105	201,015	30,255	390,375
Reapportionment of maintenance		24,204	6,051	(30,255)	0
Total		183,309	207,066	0	390,375

Task 1.5

Overhead absorption rates (OAR)

a) **Chemical mixing budgeted fixed overhead absorption rate.** Total departmental overheads (from 1.4) divided by total budgeted machine hours:

Therefore $\dfrac{£183,309}{5,237}$ = £35.00 per machine hour

b) **Solvent bottling budgeted fixed overhead absorption rate.** Total departmental overheads (from 1.4) divided by total budgeted labour hours:

Therefore $\dfrac{£207,066}{17,256}$ = £12 per labour hour

Task 1.6

	£
Overhead absorbed = 480 machine hours at £35 per hour (from 1.5 a))	16,800
Overhead now expected to be incurred	16,200
	600

Therefore there will be an over-absorption of overhead as overhead has been absorbed based on the OAR, and this is more than the actual overhead incurred.

practice exam 3 – unit 6 – answers

SECTION 2

Task 2.1

a) **Estimates of the production cost per unit of product S468 using different levels of activity**

Litres	10,000	14,000	18,000
Costs:	£	£	£
Variable costs:			
■ direct materials	1,200	1,680	2,160
■ direct labour	1,000	1,400	1,800
■ overheads	1,600	2,240	2,880
Fixed costs:			
■ indirect labour	700	700	700
■ overheads	1,600	1,600	1,600
Total cost	6,100	7,620	9,140
Cost per litre	0.61	0.54	0.51

b) **Reasons for change in cost per litre**

The **variable costs increase pro-rata to the additional litres produced** so that the variable cost per litre is the same no matter how many litres are made. **Fixed costs stay the same** so that as the number of litres produced increases the fixed cost per litre decreases. Thus the total cost per litre (fixed plus variable) decreases.

c) i) A **stepped fixed cost** is a cost **fixed** across a certain range of activity. The cost will increase once the range is exceeded and as more overheads are incurred. This will then be a new level of stepped fixed cost.

ii) Beyond the original 10,000 litres of production the fixed costs increase to a new level and remain at this until production exceeds 20,000 litres. So, at production levels of 14,000 and 18,000 litres, the **total fixed cost** remains the same.

433

practice exam 3 – unit 6 – answers

Task 2.2

a) The **budgeted breakeven sales** (stated in litres). This is fixed costs/contribution per litre:

$$\frac{£2,300}{£(0.88 - 0.38 \text{ (W)})} = 4,600 \text{ litres}$$

Working

This is $\dfrac{£3,800}{10,000 \text{ litres}}$.

b)
Forecast sales (litres)	10,000	14,000	18,000
Breakeven sales (litres)	4,600	4,600	4,600
Margin of safety (litres)	5,400	9,400	13,400
Margin of safety (%)	54	67	74

Task 2.3

a) The **cost per litre of output** is worked out by:

$$\frac{\text{(Input cost – scrap value of normal loss)}}{\text{Expected output in litres}} = \frac{(£9,000 - £(3,000 \times 0.20))}{15,000}$$

$$= £0.56$$

b) **The entries in the process account**

Description	Litres	Unit cost £	Total cost £	Description	Litres	Unit cost £	Total cost £
Input to process	18,000	0.50	9,000	Normal loss	3,000		600
				Output from process	15,000	0.56	8,400
	18,000	0.50	9,000		18,000	0.50	9,000

434

Task 2.4

Production plan to maximise profits next quarter:

Solvent	S782	S893	Total
Contribution per thousand litres (£)	400	600	
Machine hours per thousand litres	2	5	
Contribution per machine hour (£)	200	120	
Solvent ranking	1	2	
Machine hours available			6,000
Machine hours allocated to: Solvent .... Solvent	4,000	2,000	
Litres produced ('000)	2,000	400	
Total contribution earned (£)	800,000	240,000	1,040,000
Less: fixed costs (£)			640,000
Profit/loss made (£)			400,000

Task 2.5

Report

To: Chief Accountant
From: AAT student
Subject: Investment appraisal
Date: 3 December 2007

The company's stated policy for investments is a **payback period** within 3 years. The investment being considered has a payback period of 2.4 years. Based on this measure, therefore, it should go ahead.

However, the **NPV** of the project is negative and on this basis it should not go ahead. Likewise, the **IRR** is 14% which is below the company's 16% cost of capital and so the investment should not go ahead.

In summary, the investment should not go ahead because the NPV is negative. This is the dominant criterion as it is a measure of absolute wealth maximisation.

PRACTICE EXAM 4
UNIT 6

EASTERN BUS COMPANY PLC

practice exam 4 – unit 6 – answers

SECTION 1

Task 1.1

Parts a) and c) – stock record card for diesel

| | Receipts ||| Issues ||| Balance ||
Date	Quantity Litres	Cost per litre p	Total cost £	Quantity Litres	Cost per Litre p	Total cost £	Quantity Litres	Total cost £
Balance as at 22 May							22,000	6,600
24 May	100,000	32.44	32,440				122,000	39,040
26 May				80,000	32.00	25,600	42,000	13,440
28 May	50,000	32.55	16,276				92,000	29,716
30 May				80,000	32.30	25,840	12,000	3,876

b) The method used for valuing issues is AVCO (deduced from the 26 May issue).

Working

Closing stock 24 May = 122,000 litres costing £39,040 = 32p per litre. This is the average cost of the stock at that date and it is the cost attributed to the issue on 26 May.

Task 1.2

JOURNAL

Date	Code	DR (£)	CR (£)
24 May	200	32,440	
24 May	600		32,440
26 May	501	25,600	
26 May	200		25,600
28 May	200	16,276	
28 May	600		16,276
30 May	502	25,840	
30 May	200		25,840

Working

The journal for the 24 May transaction shows that £32,400 of fuel was debited to the stock account (code 200) and credited to the creditors control (code 600).

The other journals follow the same principles.

practice exam 4 – unit 6 – answers

Task 1.3

Employee: S Moss
Employee number: D104
Profit Centre: Scheduled Services
Basic pay per hour: £12.00

	Hours spent driving	Hours worked on indirect work	Notes	Basic pay £	Overtime premium £	Total pay £
Monday	6	–		72	–	72 (W1)
Tuesday	3	3	12am – 3pm customer care course	72	–	72 (W1)
Wednesday	8			96	12	108 (W2)
Thursday	6			72	–	72
Friday	6	1	2–3pm health and safety briefing	84	6	90 (W3)
Saturday	5			60	24	84 (W4)
Sunday	3			–	72	72 (W5)
Total	37	4		456	114	570

Workings

1) 6 × £12 = 72
2) (8 × £12) + (2 × £6) = £108
3) (7 × £12) + (1 × 6) = £90
4) (5 × £12) + (2 × £12) = £84
5) (3 × £12) + (3 × £12) = £72

* Alternative answer (provided by Chief Assessor) – the Sunday working is counted as 3 hours' basic and 3 hours' overtime.

Sunday	3			36	36	72

Task 1.4

	Basis of apportionment	Scheduled services £	Contract Services £	Vehicle maintenance and repairs £	Fuel and parts store £	General admin £	Totals £
Depreciation of buses	NBV of buses	2,251,620 (W1)	964,980				3,216,600
Diesel fuel and other variable overheads	Planned number of miles	1,716,000 (W2)	18,990				2,860,000
Rent and rates	Floor space			209,000 (W3)	125,400	83,600	418,000
Light, heat and power	Floor space			46,200 (W4)	27,720	18,480	92,400
Indirect labour	Allocated			404,600	96,200	308,800	809,200
Totals		3,967,620	2,108,980	659,800	249,320	410,480	7,326,200
Reapportion vehicle maintenance and repairs		494,850 (W5)	164,950	(659,800)			
Reapportion fuel and parts store		137,126 (W6)	112,194		(249,320)		
Reapportion general admin		205,240 (W7)	205,240			(410,480)	
Total overheads to profit centres		4,804,836	2,591,364				7,396,200

practice exam 4 – unit 6 – answers

Workings

1) $\dfrac{£3,216,600 \times 22,400,000}{32,000,000} = £2,251,620$

2) $\dfrac{£2,860,000 \times 34,320}{57,200} = £1,716,000$

3) $\dfrac{£418,000 \times 14,000}{28,000} = £209,000$

4) $\dfrac{£92,400 \times 14,000}{28,000} = £46,200$

5) £659,800 × 0.75 = £494,850

6) £249,320 × 0.55 = £137,126

7) £410,480 × 0.5 = £205,240

Task 1.5

Overhead absorption rates

Scheduled services rate per mile: $\dfrac{£4,804,836}{34,320}$ planned miles = £140.00

Contract services rate per mile: $\dfrac{£2,591,364}{22,880}$ planned miles = £113.26

Task 1.6

The cost per mile under:

a) **Variable (marginal) costing**

Fuel and variable overheads	£9,200
Total miles travelled	4,600
Variable cost per mile	£2 per mile

b) **Full absorption costing**

	£ per mile
Total variable cost per mile	2.00
Drivers' wages, pension and national insurance $\dfrac{£3,220}{4,600 \text{ miles}}$	0.70
Fixed overheads $\dfrac{£23,000}{4,600 \text{ miles}}$	5.00
Total absorption cost per mile	7.70

SECTION 2

Task 2.1

a) **Completed table**

Likely miles	10,000	12,000	14,000
	£	£	£
Sales revenue	100,000	120,000 (W1)	140,000
Variable costs			
■ fuel	8,000	9,600 (W1)	11,200
■ drivers' wages and associated costs	5,000	6,000 (W1)	7,000
■ overheads	6,000	7,200 (W1)	8,400
Fixed costs			
■ indirect labour	10,600	10,600	10,600
■ overheads	25,850	25,850	25,850
Total cost	**55,450**	**59,250**	**63,050**
Total profit	44,550	60,750	76,950
Profit per mile	4.455	5.063	5.496

Workings

The sales revenue and variable costs vary in proportion to the miles travelled.

Thus, the sales revenue for 12,000 miles is calculated as £100,000 × $\frac{12,000}{10,000}$ = £12,000.

The variable cost for fuel for 12,000 miles is calculated as £8,000 × $\frac{12,000}{10,000}$ = £9,600.

All the other variable costs for 12,000 and 14,000 are calculated in the same way.

practice exam 4 – unit 6 – answers

b) Reason for change in profit per mile

The variable costs and revenue increase pro rata to the additional miles travelled so that the variable cost per mile is the same no matter how many miles are travelled. Fixed costs stay the same so that as the number of miles travelled increases the fixed cost per mile decreases. Thus the total cost per mile (fixed plus variable) decreases and the profit per mile therefore increases.

Task 2.2

Forecast number of miles		12,000	14,000
Sales revenue (per 2.1)	£	120,000	140,000
Fixed costs £(10,600 + 25,850)	£	36,450	
Contribution (per 2.1: £(120,000 – 9,600 – 6,000 – 7,200))	£	97,200	
Contribution per mile £(97,200/12,000)	£	8.10	
Break-even number of miles £(36,450/8.10)	Miles	4,500	
Break-even sales revenue (4,500 × £10)	£	45,000	
Margin of safety in number of miles (12,000 – 4,500) = 7,500 and (14,000 – 4,500) = 9,500	Miles	7,500	9,500
Margin of safety in sales revenue £(120,000 – 45,000) = 75,000 and £(140,000 – 45,000) = 95,000	£	75,000	95,000
Margin of safety	%	62.5	67.9

Task 2.3

Tutorial note. All working are shown for route X; the working for the other routes are similar.

Scheduled route	X	Y	Z	Total
Contribution per mile (£) (£6,400/5,000) = £1.28 per mile	1.28	1.20	1.40	
Driver hours per mile (400/5,000 = 0.08)	0.08	0.05	0.07	
Contribution per driver hour (£) £1.28/0.08 = £16 or £6,400/400 = £16	16	24	20	
Route ranking	3	1	2	
Driver hours available				620
Driver hours allocated to each route	0	200	420	620
Number of miles in the route		4,000	6,000	
Total contribution earned (£) 4,000 × £1.20 = £4,800 6,000 × £1.40 = £8,400		4,800	8,400	13,200
Less: fixed costs (£) (see note)				6,300
Profit/loss made (£)				6,900

Tutorial note. The fixed costs must include all the fixed cost associated with the three routes even though route X is not covered – X's fixed costs are still incurred.

Task 2.4

The net present cost of machine A

	Year 0	Year 1	Year 2	Year 3
	£'000	£'000	£'000	£'000
Capital expenditure	800			
Operating costs		365	380	405
Net cash flows	800	365	380	405
PV factors	1.00000	0.87719	0.76947	0.67497
Discounted cash flows	800	320	292	273
Net present cost	1,685			

The net present cost of machine B

	Year 0	Year 1	Year 2	Year 3
	£'000	£'000	£'000	£'000
Capital expenditure	650			
Operating costs		460	470	480
Net cash flows	650	460	470	480
PV factors	1.00000	0.87719	0.76947	0.67497
Discounted cash flows	650	404	362	324
Net present cost	1,740			

Tutorial note. The net present cost is the total of the discounted cash flows of all the costs over the three years, including the initial capital expenditure.

Task 2.5

Report

To: The Management Accountant
From: AAT student
Subject: Investment appraisal
Date: 18 June 2007

a) On **purely financial grounds**, the type A machine should be bought because it has the lower net present costs. This assumes that the financial benefits arising from either machine are the same.

b) **Commercial issues** would include the ease of use of the two machines; their reliability; the need for staff training; their residual values (if any) at the end of their three-year lives and the finance options offered by the supplying companies if relevant.

c) One other method of investment appraisal is **Payback**. Another method is **Internal rate of return**. (*Only one required by the question.*)

PRACTICE EXAM 5
UNIT 6

BRECKVILLE DAIRIES LTD

SECTION 1

Task 1.1

a) and b)

STOCK RECORD CARD

Date	Receipts Quantity (litres)	Receipts Cost per litre (£)	Receipts Total cost (£)	Issues Quantity (litres)	Issues Cost per litre (£)	Issues Total cost (£)	Balance Quantity (litres)	Balance Total cost £
Balance as at 1 Nov							2,000	4,000
6 Nov	1,000	2.60	2,600				3,000	6,600
14 Nov				1,000	$\frac{6,600}{3,000} = 2.20$	2,200	2,000	4,400
22 Nov	1,000	3.40	3,400				3,000	7,800
27 Nov				2,000	$\frac{7,800}{3,000} = 2.6$	5,200	1,000	2,600

c) Another method of stock issue and valuation is LIFO (last in first out).

d) FIFO would lead to a lower valuation of the stock balance at 27 November.

Tutorial note. This is because the stock values are based on older costs which are lower than the more up-to-date costs.

Task 1.2

Date	Code	DR £	CR £
6 November	2004	2,600	
6 November	6030		2,600
14 November	7012	2,200	
14 November	2004		2,200
22 November	2004	3,400	
22 November	6030		3,400
27 November	7039	5,200	
27 November	2004		5,200

Task 1.3

		£
Normal hours	350 hours x £8	2,800
Overtime:		
Time and a half	60 hours x £12	720
Double time	40 hours x £16	640
Total direct labour cost		4,160

Task 1.4

Fixed overhead	Basis of allocation or apportionment	Total cost £	Materials Mixing £	Product Packing £	Maintenance £
Insurance of machinery	NBV (360:180:60)	33,600	20,160	10,080	3,360
Rent and rates	Floor area (550:400:50)	91,200	50,160	36,480	4,560
Indirect labour costs	Allocated	135,450	35,750	87,450	12,250
		260,250	106,070	134,010	20,170
Maintenance	Time spent (60:40)		12,102	8,068	(20,170)
Totals		260,250	118,172	142,078	0

Note. Additional workings have been shown in the above answer.

Task 1.5

a) Materials mixing fixed overhead absorption rate:

$$\frac{\text{Department fixed overheads}}{\text{Department machine hours}} = \frac{118,172}{3,940}$$

$$= £30 \text{ per machine hour}$$

b) Product packing fixed overhead absorption rate:

$$\frac{\text{Department fixed overheads}}{\text{Department labour hours}} = \frac{142,078}{10,920}$$

$$= £13 \text{ per labour hour}$$

practice exam 5 – unit 6 – answers

Task 1.6

a) i) Variable (marginal) cost per unit:

	£
Direct materials	12.20
Direct labour	27.80
Prime cost	40.00
Variable overheads (20,000/1,000)	20.00
Variable cost per unit	60.00

ii) Full absorption cost per unit:

	£
Direct materials	12.20
Direct labour	27.80
Prime cost	40.00
Variable overheads (20,000/1,000)	20.00
Fixed overheads (50,000/1,000)	50.00
Variable cost per unit	110.00

b) The closing stock of 200 units would be valued at £12,000 (200 x £60) under marginal costing, and £22,000 (200 x £110) under full absorption costing. This means that an extra £10,000 is deducted from the cost of sales, making the profit £10,000 greater under full absorption costing.

practice exam 5 – unit 6 – answers

SECTION 2

Task 2.1

a)

Units made	1,000	1,200	1,500
Costs	£	£	£
Variable costs:			
■ direct materials	3,000	3,600	4,500
■ direct labour	7,000	8,400	10,500
■ overheads	6,000	7,200	9,000
Fixed costs:			
■ indirect labour	9,800	9,800	9,800
■ overheads	19,000	19,000	19,000
Total cost	44,800	48,000	52,800
Cost per unit	44.80	40.00	35.20

b) i) Fixed costs are only fixed over a certain range of activity, and they may well rise if such a large rise in production were to occur, causing a rise in the cost per unit.

ii) Variable costs per unit might also change. For example, quantity discounts might be obtained on bulk purchases of material which would reduce cost per unit.

iii) Without further information it is not possible to extrapolate to estimate a new cost per unit as the new production level is so far beyond the current production range.

Task 2.2

a) Breakeven sales $= \dfrac{\text{Fixed costs}}{\text{Contribution per unit}}$

$= \dfrac{£28,800}{£24 \text{ (working)}}$

$= 1,200$ units

Working

Contribution per unit $= \dfrac{£3,000 + £7,000 + £6,000}{1,000 \text{ units}}$

$= £24$ per unit

454

b)

Forecast sales (units)	1,000	1,200	1,500
Break-even sales (units)	1,200	1,200	1,200
Margin of safety (units)	(200)	0	300
Margin of safety (%)	–	0%	20%

c) i) **1,000 units**

At this level of forecast sales the company is selling 200 units below what it needs to break even, so there is no margin of safety; it is already making a loss.

ii) **1,200 units**

At this forecast level of sales the margin of safety is zero as this is the break even level. Sales cannot fall below this level or else a loss will be made.

iii) **1,500 units**

At this forecast level of sales the company is making a profit. Sales could drop by 20% before a profit would no longer be made.

The company needs to sell more than 1,200 units.

Task 2.3

a) Cost per litre of output = $\dfrac{£12,000 - (200 \times £5)}{1,000 \text{ litres}}$

= £11

b)

Process account: Product T

	Litres	Unit cost £	Total cost £		Litres	Unit cost £	Total cost £
Input to process	1,200	10	12,000	Normal loss	200	5	1,000
				Output from process	1,000	11	11,000
			12,000				12,000

Task 2.4

Product	V	W	Total
Contribution/unit (£)	10	15	
Machine hours/unit	2	5	
Contribution/machine hour (£)	5	3	
Product ranking	1	2	
Machine hours available			
Machine hours allocated to: Product...V.... Product...W...	2,000	1,000	3,000
Units made	1,000	200	
Total contribution earned (£)	10,000	3,000	13,000
Less: fixed costs (£)			9,000
Profit/loss made (£)			4,000

Task 2.5

REPORT

To: Chief Accountant **Subject:** Appraisal of investment in mixing machine

From: Accounting Technician **Date:** 28 November 2007

The payback period for the purchase of the mixing machine is 3.6 years, which is within our required limit of four years. On this basis we would accept the investment.

The NPV of the investment project is negative at our cost of capital of 15%, the IRR being only 12%. On these criteria we should not accept the investment proposed.

Although the different bases appear to conflict, the correct decision will be made only if we base our decision on NPV. We should therefore reject the investment proposal as it would mean that the company would be £200,000 worse off if it were to go ahead.

AAT

SAMPLE SIMULATION
UNIT 6

QUALITY CANDLES LTD

ANSWERS

AAT sample simulation – unit 6 – answers

Task 1

STORES RECORD CARD

Materials description: Candlewick thread, 200 metre rolls
Code no: CW728

Maximum quantity: 400
Minimum quantity: 140
Reorder level: 230
Reorder quantity: 80

Date	Receipts Document number	Qty	Price per roll (£)	Total (£)	Issues Document number	Qty	Price per roll (£)	Total (£)	Stock balance Qty	Price per roll (£)	Total (£)
1 Oct									28	2.20	61.60
									26	2.30	59.80
									54		121.40
3 Oct					249	26	2.30	59.80			
						4	2.20	8.80			
						30		68.60	24	2.20	52.80
6 Oct	419	80	2.35	188.00					24	2.20	52.80
									80	2.35	188.00
									104		240.80
8 Oct					252	40	2.35	94.00	24	2.20	52.80
									40	2.35	94.00
									64		146.80
9 Oct	427	80	2.38	190.40					24	2.20	52.80
									40	2.35	94.00
									80	2.38	190.40
									144		337.20
10 Oct	75	3	2.35	7.05					24	2.20	52.80
									43	2.35	101.05
									80	2.38	190.40
									147		344.25

458

Task 2

MATERIALS REQUISITION

Department: Manufacturing

Document no: 252
Date: 08/10/2007

Code no	Description	Quantity	Cost office use only Value of issue (£)
CW728	Candlewick thread 200m rolls	40	94.00

Received by: .... Signature: ....

MATERIALS RETURNED

Department: Manufacturing

Document no: 75
Date: 10/10/2007

Code no	Description	Quantity	Cost office use only Value of issue (£)
CW728	Candlewick thread 200m rolls	3	7.05

Received by: .... Signature: ....

AAT sample simulation – unit 6 – answers

Task 3

MEMO

To: General Manager
From: Bobby Forster, Accounts Assistant
Subject: Stock levels of candlewick thread, week ending 10 October 2007
Date: 14 October 2007

The stock levels on this item have been a cause for concern during the last week.

The stock level began the week below the minimum quantity of 140 rolls and, although two deliveries brought the balance to 147 rolls by the end of the week, it is clear that the minimum level is soon to be reached once more.

This could lead to the company running out of stock before a new batch of candlewick is received from the supplier. Customer orders could be lost or it may be necessary to pay high prices to acquire urgent supplies.

I suggest that we should review the stock control levels and reorder quantity. Perhaps usage patterns have changed since the levels were set. If this is the case the levels and the reorder quantity should be recalculated, taking account of any changes in usage patterns and supply lead times.

I would be happy to discuss the problem with you at any time.

Task 4

QUALITY CANDLES LIMITED
PIECEWORK OPERATION CARD

Operative name: Mary Roberts   Department: Manufacturing

Clock number: R27

Week beginning: 6 October 2007

Activity	Monday	Tuesday	Wednesday	Thursday	Friday
Batches produced	120	102	34	202	115
Batches rejected	5	7	4	11	5
Batches accepted	115	95	30	191	110
Rate per batch	£ 0.50	£ 0.50	£ 0.50	£ 0.50	£ 0.50
Piecework payment	£ 57.50	£ 47.50	£ 15.00	£ 95.50	£ 55.00
Bonus payable	£ 2.30	£ nil	£ nil	£ nil	£ 2.20
Total payable for day*	£ 59.80	£ 50.00	£ 50.00	£ 95.50	£ 57.20

Total wages payable for week:

£

Direct wages	308.00
Indirect wages	4.50
Total wages	312.50

* Guaranteed daily wage of £50 is payable if piecework payment plus bonus amounts less than £50

Supervisor's signature: *A Peters*

Task 5

INTERNAL MEMO

To: Roy Hart, Manufacturing Department Supervisor
From: Bobby Forster, Accounts Assistant
Subject: Discrepancy on piecework operation card
Date: 10 October 2007

I have a query on a piecework operation card for the week beginning 6 October, a copy of which is attached. The employee concerned is Mary Roberts, clock number R27.

The output recorded for Wednesday is exceptionally low and correspondingly the output for Thursday is very high. It is possible that some of the output for Wednesday was recorded in error for Thursday. This distorts the wages payable because of the guaranteed daily rate.

Could you please look into this for me, to see whether there was in fact a genuine reason for the unusual pattern in output levels.

Thank you for your help.

Task 6

Production overhead analysis sheet for 2008

Production overhead item	Total £000	Manufacturing £000	Painting/finishing £000	Packing £000	Stores £000	Maintenance £000
Indirect labour	98	22	14	11	35	16
Indirect materials	40	12	2	2	12	12
Rent and rates	105	45	15	24	12	9
Protective clothing	31	31				
Power	40	20	4	12	2	2
Insurance	24	11	4	6	2	1
Heat and Light	35	15	5	8	4	3
Depreciation	48	22	8	12	4	2
Other	15	5	5	5		
Total department overheads	436	183	57	80	71	45
Apportion maintenance total	—	21	12	9	3	(45)
Apportion stores total	—	36	20	18	(74)	
Total production dept overheads	436	240	89	107		

Task 7

Working paper

Calculation of production overhead absorption rates for 2008

Manufacturing department

Machine hour rate = $\dfrac{£240,000}{200,000}$

= £1.20 per machine hour

Painting and finishing department

Labour hour rate = $\dfrac{£89,000}{28,000}$

= £3.18 per labour hour

Packing department

Machine hour rate = $\dfrac{£107,000}{90,000}$

= £1.19 per machine hour

Task 8

Sample calculations: working paper
Reversing the order of service department re-apportionments

Production overhead item	Total £000	Manufacturing £000	Painting/finishing £000	Packing £000	Stores £000	Maintenance £000
Total department overheads (from Task 6)	436	183	57	80	71	45
Apportion stores total	–	27	15	13	(71)	16
Apportion maintenance total	–	31	17	13	–	(61)
Total production dept overheads	436	241	89	106		

Task 9

INTERNAL MEMO

To: General Manager
From: Bobby Forster, Accounts Assistant
Subject: Re-apportionment of service department costs
Date: 5 November 2007

I have carried out the analysis you requested and the results are attached.

As you will see, the change in method does not result in a material difference in the total overhead for each production cost centre. Therefore I suggest that we should not change our apportionment methods since the value of the management information would not be materially affected by the change.

Task 10

Journal entry for production overheads

October 2007

Entries for overhead absorbed during the month

	Debit (£)	Credit (£)
Work in progress: manufacturing dept	18,500	
Work in progress: painting and finishing dept	7,400	
Work in progress: packing dept	8,300	
Production overhead control		34,200

Entries for overhead under-/over-absorbed during the month

	Debit (£)	Credit (£)
Overhead over-/under-absorbed (P+L)		18,400
Production overhead control	18,400	

466

INTERNAL MEMO

To: Production Manager
From: Bobby Forster, Accounts Assistant
Subject: Overhead absorption for October 2007
Date: 9 November 2007

A significant over absorption arose during the month. The total amount over absorbed was £18,400 compared with total actual expenditure of £15,800.

Could you please check the data for me to ensure that no recording errors have occurred?

The actual production overhead figure may be too low, perhaps because of miscoding of invoices. Alternatively, the activity data for the production departments may have been recorded incorrectly.

Thank you for your help.

Task 11

Workings for determination of revenue and cost behaviour patterns

Sales revenue

Selling price per case = £28,000/7,000 = £4

Check: 6,200 x £4 = £24,800; 5,900 x £4 = £23,600

Candles cost

Candle cost per case = £9,100/7,000 = £1.30

Check: 6,200 x £1.30 = £8,060; 5,900 x £1.30 = £7,670

Packing materials cost

Packing materials cost per case = £5,250/7,000 = £0.75

Check: 6,200 x £0.75 = £4,650; 5,900 x £0.75 = £4,425

Packing labour cost

Packing labour cost per case = £2,100/7,000 = £0.30

Check: 6,200 x £0.30 = £1,860; 5,900 x £0.30 = £1,770

Packing overhead cost

	Cases	£
High	7,000	5,400
Low	5,900	5,180
Difference	1,100	220

Variable cost per case = £220/1,100 = £0.20. Fixed cost = £5,400 − (7,000 x £0.20) = £4,000

Check: for 6,200 cases cost is £4,000 + (6,200 x £0.20) = £5,240

Other overheads cost

Fixed cost = £2,500 per month

AAT sample simulation – unit 6 – answers

Quality Candles Limited: mail order division
Planned results for December 2007

	December
Number of cases to be sold	6,800
	£
Candles cost (@ £1.30)	8,840
Packing materials cost (@ £0.75)	5,100
Packing labour cost (@ £0.30)	2,040
Packing overhead cost	5,360
Other overhead cost	2,500
Total costs	23,840
Sales revenue (@ £4)	27,200
Profit	3,360

Packing overhead cost

	£
Fixed	4,000
Variable (6,800 x £0.20)	1,360
	5,360

Task 12 (i)

Quality Candles Limited: mail order division
Planned results for December 2007: increased activity

	December
Number of cases to be sold	7,600
	£
Candles cost (@ £1.30)	9,880
Packing materials cost (@ £0.60)	4,560
Packing labour cost (@ £0.30)	2,280
Packing overhead cost	5,520
Other overhead cost	2,500
Total costs	24,740
Sales revenue (@ £4)	30,400
Profit	5,660

Packing overhead cost

	£
Fixed	4,000
Variable (7,600 x £0.20)	1,520
	5,520

469

Task 12 (ii)

Quality Candles Limited: mail order division

Planned results for December 2007: increased activity

Calculation of breakeven point and margin of safety: working paper

	£	£
Contribution per case:		
Selling price		4.00
Less variable costs:		
Candles	1.30	
Packing materials	0.60	
Packing labour	0.30	
Packing overhead	0.20	
		2.40
Contribution per case		1.60
Fixed overhead:		
Packing overhead		4,000
Other overheads		2,500
		6,500

Breakeven point

Number of cases to breakeven $= \dfrac{£6,500}{£1.60}$

$= 4,063$ cases

Margin of safety $= 7,600 - 4,063$ cases

$= 3,537$ cases

$= 47\%$ of planned activity

Task 12 (iii)

INTERNAL MEMO

To: General Manager
From: Bobby Forster, Accounts Assistant
Subject: Mail order division: bulk discounts for December 2007
Date: 11 November 2007

I have evaluated the proposal to increase sales and take advantage of a bulk discount for packing materials.

The planned profit will increase considerably to £5,660 for the month compared with £3,360 without the increased activity. The breakeven point will be 4,063 cases which results in a margin of safety of 47% of planned activity.

Since the company is looking for opportunities to increase profit, the high profit and the wide margin of safety mean that this represents a very attractive proposal.

However the following assumptions affect the validity of the projections.

- The increased sales volume can be achieved at the current selling price. It is possible that the selling price would have to be reduced in order to sell the greater output.

- All other unit variable costs and fixed costs will not be altered by the increase in activity. Since the volume projection is outside the range for which data is available this may not be a valid assumption. For example it may be necessary to pay overtime rates to labour in order to achieve the increased output.

- The increased volume can be achieved with the existing packing and delivery capacity.

Please let me know if you require any further information.

Task 13 (i)

Working paper for the financial appraisal of purchase of delivery vehicles

Year	Cashflow £	Discount factor @ 12%	Present value £
2007	−90,000	1.000	−90,000
2008	34,800	0.893	31,076
2009	34,800	0.797	27,736
2010	34,800	0.712	24,778
2011	39,800	0.636	25,313
Net present value			18,903

Working space for calculation of payback period

	Cumulative cashflow (£)
2007	−90,000
2008	−55,200
2009	−20,400
2010	14,400

Payback period = 2 years + (20,400/34,800) = 2.6 years

Task 13 (ii)

INTERNAL MEMO

To: General Manager
From: Bobby Forster, Accounts Assistant
Subject: Purchase of delivery vehicles for mail order division
Date: 14 November 2007

The proposal to purchase delivery vehicles is acceptable from a financial viewpoint because it returns a positive net present value of £18,903 at a discount rate of 12%. This calculation assumes that all cashflows occur at the end of each year.

The payback period is between two and three years. If we assume even cashflows during the year the payback period can be calculated as 2.6 years. This is acceptable since it is shorter than the company requirement of three years, although there is not much room for error in the cashflow calculations.

Please let me know if I can help any further with the evaluation.

PRACTICE SIMULATION
UNIT 6

HIGH HEAT LTD

Task 1

Oven 900 – contribution to fixed costs for October 2007

	£	£
Sales		78,530
Less: cost of sales		
Opening stock	13,850	
Materials issued	32,135	
Direct labour	28,200	
Variable overheads	1,970	
Closing stock	(16,830)	
		(59,325)
Contribution to fixed costs		19,205

Task 2

STOCK RECORD (STOCK CARD)

Part description: Hi-grade filters
Code: FF783
Maximum purchase price: £17.00

Maximum quantity: 100
Minimum quantity: 20
Reorder level: 50
Reorder quantity: 75

Date	Receipts Quantity	Receipts Price £	Receipts Total £	Issues Quantity	Issues Price £	Issues Total £	Balance Quantity	Balance Price £	Balance Total £
1 Oct							20	16.30	326.00
2 Oct	75	16.50	1,237.50				20	16.30	326.00
							75	16.50	1,237.50
							95		1,563.50
8 Oct				20	16.30	326.00	45	16.50	742.50
				30	16.50	495.00			
				50		821.00			
12 Oct	75	16.70	1,252.50				45	16.50	742.50
							75	16.70	1,252.50
							120		1,995.00
15 Oct				45	16.50	742.50	60	16.70	1,002.00
				15	16.70	250.50			
				60		993.00			
29 Oct	80	17.10	1,368.00				60	16.70	1,002.00
							80	17.10	1,368.00
							140		2,370.00
31 Oct				60	16.70	1,002.00	50	17.10	855.00
				30	17.10	513.00			
				90		1,515.00			

475

practice simulation – unit 6 – answers

Task 3

MEMORANDUM

To: Production Director
From: Management Accounts Assistant
Subject: Stock of hi-grade filters, October 2007
Date: 5 November 2007

A number of problems have arisen during October concerning the application of our stock control and purchasing practices to the stock of hi-grade filters, code number FF783.

Stock levels above the maximum quantity

The maximum stock level is 100 units for this item, but the level rose to 120 units on 12 October, and 140 on 29 October. It looks as though this was done in anticipation of the unusually large requisition for 90 units on 31 October.

Stock ordered before the level reached the reorder level

The order on 27 October was placed when the stock level was 60 units, whereas the reorder level is 50 units.

Order placed for an amount greater than the reorder quantity

The order of 27 October was for more than the reorder quantity of 75 units.

Order placed at too high a price and not checked by a person in authority

The order of 27 October had a number of errors which may have been picked up if it had been authorised: it was placed when the reorder level had not yet been reached, it was for more than the reorder quantity, and it was at a price that exceeded the maximum stated on the Stock Record.

Conclusion

These breaches of good practice, especially the lack of authorisation and the errors on the order on 27 October, should be thoroughly investigated. Holding too much stock is expensive, can lead to obsolescence and pilfering, and shows a lack of good control.

However, if it transpires that the levels for this part have not been updated for the apparent increase in activity then this should also be looked at as part of production planning.

Task 4

MEMORANDUM

To: Ismay Ratliff, Production Director
From: Management Accounts Assistant
Subject: Stock valuation October 2007
Date: 3 November 2007

Raw materials stock valuation

Please find attached a stock record for hi-grade filters as requested, prepared on the alternative AVCO basis.

Part-finished goods valuation

Oven 678s at 31 December 2007 (estimate)

	£
Materials: 100% x 565	565.00
Labour: 60% x £890	534.00
Variable overheads: 100% x 200	200.00
	1,299.00
Value in year-end accounts: £1,299 x 40	£51,960.00

Finished goods valuation

Absorbing fixed production overheads into the valuation of finished goods will lead to a higher value for finished goods at the year-end. This will increase profits, as expenses that would otherwise have been written off to the profit and loss account in 2007 will instead be carried forward into 2008 as stock.

Task 4 (continued)

STOCK RECORD

Part description: Hi-grade filters
Code: FF783
Valuation basis: AVCO

Date	Receipts			Issues			Balance		
	Quantity	Price £	Total £	Quantity	Price £	Total £	Quantity	Price £	Total £
1 Oct							20	16.30	326.00
2 Oct	75	16.50	1,237.50				20	16.30	326.00
							75	16.50	1,237.50
							95	16.46	1,563.50
8 Oct				50	16.46	823.00	45	16.46	740.70
12 Oct	75	16.70	1,252.00				45	16.46	740.70
							75	16.70	1,252.50
							120	16.61	1,993.20
15 Oct				60	16.61	996.00	60	16.61	996.60
29 Oct	80	17.10	1,368.00				60	16.61	996.60
							80	17.10	1,368.00
							140	16.89	2,364.60
31 Oct				90	16.89	1,520.10	50	16.89	844.50

Task 5

TIME SHEET						
Week ending 31/10/07						
Name Sanjeev Patel						
Area Machine shop			**Employee number**		M042	
Grade B						
Activity	**MON**	**TUES**	**WED**	**THURS**	**FRI**	**TOTAL**
Oven 900 machining	9		9			18
Oven 778 machining		9		3		12
Sick				4.5		4.5
Training					7.5	7.5
Hours attendance	9.0	9.0	9.0	7.5	7.5	42
Bonus hours	0.5	0.5	0.5			1.5

Employee's signature *Sanjeev Patel*

Manager's signature *Malcolm Harrison*

ANALYSIS OF HOURS

Basic rate hours	7.5	7.5	7.5	7.5	7.5	37.5
Overtime hours	1.5	1.5	1.5	0	0	4.5
Bonus hours	0.5	0.5	0.5	0	0	1.5

ANALYSIS OF GROSS PAY

	Hours	Rate £	£	£
Direct hours (25.5 + 4.5)	30	8.50		255.00
Indirect hours				
Sick	4.5	8.50	38.25	
Training	7.5	8.50	63.75	
Overtime hours at premium	4.5	4.25	19.13	
Bonus hours	1.5	17.00	25.50	
Total indirect				146.63
Gross pay				401.63

practice simulation – unit 6 – answers

Task 5 (continued)

TIME SHEET

Week ending 31/10/07
Name Jacob Ellis
Area Machine shop **Employee number** M042
Grade C

Activity	MON	TUES	WED	THURS	FRI	TOTAL
Oven 900 machining	8	7.5	8	9	9	43.5
Hours attendance	8	7.5	8	9	9	43.5
Bonus hours	1		1	1	1	4

Employee's signature *Jacob Ellis*
Manager's signature

ANALYSIS OF HOURS

Basic rate hours	8	7.5	8	9	9	41.5
Overtime hours						
Bonus hours						

ANALYSIS OF GROSS PAY

	Hours	Rate £	£	£
Direct hours	41.5	7.00		290.50
Indirect hours				
Sick				
Training				
Overtime hours at premium				
Bonus hours				
Total indirect				
Gross pay				290.50

480

Task 6

MEMORANDUM

To: Malcolm Harrison, Machine Shop Manager
From: Management Accounts Assistant
Subject: Discrepancy on Time Sheet for Jacob Ellis
Date: 2 November 2007

I have some queries on the Time Sheet for Jacob Ellis for the week ending 31 October 2007. I attach a copy of the Time Sheet.

The Time Sheet relates only to direct hours on Oven 900 machining but the hours have been added incorrectly to 43.5 hours, when the correct total is 41.5 hours. Because of this discrepancy, in line with the Payroll Guide I have calculated these 41.5 hours at his basic rate only.

In addition, the Time Sheet has not been signed by you, although Jacob has signed it. I have therefore not included the 4 hours bonus hours indicated on the Time Sheet in my calculations. These appear to have been filled in by Jacob himself.

Until the Time Sheet is signed by you I cannot proceed with any payment to Jacob. Could you please look into this as a matter of urgency therefore?

Task 7

Calculation of under-/over-absorption of production overheads

October 2007

Total number of machine hours worked	4,590.00
Pre-determined overhead absorption rate per machine hour, 2007	£13.00
Total production overhead absorbed, October 2007	£59,670.00
Actual production overhead incurred	£68,750.00
Production overhead ~~over~~/(under) absorbed, October 2007	(£9,080.00)

The amount of £9,080 has been ~~over~~/under* absorbed and will be debited/~~credited~~* to the profit and loss account.

(*Delete as applicable.)

practice simulation – unit 6 – answers

Task 8

MEMORANDUM

To: Production Director
From: Management Accounts Assistant
Subject: Production overhead absorption rates for 2008
Date: 14 November 2007

Calculation of single machine hour rate

If we continue to use the current overhead absorption basis of a single, factory-wide machine hour rate in 2008, we can calculate the absorption rate as follows.

$$\text{Machine hour rate} = \frac{\text{total budgeted production overheads}}{\text{total budgeted machine hours}}$$

$$= \frac{£855,000}{52,600}$$

$$= £16.25 \text{ per machine hour}$$

Problems with the single rate

The Assembly Shop Manager has indeed highlighted a problem with the use of a single factory-wide absorption rate: it does not reflect the different activities in the two production cost centres and therefore the different ways in which they incur overhead costs. In the Assembly Shop, there are more labour hours and fewer machine hours, as it is a labour-intensive rather than a machinery intensive operation.

If we use different rates for each area, we would begin by allocating certain production overheads directly to the cost centres that incur them, then apportioning or sharing other types of cost on an agreed basis to the cost centres so as to reflect the use of the resources. Our aim is to determine as fairly as possible the total cost of operating both the Machine Shop and the Assembly Shop, including a share for each of the Testing Centre and Staff Amenity Centre costs.

The activity data shows us that the Assembly Shop is more labour-intensive and uses fewer machine hours, so it would seem fair to absorb the overheads for this department according to labour activity, using a direct labour hour rate. The Machine Shop makes far more use of machinery, so a machine hour rate should be calculated for it.

The two separate absorption rates would then be applied to each cost unit depending on the amount of time (on machines, or on labour) spent in each area. The final absorbed overhead cost should be a more accurate reflection of the resources consumed by each cost unit.

Task 9

Overhead Analysis Sheet: Budget 2008

Rate using step down method of apportionment

Overhead expense item	Basis of allocation/ apportionment	Total £	Machine Shop £	Assembly Shop £	Testing Centre £	Staff Amenity Centre £
Primary allocations and apportionments						
Indirect labour	Indirect employees 1:1	406,600	203,300	203,300		
Manager salaries.	Allocation	82,000	41,000	41,000		
Testing Centre costs	Allocation	124,800			124,800	
Staff Amenity Centre costs	Allocation	70,500				70,500
Depreciation	Net book value	25,200	17,080	3,900	3,000	1,220
Rent, rates, etc.	Floor area	101,300	30,390	50,650	14,182	6,078
Other o'heads	Equal app'ment	44,600	22,300	22,300		
Total primary allocation		855,000	314,070	321,150	141,982	77,798
Reapportion Staff Amenity Centre	No employeed 26:41:6		27,709	43,695	6,394	(77,798)
Re-apportion Testing Centre	25:75		37,094	111,282	(148,376)	
Total production cost centre overhead allocation			378,873	476,127		

ABSORPTION RATES
FOR EACH PRODUCTION DEPARTMENT USING STEP DOWN METHOD:

Machine Shop = $\dfrac{£378,873}{41,500}$ = £9.13 per machine hour

Assembly Shop = $\dfrac{£476,127}{85,900}$ = £5.54 per direct labour hour

Task 9 (continued)

Alternative rates using direct method of apportionment

Overhead expense item	Basis of allocation/ apportionment	Total £	Machine Shop £	Assembly Shop £	Testing Centre £	Staff Amenity Centre £
Total primary allocation		855,000	314,070	321,150	141,982	77,798
Apportion Test Centre costs	25:75		19,449	58,349		(77,798)
Apportion Staff Amendity Centre costs	No employees 26:41		55,097	86,885	(141,982)	
Total production cost centre overhead allocation			388,616	466,384		

CALCULATION OF ABSORPTION RATES
FOR EACH PRODUCTION DEPARTMENT USING DIRECT APPORTIONMENT:

Machine Shop = $\dfrac{£388,616}{41,500}$ = £9.36 per machine hour

Assembly Shop = $\dfrac{£466,384}{85,900}$ = £5.43 per direct labour hour

Task 10

Working paper for calculation of payback period and net present value

Payback period

Year	Cash flow £	Cumulative cash flow £
0	(1,000,000)	(1,000,000)
1	250,000	(750,000)
2	350,000	(400,000)
3	500,000	100,000
4	650,000	750,000

Payback period = 2 years + (400,000/500,000 × 1 year)
            = 2.8 years

Net present value

Year	Cash flow £	Discount factor at 6%	Cumulative cash flow £
0	(1,000,000)	1.0000	(1,000,000)
1	250,000	0.9434	235,850
2	350,000	0.8900	311,500
3	500,000	0.8396	419,800
4	650,000	0.7920	514,800
Net present value			481,950

Task 10 (continued)

MEMORANDUM

To: Production Director
From: Management Accounts Assistant
Subject: New sites and products
Date: 25 November 2007

HIGHLY CONFIDENTIAL

I have calculated the payback period and the net present value, as requested, for the planned expansion to three sites and the development of new product ranges.

    Payback period   2.8 years
    Net present value (NPV) at company's cost of capital, 6%   £481,950

The results of the evaluation on this basis are that it should be accepted, since it returns a positive NPV when discounted at the company's cost of capital. It also achieves a payback period of less than the three year maximum set by the company. Whether the amount by which the net present value is positive is acceptable to the company is a question of considering the relative risk. It may be worthwhile calculating the internal rate of return (IRR) of the move.

Assumptions underlying the above results include the following.

- For the calculation of the payback period of 2.8 years it is assumed that cash flows occur evenly during the fourth year. If the cash flows occurred instead later on in the third year then the payback period would be even closer to the company's cut-off point of three years

- For the NPV calculation, all cash flows are assumed to occur at the end of each year

Task 11

Working paper to determine sales volume, cost behaviour patterns and projected costs and revenues

Projected sales volume

Projected sales volume = 150 dishwashers + (300/75 x 5) machines = 170 machines

Analysis of cost behaviour

Direct material cost

Variable materials cost = £880 per machine

Projected total variable materials cost = 170 x £880 = £149,600

Direct labour cost

Variable cost = £412 per machine

Projected total variable labour cost = 170 x £412 = £70,040

Production overheads cost

Machines		Total cost £
160	(× £355)	56,800
150	(× £364)	54,600
10		2,200

Variable production overhead cost per additional machine = £2,200/10 = £220

Fixed production overhead cost = £56,800 – (£220 x 160) = £21,600

Projected total overhead cost:

		£
Fixed overhead		21,600
Variable overhead	(170 × £220)	37,400
		59,000

Other (non-production) overhead cost

Total cost for 150 machines = 150 x £50.00 = £7,500

Total cost for 160 machines = 160 x £46.88 = £7,500

This is a fixed overhead cost.

Sales revenue

Projected sales revenue = 170 machines x £2,000 = £340,000

Task 11 (continued)

Projected costs and revenues for new product range next year

Output volume (machines) 170

	£	£
Sales revenue		340,000
Projected costs		
Direct material	149,600	
Direct labour	70,040	
Variable production overhead	37,400	
Fixed production overhead	21,600	
Other (non-production) overhead	7,500	
Total projected cost		(286,140)
Projected annual profit		53,860

Task 12

Working paper to calculate margin of safety, P/V ratio and maximum possible change in fixed production overheads

Margin of safety

Contribution per machine = £2,000 - £(880 + 412 + 220) = £488

$$\text{Breakeven sales} = \frac{\text{Fixed costs}}{\text{Contribution per machine}}$$

$$= \frac{£21,600 + 7,500}{488}$$

= 60 machines (rounded up to nearest whole number)

Margin of safety = forecast sales – breakeven sales = 170 – 60 machines
= 110 machines

As a percentage of projected sales volume = 110/170 x 100
= 65%

Profit/volume (P/V) ratio

Profit/volume ratio = (Contribution per unit/Sales revenue per unit) x 100
= (£488/£2,000) × 100
= 24.4%

Possible change in fixed production overheads

Forecast profit from new product range = £53,860

Forecast production overhead cost = £59,000

Possible change required to negate profit = (53,860/59,000) x 100
= 91%

Task 12 (continued)

MEMORANDUM

To: Production Director
From: Management Accounts Assistant
Subject: New large size dishwashers
Date: 29 November 2007

HIGHLY CONFIDENTIAL

I attach the calculations that I have made in response to your memo of today's date.

Analysis of dishwasher product

The projected annual profit for a selling price of £2,000 is £53,860. The margin of safety is 65 per cent of projected sales volume, which amply meets the company's criterion of a 30 per cent safety margin.

The proposal therefore would seem attractive because it achieves the company's goals of increasing profit without unacceptable risk, and it also exceeds the minimum PV ratio of 20%.

My calculations show that the forecast of fixed production overhead could increase by 91% before the new product line fails to earn a profit. Therefore there is some room for error in this difficult forecast.

Please note that I have made the following assumptions in preparing these calculations.

- The cost behaviour patterns observed for 150 machines and 160 machines will continue to apply for a volume of 170 machines. The projected volume is outside the range of data supplied, therefore this assumption might not be valid. In particular, there may be a step increase in fixed costs necessary to meet this level of production (see below).

- Variable costs behave in a linear fashion. It is possible that the unit costs may alter for higher output volumes, particularly if we obtain bulk discounts for materials and if the workforce becomes more skilled and therefore spends fewer hours per machine.

- There will be no unexpected steps in the fixed costs. Storage or financing costs may increase if the output increases, and this will affect the calculations.

Task 13

MEMORANDUM

To: Production Director
From: Management Accounts Assistant
Subject: New products at the new sites
Date: 30 November 2007

HIGHLY CONFIDENTIAL

Contracts required by Welsh consultancy

As far as the Welsh consultancy business is concerned, the calculations are as follows:

	£
Projected fixed costs	50,000
Target profit	80,000
Total contribution required	130,000
Contribution per contract	2,000
Number of contracts required	£130,000/2,000 = 65

Limiting factor on production of large electric woks in Scotland

Machine hours	2,000/14 = 142 woks can be produced
Labour hours	4,500/20 = 225 woks can be produced

Therefore machine hours are the limiting factor, meaning that only 142 woks can be produced.

AAT

SAMPLE SIMULATION
UNIT 7

HOMER LTD

AAT sample simulation – unit 7 – answers

Task 1

Sales to external customers
Manufacturing and Sales divisions combined

	Monthly totals £'000	Cumulative total for the year £'000
20X5/X6		
April	384	384
May	271	655
June	222	877
July	309	1,186
August	346	1,532
September	262	1,794
October	240	2,034
November	329	2,363
December	279	2,642
January	277	2,919
February	244	3,163
March	385	3,548
20X6/X7		
April	381	381
May	242	623
June	237	860
July	339	1,199
August	330	1,529
September	299	1,828
October	231	2,059
November	372	2,431
December	355	2,786
January	310	3,096
February	272	3,368
March	291	3,659

Notes

1) In the first column, enter the monthly total of external sales achieved by the two divisions.
2) In the second column, enter the cumulative total of external sales in the accounting year.

Task 2

Cumulative external sales 20X5/X6 and 20X6/X7

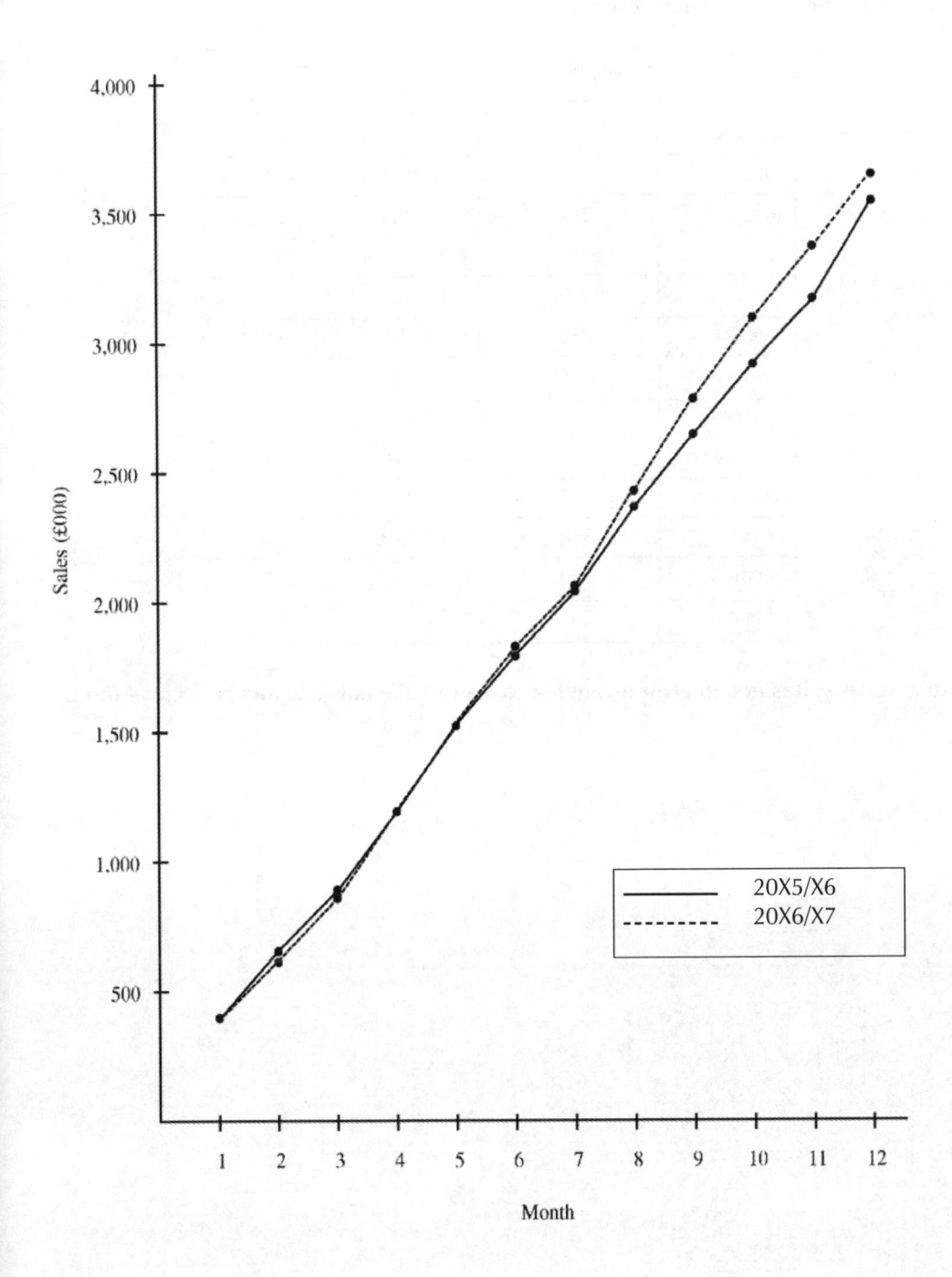

Task 3

Indexed sales to external customers
Manufacturing and Sales divisions combined

	Unadjusted totals £'000	Index factor	Indexed totals £'000
20X6/X7			
April	381	131.0/123.8	403
May	242	131.0/124.4	255
June	237	131.0/124.9	249
July	339	131.0/125.7	353
August	330	131.0/126.3	342
September	299	131.0/127.0	308
October	231	131.0/127.5	237
November	372	131.0/128.1	380
December	355	131.0/128.9	361
January	310	131.0/129.6	313
February	272	131.0/130.2	274
March	291	131.0/131.0	291

Note to assessors: it is not an error if candidates express the index factors in decimal form.

Task 4

LOAN APPLICATION (extract)

Name of applicant company	Homer Limited
Latest year for which accounting information is available	Year ended 31 March 20X7

Total sales revenue

In latest year for which accounts are available	£	3,659,000
In previous year	£	3,548,000
Percentage change (+/–)		+3.13%

Net profit after all expenses, before taxation

In latest year for which accounts are available	£	310,000
In previous year	£	278,000
Percentage change (+/–)		+11.51%
Gross profit margin (%)		40.17%
Net profit margin (%)		8.47%
Return on capital employed (%)		4.70%

Notes

1) In the case of a company with a divisional structure, all figures should refer to the results of the company as a whole, not to individual divisions within the company.

2) Unless otherwise stated, all questions relate to the latest year for which accounting information is available.

3) Figures should be actual historical values, with no indexing for inflation.

4) Return on capital employed is defined as net profit for the year before taxation, divided by total capital employed.

MEMO

To: Sonia Liesl
From: Amir Pindhi
Subject: Loan application form
Date: 14 April 20X7

I attach the completed loan application form for your approval before its submission to the bank.

If it is in order, I assume you will forward the form to the bank for processing. However, if you need further clarification please come back to me.

Task 5

MEMO

To: Sonia Liesl
From: Amir Pindhi
Subject: Ratios and performance indicators for the year ended 31 March 20X7
Date: 14 April 20X7

Here are the required ratios and performance indicators for the year ended 31 March 20X7.

Gross profit percentage: 40.17%. This has fallen from 43.15% in the previous year, possibly because of higher production costs (see 'production cost per unit' below).

Net profit percentage: 8.47%. Despite the fall in GPP, this has risen from 7.84% in the previous year, possibly because of tighter control of overheads.

Production cost per unit: (£2,190,000/199,000=) £11.01. This has risen from £10.83 in the previous year, possibly because of higher materials costs.

Value of sales earned per employee: (£3,659,000/143=) £25,587.41. This has fallen from £26,018.13, possibly because increases in sales have not kept step with increases in the number of employees.

Task 6

Value Added Tax Return
For the period
01 01 X7 to 31 03 X7

For Official Use

Registration number: 625 7816 29
Period: 03 X7

You could be liable to a financial penalty if your completed return and all the VAT payable are not received by the due date.

Due date: 30.04.X7

HOMER LIMITED
SESTOS DRIVE
PANTILE TRADING ESTATE
CV32 1AW

For Official Use

If you have a general enquiry or need advice please call our National Advice Service on 0845 010 9000

ATTENTION
If this return and any tax due are not received by the due date you may be liable to a surcharge.

If you make supplies of goods to another EC Member State you are required to complete an EC Sales List (VAT 101).

Before you fill in this form please read the notes on the back and the VAT Leaflet "*Filling in your VAT return*" and "*Flat rate schemes for small businesses*", if you use the scheme. Fill in all boxes clearly in ink, and write 'none' where necessary. Don't put a dash or leave any box blank. If there are no pence write "00" in the pence column. Do not enter more than one amount in any box.

For official use			£	p
	VAT due in this period on sales and other outputs	1	139,618	95
	VAT due in this period on acquisitions from other EC Member States	2	NONE	
	Total VAT due (the sum of boxes 1 and 2)	3	139,618	95
	VAT reclaimed in this period on purchases and other inputs (including acquisitions from the EC)	4	91,197	54
	Net VAT to be paid to Customs or reclaimed by you (Difference between boxes 3 and 4)	5	48,421	41
	Total value of sales and all other outputs excluding any VAT. Include your box 8 figure	6	873,012	00
	Total value of purchases and all other inputs excluding any VAT. Include your box 9 figure	7	520,568	00
	Total value of all supplies of goods and related services, excluding any VAT, to other EC Member States	8	75,190	00
	Total value of all acquisitions of goods and related services, excluding any VAT, from other EC Member States	9	NONE	00

If you are enclosing a payment please tick this box. ✓

DECLARATION: You, or someone on your behalf, must sign below.
I, *SONIA LIESL* declare that the
(Full name of signatory in BLOCK LETTERS)
information given above is true and complete.
Signature_____ Date _____ 20 ___
A false declaration can result in prosecution.

Task 7

HOMER LIMITED
Sestos Drive, Pantile Trading Estate CV32 1AW
Telephone: 02467 881235

14 April 20X7

H M Revenue & Customs
Bell House
33 Lambert Road
Coventry
CV12 8TR

Dear Sir/Madam

This company is considering the idea of importing raw materials from a Far Eastern supplier. We are unsure of the VAT implications of doing this.

I would be grateful if you would send me a copy of any relevant publication dealing with VAT on imports.

Yours faithfully

Sonia Liesl
ACCOUNTANT

Registered office: Sestos Drive, Pantile Trading Estate CV32 1AW
Registered in England, number 2007814

Task 8

MEMO

To: Sonia Liesl
From: Amir Pindhi
Subject: VAT on imports
Date: 14 April 20X7

I enclose a draft letter to HMRC requesting copies of publications on this topic.

Briefly, the rule is that if we import goods from a non-EC country we have to pay VAT on import at the standard rate. It will normally be possible to reclaim this as recoverable VAT.

PRACTICE SIMULATION
UNIT 7

DONALD RATHERSON & CO

practice simulation – unit 7 – answers

Task 1

	Actual 20X6 £	£	Factor	Restated 20X6 £	£
Sales					
Mail Order		1,001,456	1.04		1,041,514
Showroom		924,763	1.08		998,744
		1,926,219			2,040,258
Cost of sales					
Raw materials	125,896		1.03	129,673	
Goods for resale					
Mail Order	281,546		1.02	287,177	
Showroom	216,875		1.02	221,213	
		(624,317)			(638,062)
Gross profit		1,301,902			1,402,196
Wages					
Manufacturing Unit	169,842		1.05	178,334	
Mail Order	155,246		1.05	163,008	
Showroom	139,000		1.07	148,730	
		(464,088)			(490,072)
Expenses					
Manufacturing Unit	15,746		1.04	16,376	
Mail Order	52,463		1.03	54,037	
Showroom	55,126		1.03	56,780	
		(123,335)			(127,193)
Costs of Ascot site, including accounting and admin		(89,750)	1.05		(94,238)
Net profit		624,729			690,694

Restatement using Institute of Decorators' indices

	20X6 £	Index factor	Adj 20X6 figure £
Total revenue	1,926,219	1.02	1,957,825
Total gross profit	1,301,902	1.01	1,319,967

Note. The percentage price increases given in the memo from Ian Yates relate to price changes over the period from 1 October 20X6 to 30 September 20X7. The year 20X6 is considered as the base, with an index of 100. Showoom and Mail Order price levels, for instance, can be expressed as 108 and 104 respectively. The factor in each case is 104/100 or 1.04 and 108/100 or 1.08 respectively.

We must ensure that the Institute of Decorators' indices relate to the increase for the same period, ie from 20X6 to 20X7. The relevant indices therefore are:

$$\frac{20X7\ index}{20X6\ index} = \frac{111.5}{109.7} = 1.02 \text{ for revenue} \qquad \frac{20X7\ index}{20X6\ index} = \frac{109.6}{108.1} = 1.01 \text{ for gross profit}$$

Task 2

Donald Ratherson & Co
Consolidated statement of revenues and costs for the year ended 30 September 20X7

	£	£	£
Sales			2,238,594
Cost of sales			
Raw materials			
Opening stock	14,016		
Purchases	134,352		
Closing stock	(20,736)		
		127,632	
Goods for resale (Working 1)			
Opening stock	61,750		
Purchases	518,485		
Closing stock	(63,099)		
		517,136	
			(644,768)
Gross profit			1,593,826
Wages (Working 2)			(488,413)
Expenses (Working 3)			(131,987)
Costs of Ascot site, including			
accounting and administration costs (Working 4)			(92,500)
Net profit			880,926

Workings

1)	**Goods for resale**	Mail Order Unit	Showroom	
	Opening stock	24,130	+ 37,620	= 61,750
	Purchases	289,645	+ 228,840	= 518,485
	Closing stock	21,717	+ 41,382	= 63,099

2)	**Wages**	Manufacturing Unit	Mail Order Unit	Showroom	
		178,685	+ 165,728	+ 144,000	= 488,413
3)	**Expenses**	19,145	+ 55,242	+ 57,600	= 131,987
4)	**Costs of Ascot site**	60,125	+ 18,500	+ 13,875	= 92,500

Task 3

	MEMO
To:	Ian Yates
From:	Deputy Accountant
Subject:	Report on results for year ended 30 September 20X7
Date:	12 November 20X7

In reply to your memo of yesterday, I attach the table with my calculations of the differences in monetary and percentage terms between this year's results and those for 20X6, as adjusted for inflation.

You can see that:

- the gross profit margin has risen from 68.73% to 71.20%
- the net profit margin has risen from 33.85% to 39.35%
- return on capital employed has risen from 5.76% to 6.96%

I also attach the component bar chart and time series analysis graph you requested.

I hope this gives you what you need, but please get back to me if there is anything more I can do.

Donald Ratherson & Co
Report on the comparison of revenues and costs for the year end 31 October 20X7 with inflation-adjusted figures for 20X6

	20X7		Adjusted 20X6		Difference	
	£	£	£	£	£	%
Sales		1,146,354		1,041,514	104,840	10.07
Mail Order		1,092,240		998,744	93,496	9.36
Showroom		2,238,594		2,040,258	198,336	9.72
Cost of sales						
Raw materials	127,632		129,673		(2,041)	(1.57)
Goods for resale						
Mail Order	292,058		287,177		4,881	1.70
Showroom	225,078		221,213		3,866	1.75
		(644,768)		(638,062)	(6,706)	1.05
		1,593,826		1,402,196	191,630	13.67
Gross profit						
Wages						
Manufacturing Unit	178,685		178,334		351	0.20
Mail Order	165,728		163,008		2,720	1.67
Showroom	144,000		148,730		(4,730)	(3.18)
		(488,413)		(490,072)	1,660	(0.34)
Expenses						
Manufacturing Unit	19,145		16,376		2,769	16.91
Mail Order	55,242		54,037		1,205	2.23
Showroom	57,600		56,780		820	1.44
		(131,987)		(127,193)	(4,794)	3.77
Cost of Ascot site, inc. acc'ing & admin		(92,500)		(94,238)	1,738	1.84
Net profit		880,926		690,694	190,233	.27.54
Average capital employed		12,650,000		12,000,000		

Working

	%	%
Gross profit margin	71.20	68.73
Net profit margin	39.35	33.85
Return on capital employed	6.96	5.76

practice simulation – unit 7 – answers

Time series 20X1–X8

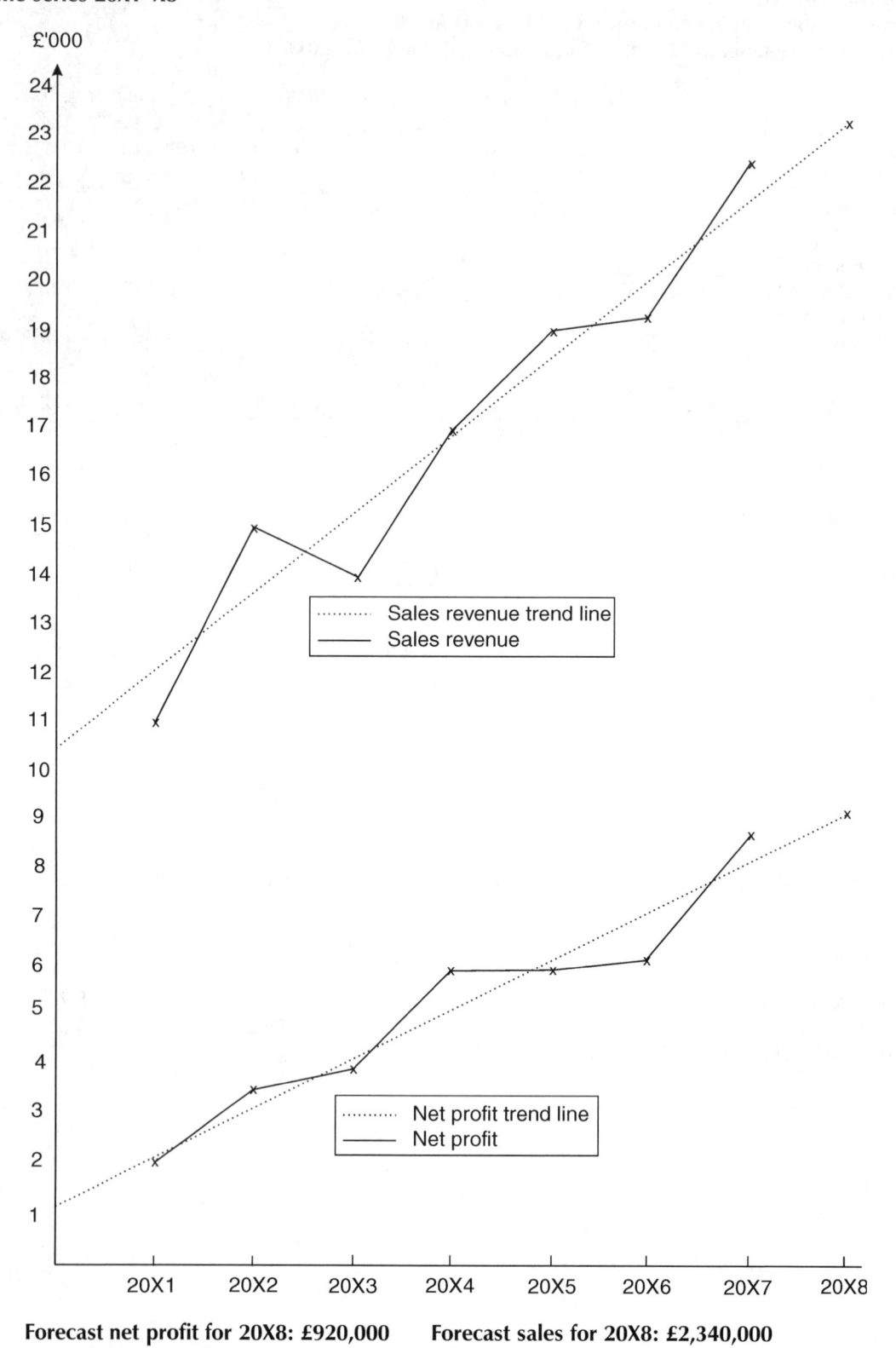

£'000

[Chart showing Sales revenue and Net profit with trend lines from 20X1 to 20X8]

Sales revenue trend line
Sales revenue

Net profit trend line
Net profit

Forecast net profit for 20X8: £920,000   **Forecast sales for 20X8: £2,340,000**

practice simulation – unit 7 – answers

Component bar chart

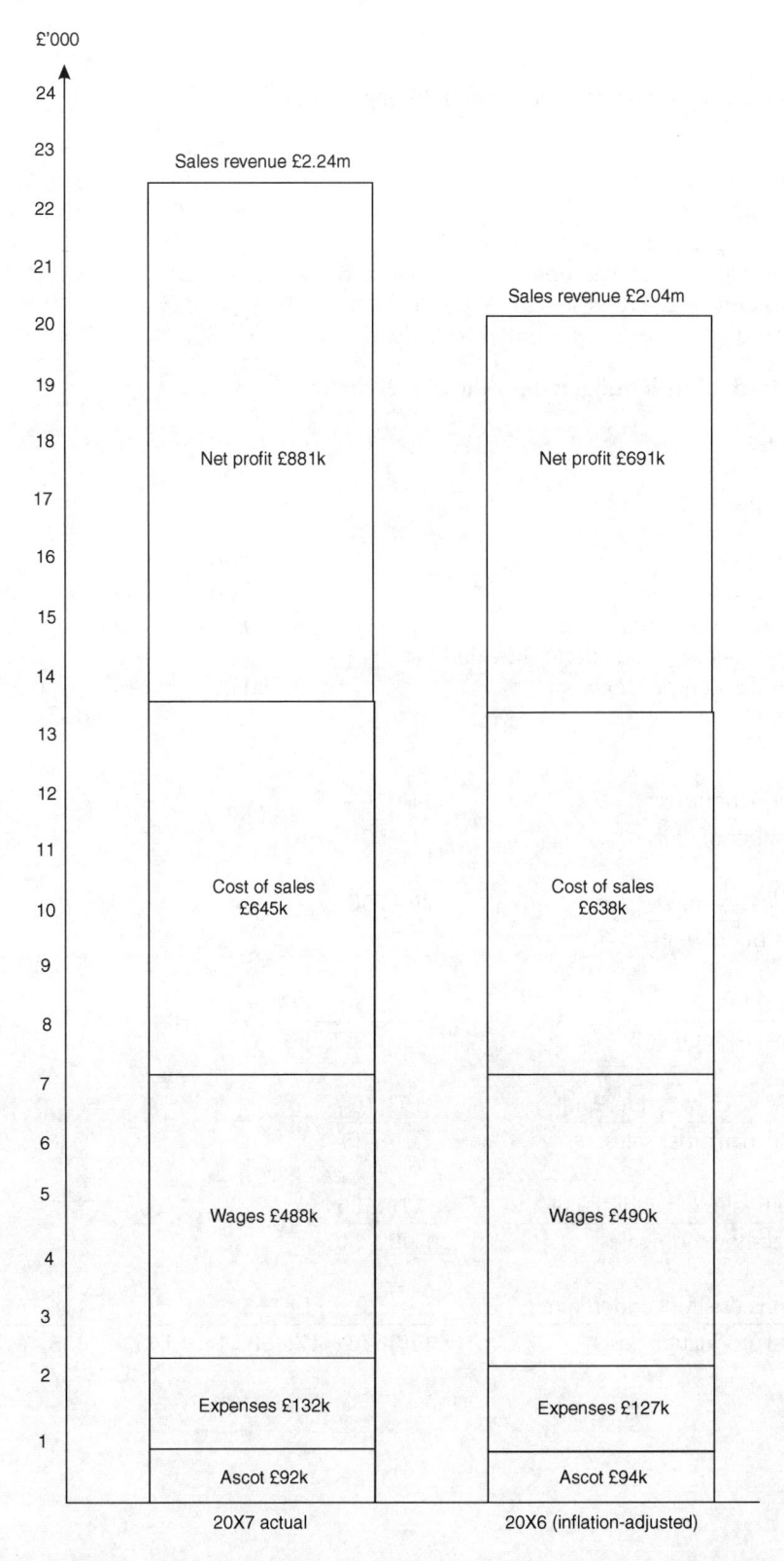

£'000

20X7 actual:
- Sales revenue £2.24m
- Net profit £881k
- Cost of sales £645k
- Wages £488k
- Expenses £132k
- Ascot £92k

20X6 (inflation-adjusted):
- Sales revenue £2.04m
- Net profit £691k
- Cost of sales £638k
- Wages £490k
- Expenses £127k
- Ascot £94k

Task 4

LadderPaint
Production and sales analysis for year ended 30 September

	20X6	20X7	Workings
Total production cost per unit	£62.30	£68.58	1
Sales value per unit	£149.00	£153.00	2
Gross profit margin per unit	58.19%	57.14%	3
Mail Order Unit sales percentage represented by LadderPaint	15.20%	13.19%	4
Showroom sales percentage represented by LadderPaint	12.85%	10.67%	5
Percentage of production costs represented by LadderPaint	35.47%	35.26%	6

Comparison of actual with budgeted production 20X6/07

Actual production	1,750	units
Actual hours	8,750	hours
Actual units per production hour	0.2	units/hr
Budgeted production	1,500	units
Budgeted hours	6,000	hours
Budgeted units per production hour	0.25	units/hr
Productivity ratio: actual production/hr divided by budgeted production per hour ×100%	80.00 %	0.2/0.25×100%

Workings

1) $\dfrac{\text{Total production costs}}{\text{Total number of units}} = \dfrac{114,765}{1,750} = £65.58$

2) $\dfrac{\text{Total sales revenue}}{\text{Total number of units}} = \dfrac{267,750}{1,750} = £153$

3) $\dfrac{\text{Gross profit}}{\text{Total sales revenue}} = \dfrac{(267,750 - 114,765)}{267,750} \times 100 = 57.14\%$

4) $\dfrac{\text{Mail order sales of LadderPaint}}{\text{Total mail order sales}} = \dfrac{151,164}{1,146,354} \times 100 = 13.19\%$

5) $\dfrac{\text{Showroom sales of LadderPaint}}{\text{Total showroom sales}} = \dfrac{116,586}{1,092,240} \times 100 = 10.67\%$

6) $\dfrac{\text{Production costs for LadderPaint}}{\text{Total production costs}} = \dfrac{114,765}{127,632 + 178,685 + 19,145} = \dfrac{114,765}{325,462} = 35.26\%$

practice simulation – unit 7 – answers

Task 5

Institute of Decorators – standard form of return 20X7

Name of business: Donald Ratherson & Co

Year ended Average no of employees	Actual current year 30 Sept X7 31	Workings	% of sales (1)	Actual prior year 30 Sept X6 32	Workings	% of sales (1)
	£			£		
Sales	2,238,594	(W1)	100	1,926,219	(W1)	
Sales per employee	72,213	(W2)		60,194	(W2)	
Gross profit	1,593,286	(W3)		1,301,902	(W3)	67.59
Net profit before taxation	880,926	(W4)		624,729	(W4)	32.43
Average capital employed	12,650,000			12,000,000		
	%			%		
Return on capital employed (2)	6.96	(W5)		5.21	(W5)	

	Inflation-adjusted prior year £	
Prior year sales revenue adjusted for inflation using Institute index	1,957,825	*
Prior year gross profit adjusted for inflation using Institute index	1,319,967	*

			Comparison % of prior year
		£	actual figure
Current year actual sales exceed prior year actual sales by	Box 1 (W6)	312,375	16.22
Amount of increase accounted for by inflation (4)	Box 2 (W1)	(31,606)	
Amount of increase in real terms	Box 1–Box 2	280,769	14.58
Current year actual gross profits exceed prior year's actual gross profits by	Box 3	291,924	22.42
Amount of increase accounted for by inflation (4)	Box 4	(18,065)	
Amount of increase in real terms	Box 3–Box 4	273,859	21.04

practice simulation – unit 7 – answers

Notes

1) All percentages are to be expressed to two places of decimals

2) Return on capital employed is the net profit, divided by the average capital employed for the year, expressed as a percentage to two decimal places

3) All entries are to be based on figures for the business as a whole, excluding any transactions between divisions or business units within the business

4) Deduct actual results from inflation-adjusted results based on Institute of Decorators' indices

* These figures are obtained from Task 1.

Workings

1) Year 20X7: Mail order unit sales + showroom sales = £1,146,354 + £1,092,240 = £2,238,594

   Year 20X6: As given in Task 1

   (£1,926,215 = £1,001,456 + £924,763)

2) Year 20X7: Sales per employee

   £2,238,594/31 = £72,212

   Year 20X6: Sales per employee

   £1,926,219/32 = £60,194

3) Year 20X7: £1,593,826 from Task 1

   Year 20X6: £1,301,902 from Task 1

4) Year 20X7: £880,926 from Task 1

   Year 20X6: £624,729 from Task 1

5) Year 20X7: £880,926/£12,650,000

   Year 20X6: £624,729/£12,000,000

6) £2,238,494 – £1,926,219 = £312,375

7) Increase due to inflation as measured by Decorators' Index

   £7,967,825 – £1,926,219

Task 6

	MEMO
To:	Ian Yates
From:	Deputy Accountant
Subject:	Institute of Decorators' return and report
Date:	11 November 20X7

I enclose the completed return and report for your authorisation prior to despatch.

Task 7

Reconciliation of business units balances as at 31 October 20X7

	£	£
Mail Order Unit balance brought forward		15,985
Add: transfer from Manufacturing		107
Closing Mail Order balance with Manufacturing		16,092
Showroom Unit balance brought forward	10,644	
Add: transfer from Manufacturing	386	
Closing Showroom balance with Manufacturing		11,030
Production cost of items transferred to Mail Order Unit and Showroom		27,122

Task 8

Donald Ratherson & Co

VAT Control Account

Administration/overheads

Date	Description	Debit £	Date	Description	Debit £
20X7			20X7		
31 Aug	Pay HMRC	49,654	1 Aug	B/d	49,654
31 Oct	Input tax – PDB	30,384	31 Oct	Output tax (SDB)	98,338
	Input tax – CB	44			
	Balance c/d	67,910			
		147,992			147,992

practice simulation – unit 7 – answers

Value Added Tax Return
For the period
01 01 X7 to 31 03 X7

For Official Use

Registration number: 482 912 5407
Period: 01/X7

You could be liable to a financial penalty if your completed return and all the VAT payable are not received by the due date.

Due date: **30 November 20X7**

Donald Ratherson & Co
Park Drive Trading Estate
Sunninghill Road
Ascot Gu8 5ZD

Your VAT Office telephone number is 01682-386000

ATTENTION

If this return and any tax due are not received by the due date you may be liable to a surcharge.

If you make supplies of goods to another EC Member State you are required to complete an EC Sales List (VAT 101).

Before you fill in this form please read the notes on the back and the VAT Leaflet *"Filling in your VAT return"*.
Fill in all boxes clearly in ink, and write 'none' where necessary. Don't put a dash or leave any box blank. If there are no pence write "00" in the pence column. Do not enter more than one amount in any box.

Box	Description	£	p
1	VAT due in this period on sales and other outputs	98,338	00
2	VAT due in this period on acquisitions from other EC Member States	NONE	
3	Total VAT due (the sum of boxes 1 and 2)	98,338	00
4	VAT reclaimed in this period on purchases and other inputs (including acquisitions from the EC)	30,428	00
5	Net VAT to be paid to Customs or reclaimed by you (Difference between boxes 3 and 4)	67,910	00
6	Total value of sales and all other outputs excluding any VAT. Include your box 8 figure	591,329	00
7	Total value of purchases and all other inputs excluding any VAT. Include your box 9 figure	193,416	00
8	Total value of all supplies of goods and related services, excluding any VAT, to other EC Member States	29,397	00
9	Total value of all acquisitions of goods and related services, excluding any VAT, from other EC Member States	NONE	00

If you are enclosing a payment please tick this box. ✓

DECLARATION: You, or someone on your behalf, must sign below.

I, ... (Full name of signatory in BLOCK LETTERS) declare that the information given above is true and complete.

Signature.................... Date .... 20....

A false declaration can result in prosecution.

0196929   IB (October 2000)

VAT 100 (Half)

515

Task 9

DONALD RATHERSON & CO

Park Drive Trading Estate, Sunninghill Road, Ascot, Berks GU8 5ZD
Telephone 01344 627896

VAT Office
Lyle House
Henry Road
Guildford
Surrey
GU8 5CM

12 November 20X7

Dear Sirs

Registration number 482 912 5407

We have recently been informed that a net sale of £15,000 to GHA Stores plc in February on 30 days credit is now a bad debt. Please confirm that the steps set out below will enable us to claim bad debt relief for the VAT element of the debt (£2,625.00) in our next VAT return.

- write off the entire debt of £17,625.00 in our accounts before 31 January 20X8

- retain a copy of the VAT invoice and the journal writing it off

- in our next VAT return, for the quarter ending 31 January 20X8 (when the debt will be more than six months overdue), add £2,625.00 to Box 4 (input tax box).

I understand that we do not need to inform GHA Stores plc that we are taking this action.

I look forward to receiving your confirmation. Thank you for your help

Yours faithfully

Deputy Accountant

Task 10

Checklist re VAT

Prepared for: Donald Ratherson

By: A N Accountant

1) The three types of supply for VAT purposes are: **standard-rated**, **zero-rated** and **exempt** supplies.

2) A taxable person who makes only zero-rated outputs **can** reclaim input tax on their purchases.

3) In a month when the VAT registration limit is exceeded, a trader must notify HMRC within **30 days of the end of that month**.

4) The effects of registration for VAT are that the trader:

   1) **must charge VAT on sales**
   2) **may reclaim VAT on purchases**
   3) **must issue VAT invoices showing the VAT registration number**

5) A VAT invoice must show:

   information about the supplier: **name, address, registration number**
   information about the invoice: **date of issue, tax point, invoice number**
   information about the customer: **name, address**

6) A less detailed VAT invoice can be issued where the total including VAT is less than **£250**.

7) The basic tax point for a VAT invoice is **the date on which goods are removed or made available to the customer, or the date on which services are completed.**

8) An earlier tax point than the basic tax point applies if **a VAT invoice is issued or payment is received earlier than the basic tax point.**

9) To find out more detail about VAT without reference to the VAT Office one should refer to **the VAT Guide.**

10) If we import raw materials from outside the EU we **must** pay input VAT on them.

11) If we export goods to buyers outside the EU we must treat them as **zero rated**.

12) We would get automatic bad debt relief if we could be part of the **cash accounting** scheme, but our annual taxable turnover is too high.

13) We would only have to complete one VAT return per year if we were part of the **annual accounting** scheme, but our taxable turnover is too high.

14) In any dispute about VAT we would need to decide between:

   1) sending further information to the Officer who issued the decision
   2) asking for a review of HMRC's decision, and
   3) asking for our appeal to be heard by an independent tribunal

15) If we submit our VAT return late, HMRC will issue us with a **surcharge liability notice**.

practice simulation – unit 7 – answers

You also asked me for some information on other matters:

16) The government body responsible for publishing government statistics is **the Office for National Statistics**.

17) An example of a regulatory body seeking a report or return is **the Financial Services Authority (FSA)**.

18) Other types of outside organisation which may seek a report or return from us are: **grant-awarding bodies, lenders, trade unions, the Office for National Statistics**.

MCQ/OT Questions

1 Costing information

1. A firm has to pay a 20p per unit royalty to the inventor of a device which it manufactures and sells.

    The royalty charge would be classified in the firm's accounts as a:

    A   Selling expense
    B   Direct expense
    C   Production overhead
    D   Administrative overhead

2. Which of the following items might be a suitable cost unit within the credit control department of a company?

    (i)   Stationery cost
    (ii)   Customer account
    (iii)   Cheque received and processed

    A   Item (i) only
    B   Item (ii) only
    C   Item (iii) only
    D   Items (ii) and (iii) only

The following information relates to questions 3 to 5

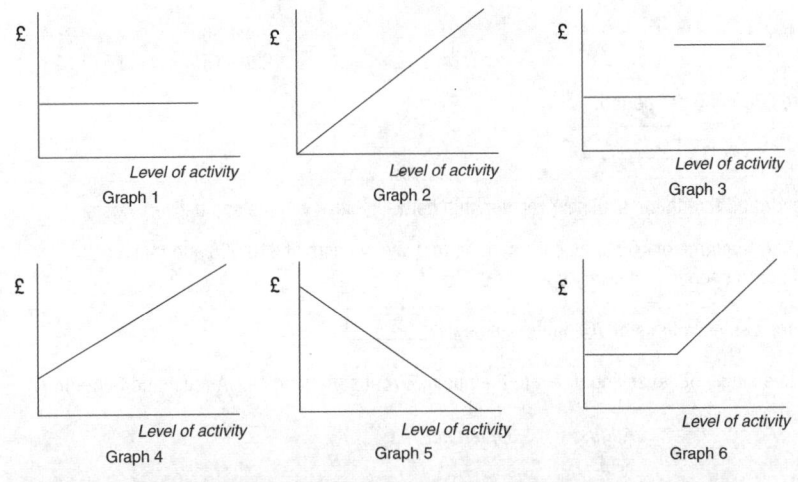

Which one of the above graphs illustrates the costs described in questions 3 to 5?

3. A linear variable cost – when the vertical axis represents cost incurred.

    A   Graph 1
    B   Graph 2
    C   Graph 4
    D   Graph 5

4. A fixed cost – when the vertical axis represents cost incurred.

    A   Graph 1
    B   Graph 2
    C   Graph 3
    D   Graph 6

MCQ/OT Questions

5 A linear variable cost – when the vertical axis represents cost per unit.

    A   Graph 1
    B   Graph 2
    C   Graph 3
    D   Graph 6

6 A company has to pay a £1 per unit royalty to the designer of a product which it manufactures and sells.

The royalty charge would be classified in the company's accounts as a (tick the correct answer):

- [ ] Direct expense
- [ ] Production overhead
- [ ] Administrative overhead
- [ ] Selling overhead

7 Fixed costs are conventionally deemed to be (tick the correct answer):

- [ ] Constant per unit of activity
- [ ] Constant in total when activity changes
- [ ] Outside the control of management
- [ ] Unaffected by inflation

8 The following data relate to two activity levels of an X-ray department in a hospital:

Number of X-rays taken	4,500	4,750
Overheads	£269,750	£273,625

Fixed overheads are £200,000 per period.

The variable cost per X-ray is £ ☐

9 An organisation has found that there is a linear relationship between sales volume and delivery costs.

It has found that a sales volume of 400 units corresponds to delivery costs of £10,000 and that a sales volume of 800 units corresponds to delivery costs of £12,000.

The delivery costs for a sales volume of 700 units will be £ ☐

10 A company operates a single outlet selling direct to the public. Profit statements for August and September 20X6 are as follows.

	August £	September £
Sales	80,000	90,000
Cost of sales	50,000	55,000
Gross profit	30,000	35,000
Less:		
Selling and distribution	8,000	9,000
Administration	15,000	15,000
Net profit	7,000	11,000

(a) The cost of sales consists of a fixed cost of £ ☐ and a variable cost of £ ☐ per £ of sale.

(b) The selling and distribution cost is a ☐ cost of £ ☐ per £ of sale.

(c) The administration cost is a ☐ cost.

522

2 Materials costs

1   Which of the following functions are fulfilled by a goods received note (GRN)?

    (i)   Provides information to update the inventory records on receipt of goods
    (ii) Provides information to check the quantity on the supplier's invoice
    (iii) Provides information to check the price on the supplier's invoice

    A   (i) and (ii) only
    B   (i) and (iii) only
    C   (ii) and (iii) only

2   There are 27,500 units of Part Number X35 on order with the suppliers and 16,250 units outstanding on existing customers' orders.

    If the free inventory is 13,000 units, what is the physical inventory?

    A   1,750
    B   3,250
    C   24,250
    D   29,250

The following information relates to questions 3 and 4

A domestic appliance retailer with multiple outlets sells a popular toaster known as the Autocrisp 2000, for which the following information is available:

Average sales	75 per day
Maximum sales	95 per day
Minimum sales	50 per day
Lead time	12-18 days
Reorder quantity	1,750

3   Based on the data above, at what level of inventory would a replenishment order be issued?

    A   600 units
    B   1,125 units
    C   1,710 units
    D   1,750 units

4   Based on the data above, what is the maximum inventory level?

    A   1,750 units
    B   2,275 units
    C   2,860 units
    D   2,900 units

5   The annual demand for a stock item is 2,500 units. The cost of placing an order is £80 and the cost of holding an item in stock for one year is £15. What is the economic order quantity, to the nearest unit?

    A   31 units
    B   115 units
    C   163 units
    D   26,667 units

MCQ/OT Questions

6 The demand for a product is 12,500 units for a three month period. Each unit of product has a purchase price of £15 and ordering costs are £20 per order placed.

The annual holding cost of one unit of product is 10% of its purchase price.

What is the Economic Order Quantity (to the nearest unit)?

- A 577
- B 816
- C 866
- D 1,155

7 A company determines its order quantity for a raw material by using the Economic Order Quantity (EOQ) model.

What would be the effects on the EOQ and the total annual holding cost of a decrease in the cost of ordering a batch of raw material?

	EOQ	Total annual holding cost
A	Higher	Lower
B	Higher	Higher
C	Lower	Higher
D	Lower	Lower

8 A manufacturing company uses 25,000 components at an even rate during a year. Each order placed with the supplier of the components is for 2,000 components, which is the economic order quantity. The company holds a buffer inventory of 500 components. The annual cost of holding one component in inventory is £2.

What is the total annual cost of holding inventory of the component?

- A £2,000
- B £2,500
- C £3,000
- D £4,000

9 The following data relates to component L512:

Ordering costs   £100 per order
Inventory holding costs   £8 per unit per annum
Annual demand   1,225 units

The economic order quantity is ⬚ units (to the nearest whole unit).

10 The following data relate to inventory item A452:

Average usage   100 units per day
Minimum usage   60 units per day
Maximum usage   130 units per day
Lead time   20-26 days
EOQ   4,000 units

The maximum inventory level was ⬚ units

3 Labour costs and expenses

1   The labour cost graph below depicts:

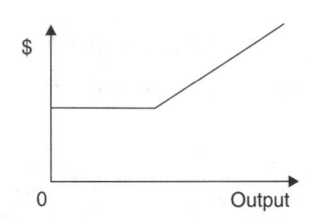

    A   A piece rate scheme with a minimum guaranteed wage
    B   A straight piece rate scheme
    C   A straight time rate scheme
    D   A differential piece rate scheme

2   The following data relate to work in the finishing department of a certain factory.

    Normal working day   7 hours
    Basic rate of pay per hour   £5
    Standard time allowed to produce 1 unit   4 minutes
    Premium bonus payable at the basic rate   60% of time saved

    On a particular day one employee finishes 180 units. His gross pay for the day will be

    A   £35
    B   £50
    C   £56
    D   £60

3   An employee is paid on a piecework basis. The basis of the piecework scheme is as follows:

    1 to 100 units   –   £0.20 per unit
    101 to 200 units –   £0.30 per unit
    201 to 299 units –   £0.40 per unit

    with only the additional units qualifying for the higher rates. Rejected units do not qualify for payment.

    During a particular day the employee produced 210 units of which 17 were rejected as faulty.

    What did the employee earn for their day's work?

    A   £47.90
    B   £54.00
    C   £57.90
    D   £63.00

4   Employee A is a carpenter and normally works 36 hours per week. The standard rate of pay is £3.60 per hour. A premium of 50% of the basic hourly rate is paid for all overtime hours worked. During the last week of October, Employee A worked for 42 hours. The overtime hours worked were for the following reasons:

    Machine breakdown: 4 hours
    To complete a special job at the request of a customer: 2 hours

    How much of Employee A's earnings for the last week of October would have been treated as direct wages?

    A   £162.00
    B   £129.60
    C   £140.40
    D   £151.20

525

MCQ/OT Questions

5 Which of the following statements is/are true about group bonus schemes?

(i) Group bonus schemes are appropriate when increased output depends on a number of people all making extra effort

(ii) With a group bonus scheme, it is easier to award each individual's performance

(iii) Non-production employees can be rewarded as part of a group incentive scheme

A   (i) only
B   (i) and (ii) only
C   (i) and (iii) only

---

6 Jane works as a member of a three-person team in the assembly department of a factory. The team is rewarded by a group bonus scheme whereby the team leader receives 40 per cent of any bonus earned by the team, and the remaining bonus is shared evenly between Jane and the other team member. Details of output for one day are given below.

Hours worked by team	8 hours
Team production achieved	80 units
Standard time allowed to produce one unit	9 minutes
Group bonus payable at £6 per hour	70% of time saved

The bonus element of Jane's pay for this particular day will be

A   £5.04
B   £7.20
C   £10.08
D   £16.80

---

7 Which one of the following groups of workers would be classified as indirect labour?

A   Machinists in an organisation manufacturing clothes
B   Bricklayers in a house building company
C   Maintenance workers in a shoe factory

---

8 (a) The following data relate to work in the finishing department.

Basic daily pay	8 hours × £6 per hour
Standard time allowed to finish one unit	12 minutes
Premium bonus payable at the basic rate	50% of time saved

On a particular day an employee finishes 50 units. His gross pay for the day will be £ ☐ (to the nearest £)

(b) An employee is paid according the following differential piecework scheme,

Weekly output Units	Rate of pay per unit £
1–25	2.30
26–40	2.40
41 and above	2.60

with only the additional units qualifying for the higher rates. In addition he receives a guaranteed weekly wage of £420. In a week when he produces 28 units, his gross wage will be £ ☐ (to the nearest penny).

MCQ/OT Questions

9 A company pays employees under a piecework scheme. An employee is paid whereby she receives £4 per piecework hour produced, plus a guaranteed weekly wage of £200. In week 12 she produces the following output.

	Piecework time allowance per unit Hours
50 units of product J	0.3
10 units of product W	4.0

The employee's gross pay for week 12 was £ **420**

---

10 A team of five employees is rewarded by means of a group incentive scheme. The team receives a basic hourly rate for output up to and including 200 units per day.

The basic rate of pay for members of the team is:

	Number of employees	Hourly rate £
Team leader	1	14
Operatives	3	10
Junior operative	1	6

For outputs exceeding 200 units per day the hourly rate for all members of the team is increased, for all hours worked that day. The increases in hourly rates, above the basic hourly rate, are as follows.

Output per day Units	Increase in hourly rate %
201 to 250	10
251 to 280	12
281 to 300	15

Due to a limitation on machine capacity it is not possible to exceed an output of 300 units per day.

Output per day Units	Hourly group remuneration £
Up to 200	A
201 to 250	B
251 to 280	C
281 to 300	D

The values that would be entered in the table above for A, B, C and D are:

A **50.00**
B **55.00**
C **56.00**
D **57.50**

4 Overheads

1 The following extract of information is available concerning the four cost centres of EG Limited.

	Production cost centres			Service cost centre
	Machinery	Finishing	Packing	Canteen
Number of direct employees	7	6	2	–
Number of indirect employees	3	2	1	4
Overhead allocated and apportioned	£28,500	£18,300	£8,960	£8,400

The overhead cost of the canteen is to be re-apportioned to the production cost centres on the basis of the number of employees in each production cost centre. After the re-apportionment, the total overhead cost of the packing department, to the nearest £, will be

- A £1,200
- B £9,968
- C £10,080
- D £10,160

The following information relates to questions 2 and 3

Budgeted information relating to two departments in a company for the next period is as follows.

Department	Production overhead £	Direct material cost £	Direct labour cost £	Direct labour hours	Machine hours
1	27,000	67,500	13,500	2,700	45,000
2	18,000	36,000	100,000	25,000	300

Individual direct labour employees within each department earn differing rates of pay, according to their skills, grade and experience.

2 What is the most appropriate production overhead absorption rate for department 1?

- A 40% of direct material cost
- B 200% of direct labour cost
- C £10 per direct labour hour
- D £0.60 per machine hour

3 What is the most appropriate production overhead absorption rate for department 2?

- A 50% of direct material cost
- B 18% of direct labour cost
- C £0.72 per direct labour hour
- D £60 per machine hour

4 Which of the following would be the most appropriate basis for apportioning machinery insurance costs to cost centres within a factory?

- A The number of machines in each cost centre
- B The floor area occupied by the machinery in each cost centre
- C The value of the machinery in each cost centre
- D The operating hours of the machinery in each cost centre

5   Factory overheads can be absorbed by which of the following methods?

   (i)   Direct labour hours
   (ii)   Machine hours
   (iii) As a percentage of prime cost
   (iv)   £x per unit

   A   (i), (ii), (iii) and (iv)
   B   (i) and (ii) only
   C   (i), (ii) and (iii) only
   D   (ii), (iii) and (iv) only

6   Which of the following is correct when considering the allocation, apportionment and reapportionment of overheads in an absorption costing situation?

   A   Only production related costs should be considered
   B   Allocation is the situation where part of an overhead is assigned to a cost centre
   C   Costs may only be reapportioned from production centres to service centres
   D   Any overheads assigned to a single department should be ignored

7   Budgeted machine hours   17,000
    Actual machine hours   21,250
    Budgeted overheads   £85,000
    Actual overheads   £110,500

   Based on the data above:

   (a) The machine hour absorption rate is £ ☐ per hour.
   (b) The overhead for the period was ☐ absorbed by £ ☐

8   A company absorbs overheads based on units produced. In one period 110,000 units were produced and the actual overheads were £500,000. Overheads were £50,000 over absorbed in the period.

   The overhead absorption rate was £ ☐ (to 2 decimal places).

9   Which of the following statements about overhead absorption rates are *not* true?

                                                                       Not true

   (i)   They are predetermined in advance for each period   ☐
   (ii)   They are used to charge overheads to products   ☐
   (iii) They are based on actual data for each period   ☐
   (iv)   They are used to control overhead costs   ☐

MCQ/OT Questions

10 A company has three main departments – Casting, Dressing and Assembly – and for period 3 has prepared the following production overhead budgets.

Department	Casting	Dressing	Assembly
Production overheads	£225,000	£175,000	£93,000
Expected production hours	7,500	7,000	6,200

During period 3, actual results were as follows.

Department	Casting	Dressing	Assembly
Production overheads	£229,317	£182,875	£94,395
Production hours	7,950	7,280	6,696

(a) The overhead absorption rate for the Casting department was £ ☐ per production hour.

(b) The overhead in the Dressing department in period 3 was ☐ absorbed by £ ☐.

5 Absorption costing and marginal costing

1 The following data is available for period 9.

Opening inventory	10,000 units
Closing inventory	8,000 units
Absorption costing profit	£280,000

The profit for period 9 using marginal costing would be:

A £278,000
B £280,000
C £282,000
D Impossible to calculate without more information

2 The overhead absorption rate for product T is £4 per machine hour. Each unit of T requires 3 machine hours. Inventories of product T last period were:

	Units
Opening inventory	2,400
Closing inventory	2,700

Compared with the marginal costing profit for the period, the absorption costing profit for product T will be:

A £1,200 higher
B £3,600 higher
C £1,200 lower
D £3,600 lower

3 In a period where opening inventories were 15,000 units and closing inventories were 20,000 units, a firm had a profit of £130,000 using absorption costing. If the fixed overhead absorption rate was £8 per unit, the profit using marginal costing would be:

A £90,000
B £130,000
C £170,000
D Impossible to calculate without more information

The following information relates to questions 4 and 5

Cost and selling price details for product Z are as follows.

	£ per unit
Direct materials	6.00
Direct labour	7.50
Variable overhead	2.50
Fixed overhead absorption rate	5.00
	21.00
Profit	9.00
Selling price	30.00

Budgeted production for the month was 5,000 units although the company managed to produce 5,800 units, selling 5,200 of them and incurring fixed overhead costs of £27,400.

4 The marginal costing profit for the month is:

- A £45,400
- B £46,800
- C £53,800
- D £72,800

5 The absorption costing profit for the month is:

- A £45,200
- B £45,400
- C £46,800
- D £48,400

6 In a period, a company had opening inventory of 31,000 units and closing inventory of 34,000 units. Profits based on marginal costing were £850,500 and on absorption costing were £955,500.

If the budgeted total fixed costs for the company was £1,837,500, what was the budgeted level of activity in units?

- A 32,500
- B 52,500
- C 65,000
- D 105,000

7 The overhead absorption rate for product M is £8 per machine hour. Each unit of M requires 6 machine hours. Inventories of product M last period were:

	Units
Opening inventory	2,400
Closing inventory	2,700

The absorption costing profit for the period for product M will be:

☐ higher
☐ lower

than the marginal costing profit. The difference between the two profit figures will be

£ ☐

8 In a period where opening inventories were 5,000 units and closing inventories 8,000 units, a firm had a profit of £130,000 using absorption costing. If the fixed overhead absorption rate was £4 per unit:

The profit using marginal costing would be £ ☐

531

MCQ/OT Questions

9 A company produces a single product. The managers currently use absorption costing, but are considering using marginal costing in future.

The fixed production overhead absorption rate is £68 per unit. There were 200 units of opening inventory for the period and 360 units of closing inventory.

If marginal costing principles were applied, the profit for the period would be [ ] than the profit reported under absorption costing. The difference between the two profits figures would be £ [ ]

10 A company has opening inventories of 825 units and closing stocks of 1,800 units in a period. The profit based on marginal costing was £50,400 and profit using absorption costing was £60,150.

The fixed overhead absorption rate per unit (to the nearest £) is £ [ ]

6 Costing systems

The following information relates to questions 1 and 2

A firm makes special assemblies to customers' orders and uses job costing.

The data for a period are:

	Job number AA10 £	Job number BB15 £	Job number CC20 £
Opening WIP	26,800	42,790	0
Material added in period	17,275	0	18,500
Labour for period	14,500	3,500	24,600

The budgeted overheads for the period were £126,000.

1 What overhead should be added to job number CC20 for the period?

   A   £65,157
   B   £69,290
   C   £72,761
   D   £126,000

2 Job number BB15 was completed and delivered during the period and the firm wishes to earn 33¹/₃% profit on sales.

   What is the selling price of job number BB15?

   A   £69,435
   B   £75,505
   C   £84,963
   D   £258,435

3 The following items may be used in costing batches.
   (i)   Actual material cost
   (ii)   Actual manufacturing overheads
   (iii) Absorbed manufacturing overheads
   (iv)   Actual labour cost

   Which of the above are contained in a typical batch cost?

   A   (i), (ii) and (iv) only
   B   (i) and (iv) only
   C   (i), (iii) and (iv) only
   D   All four of them

532

MCQ/OT Questions

4   What would be the most appropriate cost unit for a cake manufacturer?

Cost per:

A   Cake
B   Batch
C   Kg

---

5   A company makes a product, which passes through a single process.

Details of the process for the last period are as follows:

Materials	5,000 kg at 50p per kg
Labour	£700
Production overheads	200% of labour

Normal losses are 10% of input in the process, and without further processing any losses can be sold as scrap for 20c per kg.

The output for the period was 4,200 kg from the process.

There was no work in progress at the beginning or end of the period.

(a)   The value credited to the process account for the scrap value of the normal loss for the period will be £ ☐ (to the nearest £)

(b)   The value of the abnormal loss for the period is £ ☐ (to the nearest £)

---

6   A company makes a product in a single process. The following data are available for the latest period.

Opening work in progress: 300 units
Valued as follows:

	£
Material	3,600
Labour	1,600
Overhead	400

Closing work in progress: 150 units
Degree of completion:

	%
Material	100
Labour	50
Overhead	30

Units added and costs incurred during the period:

Material: 750 units	£11,625
Labour	£6,200
Overhead	£4,325
Losses	nil

WP Co uses the weighted average method of inventory valuation.

(a)   The cost per equivalent unit of material is £ ☐ (to 2 decimal places)
(b)   The cost per equivalent unit of labour is £ ☐ (to 2 decimal places)
(c)   The cost per equivalent unit of overheads is £ ☐ (to 2 decimal places)

---

7   A technical writer is to set up her own business. She anticipates working a 40-hour week and taking four weeks' holiday per year. General expenses of the business are expected to be £10,000 per year, and she has set herself a target of £40,000 a year salary.

Assuming that only 90% of her time worked will be chargeable to customers, her charge for each hour of writing (to the nearest penny) should be £ ☐

---

8   Which of the following is/are characteristics of job costing?

☐ Customer-driven production
☐ Complete production possible within a single accounting period
☐ Homogeneous products

533

MCQ/OT Questions

9 A company operates a job costing system. The company's standard net profit margin is 20 per cent of sales value.

The estimated costs for job B124 are as follows.

Direct materials   3 kg @ £5 per kg
Direct labour   4 hours @ £9 per hour

Production overheads are budgeted to be £240,000 for the period, to be recovered on the basis of a total of 30,000 labour hours.

Other overheads, related to selling, distribution and administration, are budgeted to be £150,000 for the period. They are to be recovered on the basis of the total budgeted production cost of £750,000 for the period.

The price to be quoted for job B124 is £ ☐ (to the nearest penny)

10 In which of the following situation(s) will job costing normally be used?

☐ Production is continuous
☐ Production of the product can be completed in a single accounting period
☐ Production relates to a single special order

7 Cost bookkeeping

1 A company operates an integrated accounting system. The accounting entries for the return of unused direct material from production would be:

	Debit	Credit
A	Work in progress account	Stores control account
B	Stores control account	Work in progress account
C	Stores control account	Overhead control account
D	Finished goods inventory account	Work in progress account

2 A company operates an integrated accounting system. The accounting entries for the issue to production of indirect materials from inventory would be:

	Debit	Credit
A	Work in progress account	Stores control account
B	Stores control account	Overhead control account
C	Overhead control account	Stores control account
D	Cost of sales account	Stores control account

3 A company operates an integrated accounting system. The accounting entries for absorbed manufacturing overhead would be:

	Debit	Credit
A	Overhead control account	Work in progress control account
B	Finished goods control account	Overhead control account
C	Overhead control account	Finished goods control account
D	Work in progress control account	Overhead control account

4 A company operates an integrated accounting system. At the end of a period, the accounting entries for manufacturing overhead over absorbed would be:

	Debit	Credit
A	Overhead control account	Income statement
B	Income statement	Overhead control account
C	Work in progress account	Overhead control account
D	Overhead control account	Work in progress account

5   A company operates an integrated accounting system. The accounting entries for the factory cost of finished production would be:

	Debit	Credit
A	Cost of sales account	Finished goods control account
B	Finished goods control account	Work in progress control account
C	Costing income statement	Finished goods control account
D	Work in progress control account	Finished goods control account

6   Brixon Morter Co is a manufacturing company, which is based in a single factory location. In its cost accounts, it uses an absorption costing system. 70% of the building is taken up by the production divisions, with the remainder of the space taken up by general administration (20%) and marketing (10%). The rental cost for the premises in the year just ended was £40,000.

Which one of the following bookkeeping entries would have been recorded in the company's integrated cost/financial accounts for the period?

A	Debit	Rent account	£28,000
	Credit	Production overhead control account	£28,000
B	Debit	Cash	£40,000
	Credit	Rent account	£40,000
C	Debit	Production overhead control account	£28,000
	Credit	Rent account	£28,000
D	Debit	Production overhead control account	£40,000
	Credit	Rent account	£40,000

The following information relates to questions 7 and 8

A manufacturing company uses an integrated accounting system. The production overhead absorption rate is £3 per direct labour hour. Production overhead incurred last period was £85,000 and 27,000 direct labour hours were worked.

7   The accounting entries to record the absorption of production overhead for the period would be:

	Debit		Credit	
A	Work in progress account	£85,000	Overhead control account	£85,000
B	Finished goods account	£81,000	Overhead control account	£81,000
C	Work in progress account	£81,000	Overhead control account	£81,000
D	Overhead control account	£81,000	Work in progress account	£81,000

8   The accounting entries to record the under or over absorption of production overhead for the period would be:

	Debit		Credit	
A	Income statement	£4,000	Overhead control account	£4,000
B	Overhead control account	£4,000	Income statement	£4,000
C	Work in progress account	£4,000	Overhead control account	£4,000
D	Overhead control account	£4,000	Work in progress account	£4,000

9   The material stores control account for J Co for March looks like this:

MATERIAL STORES CONTROL ACCOUNT

	£		£
Balance b/d	12,000	Work in progress	40,000
Payable	49,000	Overhead control	12,000
Work in progress	18,000	Balance c/d	27,000
	79,000		79,000
Balance b/d	27,000		

Which of the following statements are correct?

(i) Issues of direct materials during March were £18,000
(ii) Issues of direct materials during March were £40,000
(iii) Issues of indirect materials during March were £12,000
(iv) Purchases of materials during March were £49,000

A   (i) and (iv) only
B   (ii) and (iv) only
C   (ii), (iii) and (iv) only
D   All of them

10 The production control account for R Co at the end of the period looks like this.

PRODUCTION OVERHEAD CONTROL ACCOUNT

	£		£
Stores control	22,800	Work in progress	404,800
Wages control	180,400	Income statement	8,400
Expense payable	210,000		
	413,200		413,200

Which of the following statements are correct?

(i) Indirect material issued from inventory was £22,800
(ii) Overhead absorbed during the period was £210,000
(iii) Overhead for the period was over absorbed by £8,400
(iv) Indirect wages costs incurred were £180,400

A   (i), (ii) and (iii)
B   (i), (iii) and (iv)
C   (i) and (iv)
D   All of them

8 Short-term decision making

The following graph relates to questions 1 and 2

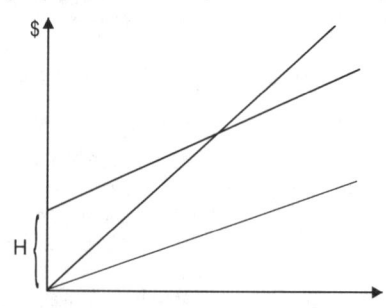

1   H on the graph indicates the value of

A   Contribution
B   Fixed cost
C   Sales value
D   Variable cost

2   This graph is known as a

    A   Contribution breakeven chart
    B   Conventional breakeven chart
    C   Profit-volume chart
    D   Semi-variable cost chart

3   The following represents a profit/volume graph for an organisation:

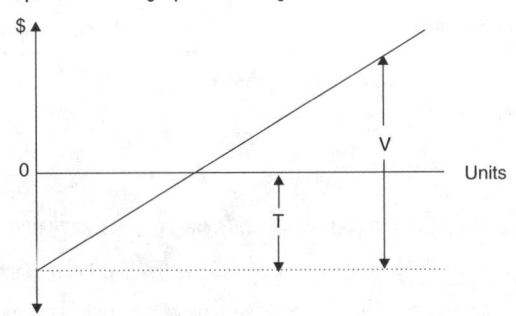

    At the specific levels of activity indicated, what do the lines depicted as 'T' and 'V' represent?

	Line 'T'	Line 'V'
A	Loss	Profit
B	Loss	Contribution
C	Total fixed costs	Profit
D	Total fixed costs	Contribution

4   A company sells a single product which has a contribution of £27 per unit and a contribution to sales ratio of 45%. This period it is forecast to sell 1,000 units giving it a margin of safety of £13,500 in sales revenue terms.

    What are the company's total fixed costs per period?

    A   £6,075
    B   £7,425
    C   £13,500
    D   £20,925

5   A company has the following budgeted information for the coming month:

    Budgeted sales revenue   £500,000
    Budgeted contribution   £200,000
    Budgeted profit   £50,000

    What is the budgeted break-even sales revenue?

    A   £125,000
    B   £350,000
    C   £375,000
    D   £450,000

6   A company sells a single product. In the coming month, it is budgeted that this product will generate a total revenue of £300,000 with a contribution of £125,000. Fixed costs are budgeted at £100,000 for the month.

    The margin of safety is ⬜ %

7   A company makes and sells a single product which has a selling price of £26, prime costs are £10 and overheads (all fixed) are absorbed at 50% of prime cost. Fixed overheads are £50,000.

    The breakeven point (to the nearest whole unit) is ⬜ units

537

MCQ/OT Questions

8 A company has calculated its margin of safety as 25% on budgeted sales. Budgeted sales are 10,000 units per month, and budgeted contribution is £40 per unit.

The budgeted fixed costs = £ ☐

9 A company wishes to make a profit of £400,000. It has fixed costs of £200,000 with a P/V ratio of 0.8 and a selling price of £15 per unit.

In order to make a profit of £400,000, Twenty Co will need to earn £ ☐ sales revenue.

10 A company sells product V, for which data is as follows.

	£ per unit
Selling price	108
Variable cost	73

Period fixed costs amount to £196,000, and the budgeted profit is £476,000 per period.

If the selling price and variable cost per unit increase by 10% and 7% respectively, the sales volume will need to ☐ to ☐ units in order to achieve the original budgeted profit for the period.

9 Long-term decision making

1 B Ltd has identified two mutually exclusive projects which have an equivalent effect on the risk profile of the company. Project 1 has a payback period of 3.7 years, an NPV of £16,100, an internal rate of return of 15% and an average accounting rate of return of 16%. Project 2 has a payback period of 4.7 years, an NPV of £14,900, an internal rate of return of 19% and an average accounting rate of return of 17%. The cost of capital is 10%.

Assuming that the directors wish to maximise shareholder wealth and no shortage of capital is expected, which project should the company choose?

- A   Project 1 because it has the shorter payback period
- B   Project 1 because it has the higher net present value
- C   Project 2 because it has the higher internal rate of return
- D   Project 2 because it has the higher accounting rate of return

2 Indicate whether or not the methods of investment appraisal listed below are based on accounting profits.

- A   NPV
- B   IRR
- C   Payback
- D   ARR

3 A project has a cash outflow of £7,000 at time 0 and cash inflows of £5,000 at time 1, £800 at time 2 and £2,700 at time 3.

Required

If the cost of capital is 15% per annum, calculate the net present value of the project.

4 Indicate by writing true or false, whether or not the following statements about the DCF approach to investment appraisal are true.

- A   The method takes account of all cash flows relating to the project.
- B   It allows for the timing of the cash flows.
- C   There are universally-accepted methods of calculating the NPV and the IRR.
- D   It is the method favoured by the majority of companies.

MCQ/OT Questions

5 Indicate whether, in a comparison of the NPV and IRR techniques, the following statements are true or false.

    A   Both methods give the same accept or reject decision, regardless of the pattern of the cash flows.
    B   IRR is technically superior to NPV and easier to calculate.
    C   The NPV approach is superior if discount rates are expected to vary over the life of the project.
    D   NPV and accounting ROCE can be confused.

6 What is the present value of £5,000 in perpetuity at a discount rate of 10%?

    A   £500
    B   £5,500
    C   £4,545
    D   £50,000

7 What are the disadvantages of the payback method of investment appraisal?

    I   It tends to maximise financial and business risk.
    II   It is a fairly complex technique and not easy to understand.
    III   It cannot be used when there is a capital rationing situation.

    A   None of the above
    B   All of the above
    C   I only
    D   II and III

8 An investment of £200,000 is required at the commencement of project X and £35,000 at the end of years 1 to 4. What is the net present value of the costs of project X if the cost of capital is 10%?

MCQ/OT Answers

MCQ/OT Answers

1 Costing information

1 B The royalty cost can be traced in full to the product, ie it has been incurred as a direct consequence of making the product. It is therefore a direct expense. **Options A, C and D** are all overheads or indirect costs which cannot be traced directly and in full to the product.

2 D It would be appropriate to use the cost per customer account and the cost per cheque received and processed for control purposes. Therefore **items (ii) and (iii)** are suitable cost units.

Stationery costs, **item (i)**, is an expense of the department, therefore it is not a suitable cost unit.

3 B Graph 2 shows that costs increase in line with activity levels
4 A Graph 1 shows that fixed costs remain the same whatever the level of activity
5 A Graph 1 shows that cost per unit remains the same at different levels of activity

6 ✓ Direct expense

The royalty cost can be traced in full to the company's product, therefore it is a direct expense.

7 ✓ Constant in total when activity changes

8 The variable cost per X-ray is £ 15.50

	X-rays No	Overheads £
	4,750	273,625
	4,500	269,750
Variable cost of	250	3,875

Variable cost per X-ray = £3,875/250 = £15.50

9 The delivery costs for a sales volume of 700 units will be £ 11,500

Using the high-low method

	Units	Total costs £
High	800	12,000
Low	400	10,000
	400	2,000

Variable cost per unit = $\dfrac{£2,000}{400}$ = £5

Total costs = fixed costs + variable costs
Let x = fixed costs
£12,000 = x + (800 × £5)
£12,000 = x + £4,000
x = £12,000 − £4,000
 = £8,000

For a sales volume of 700 units

Total costs = fixed costs + variable costs
 = £8,000 + (700 × £5)
 = £8,000 + £3,500 = £11,500

543

MCQ/OT Answers

10 (a) The cost of sales consists of a fixed cost of £ 10,000 and a variable cost of £ 0.50 per £ of sale.

Cost of sales

	£
High level	55,000
Low level	50,000
Variable cost of sales of £10,000 sales	5,000

∴ Variable cost per £ of sales £0.50

∴ Substituting at low level,

Fixed costs of sales = £50,000 – (0.50 × £80,000)

= £10,000

(b) The selling and distribution cost is a variable cost of £ 0.10 per £ of sale.

Selling and distribution costs

	£
High level	9,000
Low level	8,000
Variable distribution cost of £10,000 sales	1,000

∴ Variable cost per £ of sales £0.10

∴ Substituting at low level,

Fixed selling and distribution costs = £8,000 – (0.10 × £80,000)

= £0

(c) fixed

2 Materials costs

1 A Among other things, the GRN is used to update the inventory records and to check that the quantity invoiced by the supplier was actually received. The GRN does not usually contain price information. Therefore the correct answer is A.

2 A Free inventory balance = units in inventory + units on order from suppliers – units outstanding on customers' orders

13,000 = units in inventory + 27,500 – 16,250

∴ Units in inventory = 13,000 – 27,500 + 16,250

= 1,750

Option B is simply the difference between the units outstanding on customers' orders and the free inventory balance.

If you selected **option C** you have interchanged inventory on order and the outstanding orders. If you selected **option D** you have simply added the free inventory to the units outstanding on existing orders.

3 C Reorder level = maximum usage × maximum lead time

= 95 × 18

= 1,710 units

MCQ/OT Answers

4 C Maximum level = reorder level + reorder quantity − (minimum usage × minimum lead time)
= 1,710 + 1,750 − (50 × 12) = 2,860 units

If you selected options A, C or D you have used the correct formula, but used the incorrect reorder level as calculated in the previous question.

5 C $EOQ = \sqrt{\dfrac{2C_oD}{C_h}} = \sqrt{\dfrac{2 \times €80 \times 2{,}500}{€15}} = 163$

If you selected **option A** you have interchanged C_o and C_h.

If you selected **option B**, you have omitted the 2.

If you selected **option D** you forgot to take the square root.

6 D $EOQ = \sqrt{\dfrac{2C_oD}{C_H}}$

Where $C_o = 20$
  $D = 12{,}500 \times 4 = 50{,}000$
  $C_H = 10\% \times £15 = 1.50$

$EOQ = \sqrt{\dfrac{2 \times 20 \times 50{,}000}{1.50}}$

$= \sqrt{1{,}333{,}333}$

$= 1{,}155$ units

7 D If there is a decrease in the cost of ordering a batch of raw material, then the EOQ will also be lower (as the numerator in the EOQ equation will be lower). If the EOQ is lower, than average inventory held (EOQ/2) with also be lower and therefore the total annual holding costs will also be lower.

8 C

Annual holding cost

= [buffer (safety) inventory + reorder level/2)] × holding cost per unit

= [500 + (2,000/2)] × £2

= £3,000

9 The economic order quantity is ⎿ 175 ⏌ units (to the nearest whole unit).

$EOQ = \sqrt{\dfrac{2C_oD}{C_h}}$

$= \sqrt{\dfrac{2 \times €100 \times 1{,}225}{€8}}$

$= \sqrt{30{,}625}$

$= 175$ units

10 The maximum inventory level was ⎿ 6,180 ⏌ units.

Reorder level = maximum usage × maximum lead time = 130 × 26 = 3,380 units

Maximum level = reorder level + reorder quantity − (minimum usage × minimum lead time)
= 3,380 + 4,000 − (60 × 20) = 6,180 units

MCQ/OT Answers

3 Labour costs and expenses

1 A The graph shows a constant wage up to a certain level of output, which is payable even at zero output. This is the minimum guaranteed wage. Above a certain output the wage cost rises at a constant rate. This is the piece rate payable in addition to the minimum wage.

Graphs for the other options would look like this:

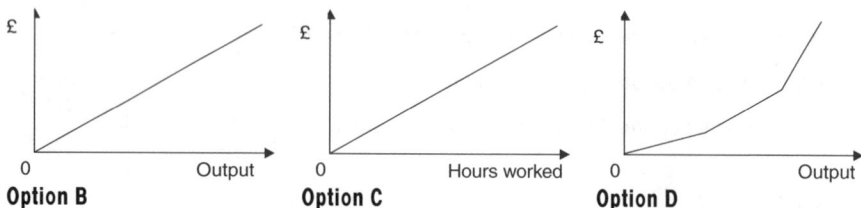

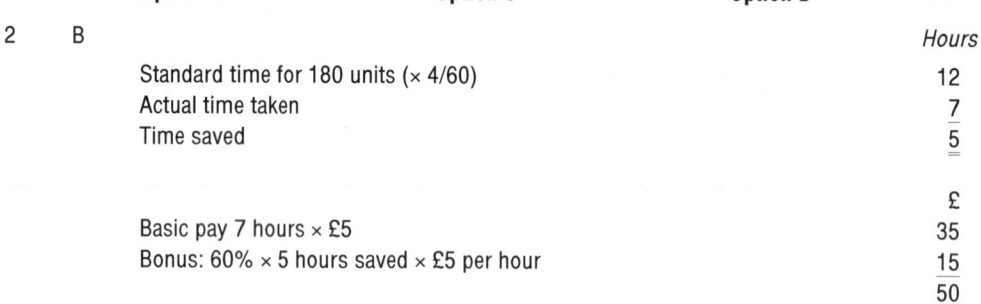

[Option B: £ vs Output, straight line from origin]
[Option C: £ vs Hours worked, straight line from a positive intercept]
[Option D: £ vs Output, flat then rising steeply]

2 B

	Hours
Standard time for 180 units (× 4/60)	12
Actual time taken	7
Time saved	5

	£
Basic pay 7 hours × £5	35
Bonus: 60% × 5 hours saved × £5 per hour	15
	50

Option A is the basic daily pay, without consideration of any bonus. If you selected **option C**, you simply added 60 per cent to the basic daily pay, so you have misunderstood how to calculate the bonus.

Option D is based on the standard time allowance for 180 units, without considering the basic pay for the seven-hour day.

3 A Number of units qualifying for payment = 210 − 17
 = 193

Piecework payment to be made:

	£
First 100 units @ £0.20	20.00
Last 93 units @ £0.30	27.90
	47.90

Option B is not correct because it includes payment for the 17 rejected units. If you selected **option C** you calculated the correct number of units qualifying for payment, but you evaluated all of them at the higher rate of £0.30 per unit. **Option D** is incorrect because it includes the 17 rejected units, and evaluates them all at the higher rate of £0.30 per unit.

4 C The overtime premium paid at the specific request of a customer would be treated as a direct cost because it can be traced to a specific cost unit.

The four hours of machine breakdown is idle time. It cannot be traced to a specific cost unit therefore it is an indirect cost.

The direct wages cost is as follows.

	£
Basic pay for active hours (38 hours × £3.60)	136.80
Overtime premium re: customer request (2 hours × £1.80)	3.60
	140.40

MCQ/OT Answers

Option A is incorrect because it is the employee's total wages for the week, both direct and indirect.

Option B is the basic pay for a 36 hour week, making no allowance for the overtime worked at the customer's request.

If you selected **option D** you calculated the basic pay for all of the hours worked, but you made no allowance for either the idle time or the overtime premium.

5   C   Group bonus schemes are useful to reward performance when production is integrated so that all members of the group must work harder to increase output, for example in production line manufacture. **Statement (i)** is therefore true.

Group bonus schemes are not effective in linking the reward to a particular individual's performance. Even if one individual makes a supreme effort, this can be negated by poor performance from other members of the group. Therefore **statement (ii)** is not true.

Non-production employees can be included in a group incentive scheme, for example when all employees in a management accounting department must work harder to produce prompt budgetary control reports. **Statement (iii)** is therefore true, and the correct option is C.

6   A

	Hours
Standard time for 80 units (× 9/60)	12
Actual time taken	8
Time saved	4

Group bonus : 70% × 4 hours saved × £6 per hour = £16.80

Jane's share of bonus   = 50% × (£16.80 × 60%)
                                = £5.04

If you selected **option B** you took all of the time saved as the bonus hours, instead of only 70 per cent. **Option C** is the bonus payable to Jane and her team-mate combined. If you selected **option D** you have calculated the group bonus correctly but have not taken the final step to calculate Jane's share of the bonus.

7   C   Maintenance workers in a shoe factory would be classified as indirect labour.

8   (a)   His gross pay for the day will be £ ⌐54⌐ (to the nearest £)

	Hours
Standard time for 50 units (× 12/60)	10
Actual time taken	8
Time saved	2

	£
Bonus = 50% × 2 hours saved × £6 =	6
Basic daily pay = 8 hours × £6 =	48
Total gross pay	54

      (b)   In a week when he produces 28 units, his gross wage will be £ ⌐484.70⌐ (to the nearest penny)

	£
Piecework earnings:	
1-25 units = 25 × £2.30	57.50
26-28 units = 3 × £2.40	7.20
Total piecework earnings	64.70
Guaranteed weekly wage	420.00
Gross wage	484.70

547

MCQ/OT Answers

9   The employee's gross pay for week 12 was £ 420

Piecework hours produced:	Piecework hours
Product J (50 × 0.3 hours)	15
Product W (10 × 4.0 hours)	40
	55

Employee's pay = £200 + (55 × £4) = £420

10

A   £50.00

B   £55.00

C   £56.00

D   £57.50

Basic hourly rate = (1 × £14) + (3 × £10) + (1 × £6) = £50.

Output per day Units	Increase %	Hourly group remuneration £
Up to 200	–	50.00
201 to 250	10	55.00
251 to 280	12	56.00
281 to 300	15	57.50

4 Overheads

1   D   Number of employees in packing department = 2 direct + 1 indirect = 3

Number of employees in all production departments = 15 direct + 6 indirect = 21

Packing department overhead

Canteen cost apportioned to packing department = $\dfrac{€8,400}{21} \times 3$

= £1,200

Original overhead allocated and apportioned = £8,960

Total overhead after apportionment of canteen costs = £10,160

If you selected **option A** you forgot to include the original overhead allocated and apportioned to the packing department. If you selected **option B** you included the four canteen employees in your calculation, but the question states that the basis for apportionment is the number of employees in each **production** cost centre.

If you selected **option C** you based your calculations on the direct employees only.

2   D   Department 1 appears to undertake primarily machine-based work, therefore a machine-hour rate would be most appropriate.

$\dfrac{€27,000}{45,000}$ = £0.60 per machine hour

Therefore the correct answer is D.

Option A is not the most appropriate because it is not time-based, and most items of overhead expenditure tend to increase with time.

Options B and C are not the most appropriate because labour activity is relatively insignificant in department 1, compared with machine activity.

MCQ/OT Answers

3 C Department 2 appears to be labour-intensive therefore a direct labour-hour rate would be most appropriate.

$$\frac{€18,000}{25,000} = £0.72 \text{ per direct labour hour}$$

Option B is based on labour therefore it could be suitable. However differential wage rates exist and this could lead to inequitable overhead absorption. **Option D** is not suitable because machine activity is not significant in department 2.

4 C The insurance cost is likely to be linked to the cost of replacing the machines, therefore the most appropriate basis for apportionment is the value of machinery.

Options A, B and D would all be possible apportionment bases in the absence of better information, but **option C** is preferable.

5 A All of the overhead absorption methods are suitable, depending on the circumstances.

Method 1, direct labour hours, is suitable in a labour-intensive environment.

Method 2, machine hours, is suitable in a machine-intensive environment.

Method 3, a percentage of prime costs, can be used if it is difficult to obtain the necessary information to use a time-based method. **Method 4**, a rate per unit, is suitable if all cost units are identical.

6 A Only production related costs should be considered when considering the allocation, apportionment and reapportionment of overhead in an absorption costing situation.

7 (a) The machine hour absorption rate is £ ⌷5⌷ per hour.

$$\text{Overhead absorption rate} = \frac{\text{Budgeted overheads}}{\text{Budgeted machine hours}}$$

$$= \frac{€85,000}{17,000}$$

$$= \underline{£5}$$

(b) The overhead for the period was ⌷under⌷ absorbed by £ ⌷4,250⌷

Overhead over-/(under)-absorbed = Overhead absorbed − Overhead incurred

$$= (21,250 \times £5) - £110,500$$

$$= \underline{£(4,250)}$$

8 The overhead absorption rate was £ ⌷5.00⌷ (to 2 decimal places)

Workings

Actual overheads = £500,000

∴ Absorbed overheads = £500,000 + £50,000
  = £550,000

Absorbed overheads = actual production × overhead absorption rate (OAR)

£550,000 = 110,000 units × £OAR

∴ OAR $= \dfrac{£550,000}{110,000 \text{ units}} = £5.00$ per unit

MCQ/OT Answers

9 (iii) They are based on actual data for each period ✓
  (iv) They are used to control overhead costs ✓

Overhead absorption rates are determined in advance for each period, usually based on budgeted data. Therefore statement (i) is true and statement (iii) is not true. Overhead absorption rates are used in the final stage of overhead analysis, to absorb overheads into product costs. Therefore statement (ii) is true. Statement (iv) is not true because overheads are controlled using budgets and other management information.

10 (a) The overhead absorption rate for the Casting department was £ 30 per production hour.

Workings

	Casting department
Production overheads	€225,000
Expected production hours	7,500
Predetermined overhead absorption rate	= £30/hr

(b) The overhead in the Dressing department in period 3 was under absorbed by £ 875

Workings

Dressing department overhead absorption rate = $\frac{€175,000}{7,000}$ = £25 per hour

	£
Overhead absorbed (7,280 hours × £25)	182,000
Overhead incurred	182,875
(Under) absorption of overhead	(875)

5 Absorption costing and marginal costing

1 D We know that the profit using marginal costing would be higher than the absorption costing profit, because inventories are decreasing. However, we cannot calculate the value of the difference without the fixed overhead absorption rate per unit.

Difference in profit = 2,000 units inventory reduction × fixed overhead absorption rate per unit

2 B Difference in profit = change in inventory level × fixed overhead per unit
= (2,400 – 2,700) × (£4 × 3)
= £3,600

The absorption profit will be higher because inventories have increased, and fixed overheads have been carried forward in inventories.

If you selected **option A or C** you used £4 per unit as the fixed overhead absorption rate, but this is the absorption rate per machine hour. If you selected **option D** you calculated the correct monetary value of the profit difference but you misinterpreted its 'direction'.

3 A Difference in profit = change in inventory level × fixed overhead per unit
= (15,000 – 20,000) × £8
= £40,000

The inventory level increased during the period therefore the absorption costing profit is higher than the marginal costing profit.

Marginal costing profit = £130,000 – £40,000 = £90,000

550

MCQ/OT Answers

If you selected **option B** you decided there would be no difference in the reported profits. If inventory levels change there will always be a difference between the marginal and absorption costing profits.

If you selected **option C** you calculated the correct monetary value of the profit difference but you misinterpreted its 'direction'.

4 A Contribution per unit = £30 − £(6.00 + 7.50 + 2.50)
                              = £14
       Contribution for month = £14 × 5,200 units
                              = £72,800
       Less fixed costs incurred = £27,400
       Marginal costing profit   = £45,400

If you selected **option B** you calculated the profit on the actual sales at £9 per unit. This utilises a unit rate for fixed overhead which is not valid under marginal costing.

If you selected **option C** you used the correct method but you based your calculations on the units produced rather than the units sold.

If you selected **option D** you calculated the correct contribution but you forgot to deduct the fixed overhead.

5 D

	£	£
Sales (5,200 at £30)		156,000
Materials (5,200 at £6)	31,200	
Labour (5,200 at £7.50)	39,000	
Variable overhead (5,200 at £2.50)	13,000	
Total variable cost		(83,200)
Fixed overhead (£5 × 5,200)		(26,000)
Over-absorbed overhead (W)		1,600
Absorption costing profit		48,400

Working   £
Overhead absorbed (5,800 × £5)   29,000
Overhead incurred   27,400
Over-absorbed overhead   1,600

If you selected **option A** you calculated all the figures correctly but you subtracted the over-absorbed overhead instead of adding it to profit.

Option B is the marginal costing profit.

If you selected **option C** you calculated the profit on the actual sales at £9 per unit, and forgot to adjust for the over-absorbed overhead.

6 B Inventory levels increased by 3,000 units and absorption costing profit is £105,000 higher (£955,500 − £850,500).

∴ Fixed production cost included in inventory increase:

$$= \frac{\$105{,}000}{3{,}000} = £35 \text{ per unit of inventory}$$

$$\frac{\text{Budgeted fixed costs}}{\text{Fixed cost per unit}} = \frac{€1{,}837{,}500}{£35} = 52{,}500 \text{ units}$$

Option A is an average of the opening and closing inventories.

Option C is the total of the opening and closing inventories. If you selected **option D** you simply calculated the difference between the two stated profit figures.

MCQ/OT Answers

7 The absorption costing profit for the period for product M will be:

☑ higher

than the marginal costing profit. The difference between the two profit figures will be
£ 14,400

Difference in profit = change in inventory level × fixed overhead per unit

$$= (2,400 - 2,700) \times (£8 \times 6)$$
$$= £14,400$$

The absorption costing profit will be higher because inventories have increased, and fixed overheads have been carried forward in inventory.

8 The profit using marginal costing would be £ 118,000

Marginal cost profit = Absorption cost profit + ((Opening inventory − Closing inventory) × Fixed overhead absorption rate)

$$= £130,000 + ((5,000 - 8,000) \times £4)$$
$$= £118,000$$

9 Lower £ 10,880

The marginal costing profit will be **lower** than the absorption costing profit because inventories increased during the period. Under the absorption costing method the amount of fixed production overhead carried forward in inventory would have increased.

Difference in profit = 160 units increase in inventory × £68 per unit

$$= £10,880$$

10 The fixed overhead absorption rate per unit (to the nearest £) is £ 10

	Units
Opening inventory	825
Closing inventory	1,800
Increase in inventory level	975

	£
Absorption costing profit	60,150
Marginal costing profit	50,400
Difference in profit	9,750

∴ Overhead absorption rate = $\dfrac{€9,750}{975}$ = £10 per unit

6 Costing systems

1 C The most logical basis for absorbing the overhead job costs is to use a percentage of direct labour cost.

$$\text{Overhead} = \dfrac{€24,600}{€(14,500 + 3,500 + 24,600)} \times £126,000$$

$$= \dfrac{€24,600}{€42,600} \times £126,000$$

$$= £72,761$$

552

MCQ/OT Answers

If you selected **option A** you used the materials cost as the basis for overhead absorption. This would not be equitable because job number BB15 incurred no material cost and would therefore absorb no overhead. **Option B** is based on the prime cost of each job (material plus labour) and therefore suffers from the same disadvantage as **option A**. **Option D** is the total overhead for the period, but some of this cost should be charged to the other two jobs.

2 C

	Job BB15 £
Opening WIP	42,790
Labour for period	3,500
Overheads ($\frac{€3,500}{€42,600} \times £126,000$)	10,352
Total costs	56,642
Profit (33 1/3% on sales)	28,321
	£84,963

If you selected **option A** you forgot to add on overhead cost. If you selected **option B** you calculated the profit as 33 1/3 % on cost, instead of 33 1/3% on sales. If you selected **option D** you charged all of the overhead to job BB15, but some of the overhead should be charged to the other two jobs.

3 C   The actual material and labour costs for a batch **((i) and (iv))** can be determined from the material and labour recording system. Actual manufacturing overheads cannot be determined for a specific batch because of the need for allocation and apportionment of each item of overhead expenditure, and the subsequent calculation of a predetermined overhead absorption rate. Therefore **item (ii)** is incorrect and **item (iii)** is correct.

4 B   Cost per cake would be very small and therefore not an appropriate cost unit. The most appropriate cost unit would be cost per batch.

5 (a) The value credited to the process account for the scrap value of the normal loss for the period will be £ ⌊100⌋ (to the nearest £)

Normal loss = 10% × input

= 10% × 5,000 kg

= 500 kg

When scrap has a value, normal loss is valued at the value of the scrap ie 20p per kg.

Normal loss = £0.20 × 500 kg

= £100

(b) The value of the abnormal loss for the period is £ ⌊300⌋ (to the nearest £)

	Kg
Input	5,000
Normal loss (10% × 5,000 kg)	(500)
Abnormal loss	(300)
Output	4,200

Cost per unit = $\frac{\text{Input costs - scrap value of normal loss}}{\text{Expected output}}$

= $\frac{€4,600^* - €100}{5,000 - 500}$

= $\frac{€4,500}{4,500}$ = £1.00

Scrap value of normal loss = 500 kg × £0.20 = £100

Value of abnormal loss = 300 × £1.00 = £300

MCQ/OT Answers

		Kg
Materials (5,000 kg × 0.5)		2,500
Labour		700
Production overhead		1,400
		4,600

6 (a) The cost per equivalent unit of material is £ ⎡14.50⎤ (to 2 decimal places)

   (b) The cost per equivalent unit of labour is £ ⎡8.00⎤ (to 2 decimal places)

   (c) The cost per equivalent unit of overheads is £ ⎡5.00⎤ (to 2 decimal places)

STATEMENT OF EQUIVALENT UNITS

	Total units	Materials	Equivalent units Labour	Overheads
Finished output*	900	900	900	900
Closing WIP	150	(100%) 150	(50%) 75	(30%) 45
	1,050	1,050	975	945

* 750 units input + opening WIP 300 units – closing WIP 150 units

STATEMENT OF COSTS PER EQUIVALENT UNIT

	Materials £	Labour £	Overheads £	Total
Opening inventory	3,600	1,600	400	
Added during period	11,625	6,200	4,325	
Total cost	15,225	7,800	4,725	
Equivalent units	1,050	975	945	
Cost per equivalent unit	£14.50	£8	£5	£27.50

7 Charge for each hour of writing (to the nearest penny) should be £ ⎡28.94⎤

Weeks worked per year   = 52 – 4 = 48

Hours worked per year   = 48 × 40 hrs

= 1,920

Hours chargeable to clients   = 1,920 × 90% = 1,728

Total expenses = £10,000 + £40,000 = £50,000

Hourly rate = $\dfrac{€50,000}{1,728}$ = £28.94 per hour

8 ✓ Customer-driven production

  ✓ Complete production possible within a single accounting period

Each job is separately identifiable, according to a customer's requirements. Therefore the first characteristic is correct.

Jobs are usually of comparatively short duration, compared to situations where contract costing is applied. Therefore the second characteristic is correct.

The third characteristic is incorrect because each job is separately identifiable.

MCQ/OT Answers

9   The price to be quoted for job B124 is £ **124.50** (to the nearest penny)

Production overhead absorption rate = £240,000/30,000 = £8 per labour hour

Other overhead absorption rate = (£150,000/£750,000) × 100% = 20% of total production cost

Job B124	£
Direct materials (3 kgs × £5)	15.00
Direct labour (4 hours × £9)	36.00
Production overhead (4 hours × £8)	32.00
Total production cost	83.00
Other overhead (20% × £83)	16.60
Total cost	99.60
Profit margin: 20% of sales (× $^{20}/_{80}$)	24.90
Price to be quoted	124.50

10 ✓ Production of the product can be completed in a single accounting period

   ✓ Production relates to a single special order

Job costing is appropriate where each cost unit is **separately identifiable** and is of relatively **short duration**.

7 Cost bookkeeping

1   B   The entries for the return of direct material to stores are the **reverse** of those made when the material is first issued to production. The **work in progress account is credited** to 'remove' the cost of the material from the production costs. The **stores account is debited** to increase the value of inventory. Therefore the correct answer is B.

If you selected option A you identified the correct accounts but your entries were reversed.

Option C represents the entries for the return of indirect materials to stores. Option D represents the entries for the transfer of the cost of completed production to finished goods inventory.

2   C   The cost of indirect materials issued is **credited to the stores account** and 'collected' in the overhead control account **pending its absorption into work in progress**. Therefore the correct answer is C.

Option A represents the entries for the issue to production of **direct materials**.

If you selected option B you identified the correct accounts but **your entries were reversed**.

Option D is not correct. The issue of materials should not be charged direct to cost of sales. The cost of materials issued should first be analysed as direct or indirect and charged to work in progress or the overhead control account accordingly.

3   D   Overhead is absorbed into the cost of production by **debiting the work in progress account** with the appropriate amount of overhead based on the predetermined overhead absorption rate. The credit entry is made in the **overhead control account**, where the overhead has been 'collected' in the debit side. Therefore the correct answer is D.

If you selected option A you identified the correct accounts but your **entries were reversed**. Option B is incorrect because the cost of production must first be 'collected' in the **work in progress account** before the final transfer of the cost of completed production to the finished goods account. If you selected option C you made the same mistake and your entries were reversed.

4   A   Over-absorbed overhead means that the overhead charged to production was too high therefore there must be a **credit to income statement**. The debit entry is made in the **overhead control account**. Therefore the correct answer is A.

If you selected option B you identified the correct accounts but your **entries were reversed**. These entries represent those that would be made for **under-absorbed** overhead.

Options C and D are incorrect because the only overhead charge made to work in progress (WIP) is the overhead **absorbed into production based on the predetermined rate**. Under or over absorption does not affect WIP.

MCQ/OT Answers

5 B The factory cost of finished production is transferred as a **debit to the finished goods account** and **credited from the work in progress account**.

Option A describes the double entry for the production cost of goods **sold**. Option C describes the same thing, where a **cost of sales account is not in use**. Option D uses the correct accounts but **the entries are reversed**.

6 C The rent account for the period would look like this.

RENT ACCOUNT

	£		£
Cash	40,000	Production overhead	28,000
		Admin overhead	8,000
		Marketing overhead	4,000
	40,000		40,000

The debit balance in the rent account is analysed between the various functional classifications of overhead. Therefore the correct answer is C.

Option A uses the correct accounts but the entries are reversed. Option B is the reverse of the entries that would be used to record the original rent payment. Option D uses the correct accounts but only 70% of overhead should be charged to production.

7 C Overhead absorbed = 27,000 hours × £3 = £81,000. This amount is **debited in the work in progress account** as part of the cost of production for the period. The credit entry is made in the **overhead control account**.

If you selected option A you identified the correct accounts but you used the figure for **actual overheads incurred**. Option B is incorrect because the cost of production must first be 'collected' in the **work in progress account** before the final transfer of the cost of completed production to the finished goods account. Option D uses the correct values and accounts, but the **entries are reversed**.

8 A

	£
Overhead absorbed	81,000
Overhead incurred	85,000
Under-absorbed overhead	4,000

This means that the overhead charged to production was too low therefore there must be a **debit to income statement**. The credit entry is made in the **overhead control account**.

Option B demonstrates the entries for **over-absorbed overhead**.

Options C and D are incorrect because under or over absorption of overhead does not affect work in progress (WIP). The only overhead charge made to WIP is the **overhead absorbed based on the predetermined rate**.

9 C Statement (i) is not correct. A debit to stores with a corresponding credit to work in progress (WIP) indicates that **direct materials returned** from production were £18,000.

Statement (ii) is correct. **Direct costs of production** are 'collected' in the WIP account.

Statement (iii) is correct. **Indirect costs of production or overhead** are 'collected' in the overhead control account.

Statement (iv) is correct. The purchases of materials on credit are credited to the suppliers account and debited to the material stores control account.

Therefore the correct answer is C.

MCQ/OT Answers

10   C   Statement (i) is correct. The cost of indirect material issued is 'collected' in the overhead control account **pending absorption into work in progress**.

Statement (ii) is incorrect. The overhead cost **incurred** was £210,000. The overhead **absorbed into work in progress** during the period was £404,800.

Statement (iii) is incorrect. The £8,400 is **debited to income statement**, indicating an extra charge to compensate for the overhead **under absorbed**.

Statement (iv) is correct. The indirect wage cost is 'collected' in the overhead control account **pending absorption into work in progress**.

Therefore the correct answer is C.

8 Short-term decision making

1   B   The distance H is the total cost at zero activity, ie the fixed cost. **Option A**, contribution, is the distance between the sales line and the variable cost line, which are the two lines that pass through the origin. Sales value (**option C**) is represented by the steepest of the two lines passing through the origin. Variable cost (**option D**) is represented by the less steep of the two lines passing through the origin.

2   A   The chart shows the variable cost line and the contribution can be read directly as the distance between this and the sales value line. Therefore this is a contribution breakeven chart.

A conventional breakeven chart (**option B**) shows the fixed cost line instead of the variable cost line. A profit-volume chart (**option C**) plots a single line to indicate the profit at any level of activity. **Option D** is not a generally recognised description of a chart used for breakeven analysis.

3   D   Line 'T' = Total fixed costs
Line 'V' = Contribution

4   D

$$\text{Selling price} = \frac{\text{Contribution per unit}}{\text{C/S ratio}}$$

$$= \frac{€27}{0.45}$$

$$= £60$$

Margin of safety (revenue) = £13,500

$$\text{Margin of safety (units)} = \frac{€13,500}{€60}$$

$$= 225 \text{ units}$$

∴ Breakeven point = (1,000 − 225 units)

= 775 units

$$\text{Breakeven point} = \frac{\text{Fixed costs}}{\text{Contribution on per unit}}$$

$$775 = \frac{\text{Fixed costs}}{€27}$$

∴ Fixed costs = 775 units × £27

= £20,925

MCQ/OT Answers

5 C Budgeted breakeven sales revenue

Budgeted contribution − fixed costs = budgeted profit

£200,000 − fixed costs = £50,000

Fixed costs = £200,000 − £50,000

Budgeted breakeven sales revenue = $\dfrac{\text{Fixed costs}}{\text{C/S ratio}^*}$

$$= \dfrac{€150,000}{0.4}$$

$$= £375,000$$

*C/S ratio = $\dfrac{\text{Contribution}}{\text{Sales revenue}}$ = $\dfrac{€200,000}{€500,000}$

6 The margin of safety is 20%

Workings

P/V ratio = $\dfrac{\text{Contribution}}{\text{Selling price}}$

$$= \dfrac{125,000}{300,000} = 0.4167$$

Sales revenue at breakeven point = $\dfrac{\text{Fixed costs}}{\text{P/V ratio}}$

$$= \dfrac{€100,000}{0.4167} = £240,000$$

Margin of safety = $\dfrac{\text{Budgeted sales - breakeven sales}}{\text{Budgeted sales}}$

$$= \dfrac{300,000 - 240,000}{300,000} \times 100\%$$

$$= 20\%$$

7 The breakeven point (to the nearest whole unit) is £ 3,125 units

Working

Breakeven point = $\dfrac{\text{Fixed cost}}{\text{Contribution per unit}}$

$$= \dfrac{50,000}{26 - 10}$$

$$= \dfrac{50,000}{16}$$

= 3,125 units

MCQ/OT Answers

8   The budgeted fixed costs = £ ⌐300,000⌐

Working

$$\frac{\text{Margin of safety}}{\text{Budgeted sales}} = 25\%$$

∴ Margin of safety = 25% × 10,000 units
                            = 2,500 units

Margin of safety	= budgeted sales volume – breakeven sales volume
2,500 units	= 10,000 units – breakeven sales volume
∴ Breakeven sales volume	= 10,000 units – 2,500 units
	= 7,500 units

$$\text{Breakeven sales volume} = \frac{\text{Budgeted fixed costs}}{\text{Contribution per unit}}$$

$$\therefore 7{,}500 \text{ units} = \frac{\text{Budgeted fixed costs}}{€40}$$

∴ Budgeted fixed costs   = 7,500 units × £40 per unit
                                   = £300,000

9   In order to make a profit of £400,000, Twenty Co will need to sell ⌐750,000⌐ units.

Working

Total contribution required for a target profit of £400,000 = Target profit + fixed costs
                                                                         = £400,000 + £200,000
                                                                        = £600,000

Target profit is achieved by earning $\dfrac{€600{,}000 \text{ (required contribution)}}{0.8 \text{ (P/V ratio)}}$ = £750,000 sales revenue.

10   If the selling price and variable cost per unit increase by 10% and 7% respectively, the sales volume will need to ⌐decrease⌐ to ⌐16,515⌐ units in order to achieve the original budgeted profit for the period.

Current contribution per unit = £(108 – 73) = £35

$$\text{Current sales volume} = \frac{€(196{,}000 + 476{,}000)}{€35}$$

                            = 19,200 units

Revised contribution per unit:

	£ per unit
Selling price £108 × 1.10	118.80
Variable cost £73 × 1.07	78.11
Contribution	40.69

$$\text{Required sales volume} = \frac{€(196{,}000 + 476{,}000)}{€40.69}$$

                              = 16,515 units

MCQ/OT Answers

9 Long-term decision making

1 B Net present value is the appraisal method to adopt when mutually exclusive projects exist.

2 NPV   – **not based on accounting profits**
   IRR   – **not based on accounting profits**
   Payback – **not based on accounting profits**
   ARR   – **based on accounting profits**

3 The NPV = £((7,000) × 1,000 + £5,000 × 0.870 + £800 × 0.756 + £2,700 × 0.658) = –£268.60.

4 A   The method takes account of all cash flows relating to the project – **true**
   B   It allows for the timing of the cash flows – **true**
   C   There are universally-accepted methods of calculating the NPV and the IRR – **true**
   D   It is the method favoured by the majority of companies – **false**

   A: The method takes into account all the relevant cash flows that arise as a result of the project being undertaken.

   B: The use of discount rates incorporates the effects of the time value of money into the calculations.

   C: The universality of methods used means that projects can be compared widely.

   D: Although many companies do use DCF techniques, the most universally-favoured approach is still the payback method.

5 A   Both methods give the same accept or reject decision, regardless of the pattern of the cash flows – **false**

   B   IRR is technically superior to NPV and easier to calculate – **false**

   C   The NPV approach is superior if discount rates are expected to vary over the life of the project – **true**

   D   NPV and accounting ROCE can be confused – **false**

   A: The methods only give the same accept or reject decision when the cash flows are conventional. When the cash flow patterns are non-conventional, there may be several IRRs that decision makers must be aware of to avoid making the wrong decision.

   B: On the contrary, NPV is technically superior to IRR and easier to calculate.

   C: Variable discount rates can be incorporated easily into NPV calculations, but not into IRR calculations.

   D: NPV is dissimilar to accounting ROCE, but IRR can be confused with ROCE since both measures are expressed in percentage terms.

6 D   The present value of £5,000 in perpetuity is calculated as £5,000/0.1.

   If you selected **option A,** you might have calculated £5,000 × 10%.

   If you selected **option B,** you might have calculated £5,000 × 110%.

   If you selected **option C,** you might have calculated £5,000/110%.

7 A   I is not a disadvantage because the fact that it tends to bias in favour of short-term projects means that it tends to minimise both financial and business risk.

   II is untrue. It is simple to calculate and simple to understand, which may be important when management resources are limited.

   III is not a disadvantage because it helps to identify those projects which generate additional cash for investment quickly.

8   The NPV is (£200,000 × 1.000) + (£35,000 × 3.170) = £310,950.

Notes

Notes

Notes

Notes

Notes

Notes

Notes

Notes

Notes

Notes